THE KAILÂSA TEMPLE, ELLORA (SOUTH SIDE)

THE ANCIENT AND MEDIEVAL ARCHITECTURE OF INDIA: A STUDY OF INDO-ARYAN CIVILISATION

THE ANCIENT AND MEDIEVAL ARCHITECTURE OF INDIA: A STUDY OF INDO-ARYAN CIVILISATION

by

E. B. HAVELL

AUTHOR OF
"INDIAN SCULPTURE AND PAINTING,"
"THE IDEALS OF INDIAN ART"
"INDIAN ARCHITECTURE: ITS PSYCHOLOGY, STRUCTURE, AND HISTORY"
ETC.

WITH 176 ILLUSTRATIONS AND MAP

GYAN

Published by

Gyan Publishing House
5, Ansari Road
Daryaganj, New Delhi-110002
Phone: 011-47034999, 9811692060
E-mail: books@gyanbooks.com

Distribution Network
gyanbooks.com
India, USA, Canada, UK, Australia, France

ISBN : 978-81-212-6000-8 (PB)
First Published, 1915

2nd Impression 2021

Printed at: Gyan Press, Delhi.

**The Ancient and Medieval Architecture of India:
A Study of Indo-Aryan Civilisation**
Author: E. B. Havell

THE ANCIENT AND MEDIEVAL ARCHITECTURE OF INDIA: A STUDY OF INDO-ARYAN CIVILISATION

BY E. B. HAVELL

AUTHOR OF
"INDIAN SCULPTURE AND PAINTING," "THE IDEALS OF INDIAN ART"
"INDIAN ARCHITECTURE: ITS PSYCHOLOGY, STRUCTURE, AND HISTORY"
ETC.

WITH 176 ILLUSTRATIONS AND MAP

1915

TO

ABANINDRO NATH TAGORE

WITH HIS GURU'S GREETINGS

PREFACE

All but the last three chapters of this book were written before the fateful days of August which saw Great Britain once more engaged in fighting for the liberties of Europe against a hateful military despotism. The splendid demonstration of Indian loyalty which the war has called forth should not blind the British nation to the fact that the work of building up our Empire in the East, so far from being finished, will inevitably grow more difficult year by year and demand more watchful care from British statesmen.

It will certainly be impossible for Great Britain to continue to refuse India privileges which our ally, Russia, is willing to grant to her Asiatic subjects; and the problem of reconciling Indian aspirations with the vital interests of the Empire can only be solved satisfactorily by avoiding the dangers into which we have drifted with regard to the government of Ireland. The root of the Irish difficulties has lain in ignorance of Irish sentiment and Irish history. Similar causes will sooner or later produce similar effects on a far larger scale in India. It is therefore that I believe myself to be fulfilling a patriotic duty in endeavouring to remove the misconceptions of Indian civilisation which have so largely governed Anglo-Indian policy. It is good to remind ourselves how history is repeating itself—that our Indian comrades-in-arms are of the same stock as those who fifteen hundred years ago were fighting on Indian soil the same battles for liberty and for Aryan civilisation against those who, like the modern Huns, knew no right but might, as we are fighting together in Europe to-day. It is good for us to know that Indian civilisation is a branch of the same tree which we are proud to call our own. And this very feeling of comradeship makes it imperative for us to try to understand the political and social ideals which India herself has cherished for so many centuries, rather than impose upon her those which we, from our Western experience, judge to be best for her.

Great Britain could grant India no greater boon than the restoration or reconstruction of her ancient Aryan constitution. None would accord better with Indian popular sentiment or do more to strengthen the ties of Imperial unity.

The present volume is supplementary to my "Indian Architecture: its Psychology, Structure, and History," which dealt with the Muhammadan and British periods, but it has a wider scope as a study of the political, social, religious, and artistic aspects of Indo-Aryan civilisation, as revealed in the ancient and medieval monuments of India. For the chronological and statistical framework of it I have mostly used the data furnished by such well-known authorities as Professor T. W. Rhys Davids' "Buddhist India," Mr. Vincent Smith's "Early History of India," and Dr. Barnett's "Antiquities of India." The interpretation of Indian history and mythology through the reading of the symbolism of Indian art is my own, and my authorities the architecture, sculpture, and painting here illustrated. If my reading is wrong, my critics will convict me of error from the same sources.

The reasons for rejecting entirely Fergusson's classifications of styles and some of the chronological estimates which have hitherto been adopted by all archæologists are stated in the text. Owing to the fact that for the last fifty years archæological research in India has been conducted entirely on the lines laid down by Fergusson, it has been sometimes difficult for me, not having had the opportunities of collecting material for myself which officers of the Archæological Survey of India enjoy, to give a sufficiently clear demonstration of various statements. The position of unquestioned authority which Fergusson's works have hitherto obtained has unfortunately had the effect of preventing the collection and publication of much material which would demonstrate the fallacies of his theories; but I have not the least doubt that a great deal more will be forthcoming when the clues I have given are carefully followed up. In the meantime I must content myself with making the most of the material at my disposal. At some future time I hope to be able to deal with the subject more effectively in every respect.

I have to acknowledge the valuable assistance rendered me by the Secretary of State for India in granting me permission to use illustrations from official publications. In etymological questions Professor T. W. Rhys Davids and Mr. F. W. Thomas have freely given me the aid of their accomplished scholarship. Dr. J. H. Marshall, C.I.E. (Director-General of the Archæological Survey of India), Mr. Abanindro Nath Tagore, C.I.E., Mr. Nanda Lal Bose, M. Victor Goloubeff and the Editor of *L'Art Decoratif*, Paris, have helped me much with the illustrations. I am indebted to Mr. Ratan Tata for placing at my disposal reports on the excavations now in progress on the site of Pâtaliputra, and to Mr. Murray for allowing me the use of blocks from Fergusson's works. Messrs. Johnston & Hoffmann, Calcutta, have permitted me to reproduce one of their copyright negatives, and I have to thank Mr. J. Marshall for some useful references.

E. B. H.

CONTENTS

CHAPTER VII

CHAPTER VIII

CHAPTER IX

CHAPTER X

CHAPTER XI

CHAPTER XII

CHAPTER XIII

CHAPTER XIV

CHAPTER XV

CHAPTER XVI

LIST OF PLATES

ABBREVIATIONS.—I.O., India Office. A.S.I., Archæological Survey of India.

LIST OF PLATES

LIST OF TEXT ILLUSTRATIONS

INTRODUCTION

ONCE upon a time a Botanist, very learned but with rather defective eyesight, went travelling in far-distant lands. And he came to a great primeval forest with lordly trees, to whose branches many kinds of creepers and curious plants were clinging. Wishing to know what kind of trees these were, he began to gather the leaves and flowers of the creepers and parasites which had intertwined themselves with the branches, without noticing that they were not the real growth of those great forest trees. And he brought them home and dried them carefully, gave them long Latin names, and sent them to other men of science as leaves and flowers of the very rare and curious trees which he had found. So he became famous as a great discoverer.

But soon afterwards another traveller, not learned but loving the beauty of the forest, went the same way and saw the same lordly trees. And at first he too thought he had never seen such trees before; but, looking at them closer and pulling the creepers and undergrowth aside, he saw that the trees were really of the same species as those which grew in his native land—such as the oak, chestnut, the elm and ash tree—only in a tropical climate they grew larger and more luxuriantly. The Botanist, when he heard of this, smiled scornfully and said: "That fellow knows nothing about trees. Did I not examine every branch and give the trees their proper names? Of course, the leaves and flowers I took were of the creepers and parasites; but the trees themselves are rotten and useless. The forest should be cut down, so that the soil may be ploughed and used for growing things that are useful and good for food."

And the King who ruled over all those lands, wishing to know the truth, for he was building a new city and wanted good timber for it, sent some of his servants who were learned in forest lore to inquire into the matter. And they came back to the King and said: "It is true, O King, that these trees are of the same kind as those we have always used for building in our country: they are very old, but sound and fit for use. The forest should not be cut down, for if the parasites, creepers and undergrowth which are spoiling the trees are removed, the forest will be of great value to the State and give good timber for building many cities." What the King did belongs to another story; but as he was a good and wise King, I do not think he had the forest cut down as the Botanist advised.

I must leave the interpretation of the parable to my readers. The present work only deals with city building incidentally, as part of a much greater subject—the history of the civilisation introduced into India by the Aryan race and its relation to empire-building. It does not profess to give more than an outline of its fundamental ideas. The materials dealt with are mainly those furnished by the ancient and medieval monuments of India—an open book for those who can read it, but one which has remained closely sealed for Europeans even to the present day. Fergusson, in his great pioneer work, "The History of Indian and Eastern Architecture," made an attempt to interpret it at a time when the difficulties of the subject were immeasurably greater than they are now. It says much for his genius as a historian that he seized at once the great cardinal truth stated so admirably in his introduction—one that cannot be repeated too often: "Architecture in India is still a living art, practised on the principles which caused its wonderful development in Europe in the twelfth and thirteenth centuries; and there, consequently, and there alone, the student of architecture has a chance of seeing the real principles of the art in action. In Europe, at the present day, architecture is practised in a manner so anomalous and abnormal that few, if any, have hitherto been able to shake off the influence of a false system and to see that the art of ornamental building can be based upon principles of common sense; and that when so practised the result not only is but must be satisfactory. Those who have an opportunity of seeing what perfect buildings the uneducated natives of India produce, will easily understand how success may be achieved; while those who observe what failures the best educated and most talented architects in Europe frequently perpetrate, may by a study of Indian models easily see why this must inevitably be the result. It is only in India that the two systems can be seen practised side by side—the educated and intellectual European failing because his principles are wrong, the feeble and uneducated native as invariably succeeding because his principles are right."

Fergusson did not always rise above prejudices which are as strong now as in his own day, and the keynote of his writings on Indian art was that "it cannot, of course, be for one moment contended that India ever reached the intellectual supremacy of Greece or the moral greatness of Rome." But, making allowances for this, the statement quoted above is as profoundly true in every respect now as when it was written over fifty years ago. If Fergusson's followers had taken it for their starting-point, they might have added much to our knowledge of one of the most important chapters of the world's history. But with a blindness characteristic of imitators they have quietly buried with his bones the one vital truth which illumines Fergusson's pages, and have only taken for their texts the fallacies which

Fergusson, if he had lived in the present day, would have been the first to reject—his classifications of "styles." The history of Indian architecture has therefore remained where Fergusson left it—not a history of Indian life, but a Museum of Antiquities wrongly labelled.

"Bureaucracy to me in India," said a distinguished historian of English politics, formerly Secretary of State for India, "is a great and splendid machine performing the most difficult task ever committed to the charge of any nation. Show me where it fails—no sensible man would hold it perfect in every respect—show me from day to day any point where bureaucracy has been at fault, and do you suppose I will not show my resentment at the fault and will not do all I can to remedy it?"[1]

There is much food for reflection in the fact that the abiding cause of the failings—such as they are—of bureaucracy in India has always been, and still is, its complete ignorance of Indo-Aryan history—the only history of India which really matters. It is an axiom in British Imperial administration to trust the man on the spot. In India he is the District Officer, the eyes and ears of the Government of India, dispensing British justice under the village banyan tree. His knowledge of India is certainlyextensive and peculiar—only his India is not Aryan India. It is aboriginal or prehistoric, Muhammadan India, and the India of the Government files. The India which counts most in history, Aryan India, is not on the file, and under these circumstances the District Officer would be more than human if he knew much of it.

It might be supposed that the educated Indian, born in an Indian village, must know his India if any one does. But neither is his point of view, as a rule, Indo-Aryan India. He does not read the open book of Indian art for himself—he trusts to the

[1] Mr. John Morley, M.P. (Lord Morley of Blackburn), *The Times* Parliamentary Report, Feb. 1, 1908.

Anglo-Indian interpretation of it. He learns his history mostly from official text-books, and if he is an official, from the Government files.

A bare recital of the historical fallacies which form the basis of European histories of India would fill a large volume, and the omission of essential facts another one. Perhaps one illustration will be sufficient. In the Session of 1913 the Under-Secretary of State for India, when presenting the Indian Budget to Parliament, explained that the chief difficulty of British government in India lay in the fact that the great mass of the people "still lived in the fifth century A.D." These words may express a profound historical truth, but only when taken in a sense the very opposite of that which they were intended to convey. Mr. Montagu wished to paint a picture of the Cimmerian darkness in which the Indian masses dwelt, but not to revive memories of the time when Indo-Aryan civilisation reached its zenith; when Vikrâmaditya, the hero of Indian romance and legend, had saved the liberties of Aryan India from the savage barbarians who were ravaging Europe; and when Indian culture was the inspiration of the civilised world. An impartial historian might well consider that the greatest triumph of British administration would be to restore to India all that she enjoyed in the fifth century A.D.

Many explanations have been given of the causes of Indian unrest, but none seem to take into account that which has always been the great disturbing cause in the history of India. It has never been a racial question. India has been as happy and contented under Scythian or Mogul rulers as under those of Aryan race. It has not been a religious question, for no people have been more open-minded in religious thought than Indians. But ever since the Aryans made India prosperous and content with the wonderful organization of their village communities and the splendid culture which grew out of them, those who have tampered with it, knowingly or ignorantly, have had to meet the active or passive resistance of all—to whatever race or sect they might belong—who had learned to love the freedom of Indo-Aryan institutions.

It may seem paradoxical to those who have been taught as schoolboys that the basis of Indian polity has always been what is called "oriental despotism," to speak of India as a land of freedom. "Oriental despotism" is one of those historical fallacies upon which British administrators of India are nurtured. Of despotism like that of Imperial Rome, or of the Greek Tyrants, there are very few recorded instances in Indian history, either before Muhammadan times or after. One was the Hun king, Mihiragula, but his tyranny was short-lived. His freedom-loving Aryan subjects rebelled and escorted him beyond the confines of India. Aurangzîb was a tyrant of the Western pattern. He threw India into chaos and shattered the Mogul Empire.

There were two things which most impressed the Greek Megasthenes in what he learnt of Indian politics as ambassador at the Court of Chandragupta Maurya—first, that "it was a great thing in India that all Indians were free," and, secondly, that the power of Indian kings was restrained by the "Five Great Assemblies" of the people. Taking into consideration that the Indian franchise was the franchise of intellect, not of wealth or physical force, and that it was limited to those who wore the sacred thread, *i.e.* the three highest castes and skilled craftsmen attached to the temple service, India, down to the time of Aurangzîb, probably enjoyed as much political liberty as any European country before the eighteenth century. Evidently the Indian system of serfdom seemed to Megasthenes like freedom compared with the helotage of Greece, and at its worst it may be questioned whether it was more cruel and tyrannical than the feudal system of Europe.

It is true that Indo-Aryan liberty was not of the crude Western type represented by the formula "Liberté, Égalité, Fraternité." It was liberty for every man, whether king or peasant, to follow his own Dharma—the Dharma being that which long tradition and the wisest of Aryan law-givers, who knew Indian history and the Indian people, had taught every man within the Aryan pale to regard as his duty to God, the State, his household, and himself. And the constitution which preserved this fine ideal of liberty was the Aryan miniature Republic, with its Council of Five, which was the political unit of Indo-Aryan Government.

The Dharma of Indian Emperors and Kings was to maintain this constitution. Those who did so were honoured as Aryans, whatever their race or religion might be. Those who trampled it underfoot, even those of the purest Aryan stock, were written down in Indian history as Mhlechchas—barbarians, and enemies of God and man. The Kshatriya warriors fought for this freedom—not merely for their cattle and pastures—as valiantly as their Western brothers fought at Marathon. No people were more willing to accept alien rule under these conditions. The Rajputs who defended Chitor heroically against Akbar, believing him an enemy of Aryan traditions, built him a throne as Vishnu's Vicegerent on Earth[1] when they knew him as their friend; and the Mogul dynasty had no more staunch and devoted adherents so long as it remained true to its Dharma.

The history of India is the history of Aryan institutions, traditions, and culture. But what does the Anglo-Indian historian say about them? He digs up the names of forgotten dynasties—of those who failed in their Dharma—but the "Imperial Gazetteer of India," in its summary of Indian

[1] In the Diwân-i-Khâs at Fatehpur-Sikri. See "Handbook to Agra and the Taj," by the author (Longmans).

history, does not even mention the Aryan village community. Indo-Aryan history has dropped off the official files. The same authority declares that there is little Indian sculpture to be called art after the fourth century A.D. Similarly in its history of Indian architecture, all of Fergusson's archæological categories of "styles" are cited as he arranged them, but the one vital truth which he told in his history—which should be written up in every Public Works Office and inscribed in letters of gold over the doors of Indian universities—that the Aryan tradition of building is still a living art in India—is suppressed.

Anglo-Indian bureaucracy is indeed a great and splendid machine, but the familiar proverb, *Humanum est errare*, is not yet written in its code. Sir George Birdwood, who for thirty years kept the conscience of the India Office in artistic matters, revealed the true spirit of bureaucracy when he declared that Fergusson had fixed "past all gainsaying"[1] the classification of Indian styles of architecture. Any official, unless he be of the highest rank, who impugns the accuracy of Indian history, as it is written officially, is viewed with suspicion and risks his prospects in Government service. My first venture on that desperate enterprise was to question the theory, asserted in official handbooks and propagated by Government museums and schools of art, that India never had a "fine art." This suggestion was received with mild surprise and scepticism, for the highest medical authorities had said that Indian artists were totally ignorant of anatomy and perspective. But as art teaching is never taken very seriously by British statesmen, it was not considered a very dangerous doctrine. So after many years Indian fine art has at last been put on the official file, and Mr. Abanindro Nath Tagore's recent discovery that India has a very perfect and practical system of artistic

[1] "Journal of the East India Association," January 1913, p. 22.

anatomy[1]—more practical than that which is taught in Western academies—has finally disposed of the old European misconceptions of that subject. Yet Western anatomy and perspective are still taught in Government schools as the correct formulæ for art education in India.

With greater rashness I called attention in 1901 to another error in the summary of the District Officer's knowledge of India, the statement in the then current edition of the "Imperial Gazetteer" that "the greatest industry in India, after agriculture, is the spinning and weaving carried on in power-loom mills." I showed, by facts and figures taken from the census of India, that this industry was of infinitely less economic importance to India than one which was omitted altogether from official statistics of industry, although carried on under the eyes of every District Officer—the village hand-weaving industry. That brought me into departmental disgrace at once. Only a sentimentalist and idealist would think of mentioning an industry which was moribund and doomed to disappear before the march of Western progress. What did 5,000,000 village hand-weavers matter when 350,000 coolies were working the latest Western machinery in the mills of Bombay and Calcutta? However, as the result of my indiscretion, during the last thirteen years some knowledge of the economics of Indian village life has been slowly trickling on to the official files.

Two years ago I made another offering at the shrine of Truth by calling public attention to the work of the living Indian master-builder, whose existence is ignored by the "Imperial Gazetteer." Departmentalism became seriously alarmed. He was not on the file—the District Officer had not seen him. He must be extinct, for Sir Lepel Griffin, K.C.S.I., when Agent to the Governor-General for Central India, had written that

[1] "Some Notes on Indian Anatomy," by Abanindro Nath Tagore, C.I.E. Published by the Indian Society of Oriental Art, Calcutta.

"the love for and practice of noble and beautiful architecture seems to have died out of India previous to the advent of the English."[1] Official experts said he was a figment of my imagination. And so he remained officially, until last year the Report of special investigations into the conditions of modern Indian architecture, undertaken at my suggestion before the question of the building of the new Delhi came into the arena, was published. The inquiry, though admittedly only a very superficial one, had proved that, so far from exaggerating the facts, I had understated the capacity of the modern Indian master-builder; for besides a quantity of fine building work in many different parts of the north of India, the Report revealed the fact that, under favourable conditions, Indian master-builders can build as well as, and better than, their forefathers did in the days of Shah Jahân. For in the very district which was Sir Lepel Griffin's field of observation, a mosque larger than the famous Jâmi' Masjid of Delhi, and, so far as it is completed, a finer work of art, is now in progress, designed and carried out entirely by Indian craftsmen.

Departmentalism, *more suo*, of course will belittle the importance of the revelation, as it did in the case of the hand-weaving industry; but the living Indian master-builder is now on the official file, though only as a "controversial subject"—for departmentalism is still incompetent to weigh artistic evidence, however convincing it may be to those who are able to do so.

Just as an Act of Parliament, however bad it may be, is law to all good citizens until it is amended or repealed, so the Indian Public Works system of building, based only upon inefficiency, ruinous to Indian craftsmanship and otherwise economically vicious—equally bad in art and science—will be defended by officials, as good officials, until the order is given

[1] Preface to "Famous Monuments of Central India."

to revise it. By the irony of fate, it seems quite probable that the *deus ex machinâ* who will secure this long-deferred reform for India will be the English craftsman who is now in revolt against a system which, as Ruskin said, makes him the most pitiful form of slave—a mere machine with its valves smoothed with heart's blood instead of oil, when he might be a living, progressive, and happy human being.[1]

In questioning the soundness of the historical basis upon which the statecraft of the British Raj is built, I am now venturing still further into the depths. The Indo-Aryan village community, which has dropped off the Government file, was many years ago a very thorny question. The agents of the East India Company were the first European officials to come into direct relations with the political organisation of Aryan India, so far as it had survived the chaos which followed the disruption of the Mogul Empire. It occupied the close attention of British officials until long after the events of 1857 brought India under the direct control of the Government of Great Britain. But during all the years it remained on the Government file, it was only regarded from one standpoint—the collection of revenue. The officials who occupied themselves with the subject knew as much, or as little, of Indian political history before Muhammadan rule as they do now. The religion and culture of the people they were dealing with were even less understood. Hinduism was to them an idolatrous superstition which all good Christians must wish to uproot, though as officials it was expedient to be tender with the feelings of the heathen. Indian art seemed strange and wonderful in its heathen way, but wholly incompatible with the ideas of decent, cultured, Christian gentlemen. It never occurred to them that the very institution with which they were tampering in a British businesslike way (and only with an eye to business) was the

1 "Lectures on Architecture and Painting," p. 128.

most sacred thing in India—the fountain head of all her culture and religion, that its plan was built into the fabric of Indian temples, and that its daily life and very name were consecrated in Indian religious ritual by the tradition of five thousand years.

And it has never since occurred to Anglo-Indian historians that the great upheaval of 1857, when Hindu and Musalmân joined in a desperate effort to overthrow the British Raj, probably had its root cause, not in greased cartridges, but in what seemed to the British official purely a matter of business. Or was it a mere coincidence that the years immediately before the Mutiny were those in which the agents of the East India Company were most active in dealing with this question, and when the effects of their activities were most keenly felt?

The net result of the organisation of Anglo-Indian administration effected since 1857 is that British officers, giving up their lives to India, working honestly and whole-heartedly for her good, according to their lights, rarely come into touch with Indo-Aryan civilisation except in the process of uprooting it, in which most of them are engaged. And the political reforms of recent years, from the grant of municipal self-government to the establishment of Legislative Councils, have been conceived in the same profound ignorance of the Indian point of view with which the art which reveals the people's innermost soul has been always regarded. Is it necessary to look further for the cause of Indian unrest? Is not that unrest merely a symptom that the ancient spirit of India—which by the law of heredity runs in the blood of every Indian man, woman, and child, though they may be unconscious of it—reviving under the benign influence of the *pax Britannica*, is beginning to reassert itself? If so, are legislative machines of Western pattern, constructed with a total disregard of Indian conditions, likely to allay Indian unrest, or to add fuel to the fire?

The fact that Indians who come into closest touch with

Europeans like these machines, just as they like gramophones, pianolas, oleographs, and other mechanical devices, may be taken too seriously. The renaissance of Indian culture, of which there are many evident signs, is indirectly the effect of British administration. It might become its greatest strength, if instead of the pinchbeck Imperialism and spurious Nationalism which are now so rampant everywhere, a wiser policy informed by the sympathetic study of Indian history and Indian traditions ruled the Councils of the Empire. At present both Anglo-India and Nationalist India are equally out of touch with the spirit which has ruled India for five thousand years, and still remains unaffected by two centuries of contact with Western materialism. If Anglo-India or the Calcutta University had awarded a prize for literature, open to the world, neither would have discovered a Bengali poet.

Lord Curzon at the end of his Viceroyalty, in an eloquent speech, declared that the highest aim of the Government of India was and had been the interest of the Indian peasant. That must be taken to be more a matter of intention than of achievement, otherwise the interest of the Indian village would have been considered before the interest of the town and city; the interest of the handicraftsman before the interest of the mill-owner; village culture before town culture; and the restoration of the real Constitution of India—the most perfect organisation of village life the world has known—would have been considered before the grant of Western forms of government which neither satisfy Indian aspirations nor are adapted to the genius of Aryan civilisation.

The Anglo-Indian argument against the extension of self-governing powers to the people of India is the so-called "illiteracy" of the Indian masses—another of the fallacies arising from the misapplication of Western standards to Eastern conditions. A people who have for thousands of years handed down an oral tradition of the highest philosophy and the finest literature are not illiterate; though they use not pen and ink, they are not less cultured or intelligent than the majority of those who enjoy the franchise in Western countries. But when their own instruments of culture are taken from them, and replaced by others which they cannot or will not use, they tend to become illiterate and uncultured both in an Eastern and Western sense. The Anglo-Indian pedagogue has been sterilising Indian soil, so that he may plant in it seeds of a Western culture which will not grow. The Anglo-Indian statesman digs up the roots of Indian civilisation and expects to maintain law and order upon principles totally foreign to the Indian mind. The Indian masses are unfitted for Western forms of self-government, and will remain so as long as the British Raj endures; but they are not unfitted for self-governing functions which their fathers (and mothers) exercised for countless generations while the British Raj was yet unborn.

The study of Indo-Aryan civilisation throws much needed light upon another vital question—Indian religion. Christianity will not suffer by a sympathetic attitude towards Indian religious convictions. Can the Christian teacher who regards his duty otherwise be said to be fulfilling his Master's mission in the Vineyard where Christ Himself laboured? It is a fatal misconception to consider Aryan India as idolatrous or polytheistic. No religion has been more careful to discriminate between the Symbol and the Reality behind it than that which has been taught by Indo-Aryan teachers; and if its principles have not been fully understood by the masses of the people, can it be said that Christianity has been more successful in this respect in its own special field? But that the teachings of Aryan India have been far more successful than is generally supposed is proved by a remarkable paragraph in the Indian

Census Report for 1901, one of those flashes of insight which occasionally appear in Anglo-Indian records. The Census Commissioner had asked the Superintendents to make special inquiries into the actual beliefs of the ordinary man, his standards of right and wrong, and his ideas of a Supreme Deity. The result is summarised in the words of Mr. Burn, I.C.S., one of the Superintendents, as follows:

"The general result of my inquiries is that the great majority of Hindus have a firm belief in One Supreme God, called Bhagwan, Parameshwar, Ishwar, or Narain. Mr. Baillie made some inquiries which showed that this involved a clear idea of a single personal God, and I am inclined to think that this is distinctly characteristic of Hindus as a whole."[1]

If Indian art throws any light upon Indian history, religion, sociology and the inner working of the Indian mind, it demands the careful study of all who are concerned in the administration of India, whatever their functions may be. One of the greatest artists of our age, M. Rodin, has truly said that the word "artist" in its widest acceptation means the man who takes pleasure in his work. My aims as an art teacher will be fulfilled if through my interpretations of Indian art I succeed in adding a new intellectual pleasure to Anglo-Indian work and in strengthening the bonds of sympathy between the Eastern and Western branches of that great Aryan family which has done so much for the advancement of civilisation.

June, 1914.

[1] Census Report for 1901, vol. i. p. 363.

Map of
INDIA
Shewing the Principal
Buddhist Localities.
Miles
KASHMIR
TIBET
Brahmaputra R.
Lhasa
SINDHU
GUJARAT
KACHH
SAURASHTRA
MALAVA
KOSALA
MAGADHA
KAMRUP
UTKALA
KALINGA
ANDHRA
MAHARASHTRA
KONKAN
CHOLA
KERALA
DRAVIDA
PANDYA
SINHALA
Kabul
Peshawar
Multan
Delhi
Benares
Patna
Tropic of Cancer
Rangoon
Pagan

THE ANCIENT AND MEDIEVAL ARCHITECTURE OF INDIA: A STUDY OF INDO-ARYAN CIVILISATION

CHAPTER I

THE MAURYAN DYNASTY AND THE FOUNDATIONS OF INDIAN CIVILISATION—INDIAN VILLAGE AND TOWN PLANNING

It is almost as difficult now as it was when Fergusson wrote to carry the starting-point of Indian architectural history much farther back than the reign of Asoka, 263-226 B.C., the famous emperor, missionary, and saint, who, after his conversion to Buddhism, then only one of many contending schools of Hindu thought, made it the state religion, and began that zealous propaganda of its doctrines which spread over Asia to the farthest east, and as far westwards as Alexandria. His grandfather Chandragupta, nearly sixty years earlier, had founded the Mauryan dynasty by consolidating the numerous republican confederations and petty kingdoms of Northern India, whose quarrels had made Alexander's opportunity, into an empire strong enough to bar further invasions from the north-west for many generations. Seleukos, Alexander's general, who seized the eastern portion of the Macedonian conquests after the death of the latter, made a vain attempt to repeat the glorious campaign in which he had assisted. Chandragupta Maurya not only drove him back across the Indus, but extended the north-western boundary of his own dominions so far as to include Kabûl, Herât, and Kandahâr, which formerly belonged to the empire

Alexander had wrested from Darius. This disaster made Seleukos anxious to come to terms with his Indian antagonist, and after sending one of his officers, Megasthenes, as an envoy to the Mauryan Court, he turned his arms westwards.

The account which Megasthenes has left of the splendour of Chandragupta's imperial capital, Pâtaliputra, the modern Patna in Eastern Bengal, are of little practical value to the architectural student.

The excavations recently undertaken, through Mr. Ratan Tata's public-spirited liberality, on the site of Pâtaliputra will doubtless produce material of great archæological interest, but they will never establish any new theory or confirm any old one concerning the origins of Indian art. These are already so decisively indicated by the great mass of material accumulated in many other places in India that the question whether Asoka or Chandragupta Maurya planned their palaces on Persepolitan models, or built them with foreign craftsmen, becomes entirely a side-issue and a matter of local interest only. It will doubtless be used as an argument for British architects in India importing modern Western methods of building—though there is a difference between those which stimulate the craftsman's ideas and those which sterilise them; but it is foolish to argue that Persepolitan fashions at Pâtaliputra prove that all the great art of India in early Buddhist times was inspired by foreigners—unless all Indians of Aryan race are to be classed as such.

We learn from Megasthenes that the imperial palace was planned on a grand scale like those of Sûsa and Ekbatana, that it was gorgeously decorated with gold and silver and placed in the midst of a fine garden with numerous water-ponds—a description which might apply equally well to the palaces of the Great Moguls. It is highly probable that Chandragupta, like his grandson, made considerable use of craftsmen from Persepolis or from Mesopotamia. Indeed, the latest discoveries of

Western scholars seem to make it necessary to abandon the theory that the early Aryan invaders of India were only nomads whose practice in the arts was chiefly confined to war and agriculture. If it be true—as the Russian scholar, Sheftelovich, asserts—that the Kassites, who took Babylon in 1746 B.C., and established a dynasty there which lasted 600 years, were Aryans speaking Vedic Sanskrit, whose chief god was Sûryas, Babylon must be regarded as a half-way house of the Aryan race in its march towards the Indus Valley, and some at least of the early Aryan tribes must have acquired, before they entered India, not only the high spiritual culture which is reached in the Rig Veda, but a prolonged experience of the civic arts, including architecture.

Recent German excavations on the site of Babylon show that the science of building in Vedic times had advanced much farther than has hitherto been suspected. The Babylonians had apparently perfected the construction of radiating arches centuries before Rome was founded, and it is probable that both Roman and Indian builders derived their knowledge of it from the same source in Western Asia. When the seat of imperial power was transferred from Persia to Eastern India in the fourth century B.C., it must have been as natural an inclination for Chandragupta Maurya to supplement local architectural talent at Pâtaliputra by bringing experts from Persepolis as it is for Anglo-Indian rulers in the present day to supersede it by experts from London—for Western Asia was the great culture-centre of the Indo-Aryan race.

But it is a great mistake of Anglo-Indian writers to assume that Indian building under the Mauryan dynasty was wholly, or even to a large extent, an importation of "styles" borrowed from Persepolis. Chandragupta and Asoka might set Persepolitan fashions in their palaces, just as Indian princes of to-day try to imitate the fashions of London and Paris; but

Indo-Aryan culture had already for many centuries planted itself deep in Indian soil, and Indo-Aryan building had acquired an Indian character as distinctive as that of Indo-Aryan philosophy and religious teaching. Just as at the present day one must look for all that is truly typical of Indian life and character in the village rather than in the town, in the same way the essential derivations of Indian architecture, in construction and in decoration, will be found not in imperial palaces, but in the life of the village folk.

The village in ancient India represented a highly organised social community, far removed from the decadent modern type. The Aryan, jealous of his tribal honour and proud of his social privileges, was, as the name implies, a born aristocrat; but his ideal of government was essentially democratic. Only the urgent necessity of national or racial preservation reconciled him to the life of great towns and a centralised form of government. The philosophy of the Vedas proclaimed the highest ideal of self-government, and Aryan philosophy was not an abstract speculative theory, but a practical formula of life. The teaching of Buddha, though it disputed the divine authority which the orthodox attributed to the Vedas, only gave to this formula a different interpretation and a wider application. It was a protest against sacrificial rites and the debasing practice of physical self-torture, through which certain Brahmanical sects sought to acquire spiritual wisdom and to inculcate habits of self-control; but it was in no way opposed to the esoteric teaching of Aryan philosophy. On the contrary, it laid the foundations of the latter on a wider footing and opened its doors to the whole world, instead of reserving it as the exclusive property of the Aryan race.

The great bulk of the population in early Buddhist times, says Professor Rhys Davids, or at least 70-80 per cent., lived in villages, and the entire literature of early Buddhism mentions hardly a score of towns of any considerable size as existing in the whole vast territory, from Kandahâr nearly to Calcutta, and from the Himâlayas southwards to the Run of Kutch.[1] Buddhism did not succeed any more than Christianity has done in effacing social and racial distinctions. The four varnas, or colours, representing so many ranks of social precedence, were recognised distinctions in early Buddhist village communities,[2] though the rigid barriers of the caste system did not exist. In spite of the colour bar, however, India's melting-pot long before the third century B.C. had profoundly altered the social and political conditions which prevailed when the Aryans were disputing with Dravidians, Kolarians, and with wild aboriginals classed as Rakshasas, or demons, for possession of the soil. The former had adapted themselves perfectly to their Indian environment, and had intermarried to such an extent with the civilised tribes which had preceded their immigrations or invasions, that it only needed the moving of a common spiritual impulse to make India a nation. And this impulse came from Asoka's propaganda of the teaching of Buddha.

We must, however, guard ourselves from the error of supposing that "Buddhist art," as Westerners call it, was purely sectarian, or anything else than Indian art during the ascendancy of Buddhism. Fergusson's classification of Buddhist, Jain, and Hindu temples as representing different epochs of art or different schools of artistic expression is entirely fallacious. In a village or town where Buddhists were in the majority, Buddhist shrines would naturally be the most numerous. In other localities, at the same time, Jains or followers of other sects would build similar shrines dedicated to their special divinities. Whatever school of religious doctrine the buildings might represent, the craftsmanship and principle of construction remained the same, and even the symbolism was a common vernacular language

[1] "Buddhist India," p. 50. [2] *Ibid.* chap. v.

employed by different sects to explain the special tenets of their respective cults. When a great ruler like Asoka exercised supreme political power over the greater part of India, the wealth of the state was naturally devoted to making the buildings of his especial sect of better and more expensive materials than those of others, and consequently the record of Buddhist building which survives to this day is more complete than that of the rival schools of religious thought which had to be content with less costly and less permanent building materials. But a town or village and the buildings therein, inhabited by Buddhists, Jains, or Brahmans, were never at any time in Indian history entirely differentiated by special characteristics of style. Buddhist art was at the same time and place also Jain art and Hindu or Brahmanical art. India has never known any style that can be called architectural but one—and that is Indo-Aryan.

Asoka's religious propaganda was no violent disturbance of the established customs and beliefs of his subjects: it was a policy of peaceful penetration in strict accordance with the spirit of Aryan philosophy, which proclaimed Truth to be a temple open on all sides to devout worshippers, who might choose the approach most accessible to them. Whatever Buddhism might have been as a school of philosophic speculation, Indian art of Asoka's time shows that as a popular religion it was a synthesis of contemporary Hinduism, as complete for the age to which it belonged as medieval Hinduism was for its own time. But as religion has always been essentially a part of Indian daily life, we must begin an account of the great religious architecture of India by trying to reconstruct, out of the meagre architectural records of the third century B.C., the practical planning and building of a typical Indian village. This can be done to some extent by making use of the clues given in the Hindu Silpa-sâstras, and in the sculptured representations of Indian buildings on the monuments of Asoka's time, and by comparing them with descriptions in Pâli records which Professor Rhys Davids has collected.[1]

We may take it for granted that just as the types of houses represented in the sculptures of Bharhut and Sânchî resemble in many respects the domestic buildings of modern India, so the planning of Indian villages laid down in the Mânasâra, the Silpa-sâstra[2] of which Râm Râz has given too brief a summary in his valuable essay on the architecture of the Hindus, does not differ in essential points from that which was followed in the third century B.C.

The Mânasâra Silpa-sâstra, anticipating Vitruvius, first insists upon the high intellectual and moral culture necessary for a master-builder (*stapathi*). "He should be conversant with all the sciences; always attentive to his work; of an unblemished character; generous, sincere, and devoid of enmity or jealousy." His first assistant, who might be his son or an apprentice, was the surveyor, or *sûtragrahi*, who must be particularly skilled in mathematics and obedient to his master. The next was the *vurdhaci*, or joiner, dexterous in joining wood and in combining other constructive materials with it. "He should be of a calm disposition, and acquainted with drawing and perspective."

It will probably be a revelation to modern architects to know how scientifically the problems of town planning are treated in these ancient Indian architectural treatises. Beneath a great deal of mysticism, which may be scoffed at as pure superstition, there is a foundation of sound common sense and scientific knowledge which should appeal to the mind of the European expert. The most advanced science of Europe has

[1] "Buddhist India," chaps. iii. and iv.

[2] The Silpa-sâstras were possibly compiled about the fifth or sixth century A.D., but the traditions they embody are of far greater antiquity.

not yet improved upon the principles of the planning of the garden cities of India based upon the Indian village plan as a unit.

For choosing the site of a village, the Mânasâra declares that a careful examination of its position and soil is first necessary. The best site is that which slopes towards the east, so as to get the full benefit of the first rays of the morning sun : those who have cultivated an Indian garden will appreciate the truth of this axiom. It should be near a stream running from left to right—the auspicious direction in which the sun moves across the sky—and the well-digger should be able to find water at a depth of about seven feet.[1]

The soil must be tested by its colour, smell, taste, appearance, and feel. Four different qualities were recognised—the first would be firm, of an agreeable odour, suitable for growing various kinds of shade and fruit trees, vegetables and flowers. Sites to be avoided were those inclined to the intermediate points, as N.E., N.W.; stony ground; that in which human graves, disused wells, caves, or refuse of any kind were found.

A rough practical means of testing the soil for the foundations was to dig a pit one *hasta* in depth, and then return the excavated soil into it. A stable foundation would be indicated by the soil at the top being higher than it was before; an indifferent one, if it were of the same level; a bad one, which must on no account be used, if the surface were lower.

When the site had been determined, the ground was ploughed over. A pair of oxen, of equal size and of the same colour, strong and without blemish, was chosen for the purpose. If they were to be found, oxen with white spots on the head and knees were particularly auspicious. They were decorated with gay trappings, and gold or silver rings were placed on

[1] It may be presumed that the time of the year would be during the monsoon or in the cold season.

the horns and hoofs. Then the master-builder himself, garlanded and dressed in clean garments, turned the first furrow. The rest of the work was done by labourers, or *sûdras*, hired for the purpose.[1] The oxen and the plough to which they were attached were the *stapathi's* perquisite.

The true position of the cardinal points having been carefully ascertained by means of the shadow of a gnomon, rules for the construction of which are given in the Silpa-sâstras,[2] the alignment of the main street of the village was marked out. The general planning of the larger villages followed that of the cosmic cross, and the so-called magic square, representing the four quarters of the universe; but the reader must not misunderstand this association of mysticism with the practical business of the Indian craftsman. All art in ancient India was held to be magic, and the magical virtues of these figures simply lay in the fact that the experience of many generations had proved that they were the best for purposes of defence and gave the most healthy, pleasant, and practical lay-out for an Indian village or town. The easterly axis of the plan ensured that the principal streets were purified by the rays of the sun sweeping through them from morning till evening; while the intersection of main streets by shorter ones running north and south provided a perfect circulation of air and the utmost benefit of the cool breezes.

The two principal streets which formed the arms of the

[1] The distinction made in the Mânasâra between the *stapathi* and *sûdras* is one of the many evidences which might be cited to show that skilled craftsmen in ancient and medieval India took a much higher social position than that assigned to them in modern times. Literary references to handicraftsmen as *sûdras* must be taken to mean unskilled labourers only. The *stapathi*, in this case, was the officiating priest, and it is significant that the hereditary caste craftsmen of Southern India, who add "Achary" (religious teacher) to their name, wear the sacred thread and do not employ Brahmans for their religious ceremonies. The Râmâyana also states that the craftsmen who carved the sacrificial posts at the Vedic sacrifices were honoured equally with the officiating priests.

[2] See Râm Râz, pp. 19-22.

cosmic cross were broad avenues, probably planted with umbrageous trees. The long one, running east and west, was called *Râjapatha*—King's Street; the short one, which pointed north and south, was *Mahâkala*—Broad Street, or otherwise *Vamana*—South Street—from the name of the mythical ele-

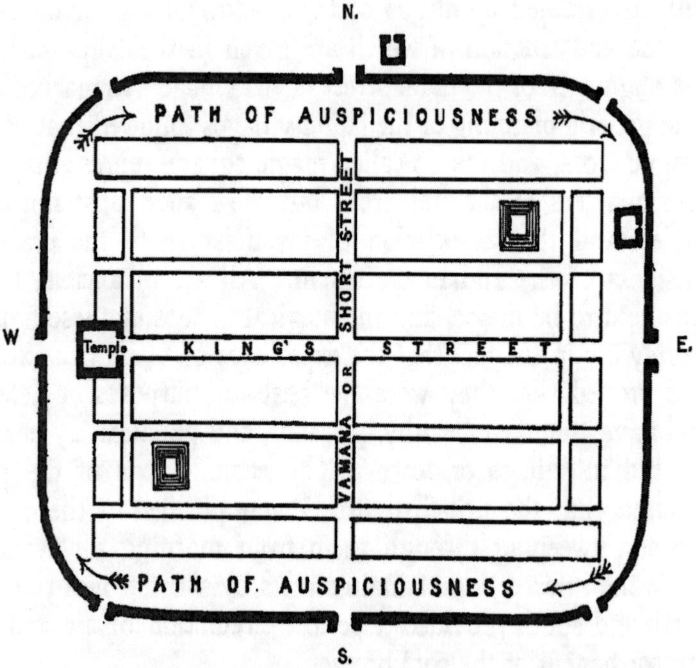

FIG. 1.—Village Plan called *Dandâka* (corrected from Ram Raz, Pl. XLIII).

phant which represented the south quarter.[1] The road or wide path running round the village inside the wall or stockade was called *Mangala-vîthî*—the Way of Auspiciousness, or Good

[1] The elephant was the rain-cloud which came with the south-west monsoon. Vamana was also the short arm of the cosmic cross—otherwise Vishnu's dwarf incarnation—the apparent distance between the sun at its zenith and its nadir being less than that between sunrise and sunset, or the long arm of the cross. This street could, therefore, also be anglicised as "Short Street."

Fortune; this being the path by which the village priests went daily in performance of the rite of *pradakshinâ*, or circumambulation. *Mangala* has also a secondary meaning as an epithet of Karttikeya, the god of war. In this sense the name refers to the use made of the road by the village or town sentinels whose watchfulness ensured the safety of its inhabitants from hostile attacks.

The centre of the village, at the intersection of the two main streets (fig. 2), was the recognised meeting-place for the Council of Elders which regulated local affairs. A banyan or a pîpal tree planted on a mound sufficed for the mote-house or assembly-hall, except when the village was a large one, and could afford a pillared *mandapam*, or a pavilion of wood, brick, or stone.

In this ancient Aryan village custom one can trace the root of the idea of the Bodhi tree, or Tree of Knowledge; for the tree of the village elders must have been associated with the wisdom of sages long before the forest tree became the place of meditation for the yogi who sought spiritual enlightenment. A symbolic or mystic meaning also attached itself to the Council tree; for, planted at the centre of the cosmic cross, it was the Tree of Vishnu—the sun at noon and the all-pervading cosmic force. It stood for the mystic tree of which the sun and moon and stars were fruits and the blue vault of heaven the foliage.

In a small village the Council tree, or Tree of Justice, would give sufficient shelter for the general meeting of the householders, who formed the Parliament of the Indo-Aryan village. They had the power of nominating all the Ministers—the Council of Five—except the headman, whose office was hereditary, but who could be deposed by the Râja, the head of the clan, in case of any grievous offence against the laws of the Aryan community. In larger villages and towns the meeting-place of this general assembly would be in the parks or groves of sacred trees planted near the gates.

The Mânasâra gives the maximum width of the main village streets as 5 *dandas.*[1] The others varied in width from 1 to 5 dandas. The size of a single cottage was reckoned as from 24 feet by 16 feet to 40 feet by 32 feet. They were generally grouped together by fours, so as to form an inner square or quadrangle: the "magic" of the square depending on the fact that it afforded the best protection for the cattle of the joint household when they were driven in from the pastures every evening.

Four cottages combined into a single habitation, with its own inner courtyard, was the next step in the evolution of the Indian house-plan. Such a house might belong to the chief herdsman, who was an important personage in the Aryan village communities, or to the headman of the village, both of which positions were hereditary. This was the derivation of a house-plan, eminently practical and suitable for a tropical climate, which is still universal in India for all classes, from the well-to-do ryot to the Maharajah, except when Indians prefer to make their surroundings uncomfortable and insanitary by adopting building fashions appropriate only for European climatic and social conditions.

Just as the single cottage, or village hut, formed the unit of house-planning, so the village plan was the unit used to form the *mahalla*, or ward, in town planning.[2] The Mânasâra recognises forty different classes of villages and towns, according to the extent of the lands owned by them; commencing with a village-unit which was 500 dandas, or 4,000 feet square, so that

[1] A *danda*, rod or pole = 8 feet.

[2] The city of Jaipur, laid out by a Bengali architect in the eighteenth century, is the best known example of a modern Indian city planned in accordance with the ancient Hindu traditions. See "Indian Architecture: its Psychology, Structure, and History," p. 216, fig. 49.

the extent of the largest cities would be 20,000 dandas, or about 30 English miles square. Of this area about one-third was devoted to building space, and the rest to the agricultural lands owned by the community, It should be observed that neither a village nor a town was usually square in plan, but a rectangle, with the long sides running east and west, so as to secure a proper circulation of air even in the largest cities. In the description of Ayodhya given in the Râmâyana, the proportion between its breadth and length is as one is to four. Pâtaliputra was about 9 miles in length and 1½ miles in breadth. Hindu Gaur was also a long rectangle. One of the long sides generally faced a lake or river, an arrangement which provided bathing facilities for all the inhabitants, and obviated the necessity of building defensive works all round.

It will be interesting to examine in detail some of the village plans, of which eight standard types are given in the Mânasâra.[1]

The simplest one (fig. 1), called *Dandâka*, after the staff carried by *sannyâsins*, was specially intended for a hermitage (*asrâm*) or other religious community. It consisted of from one to five long parallel streets running east and west, with three shorter ones intersecting them in the middle and at the two ends. There were two bathing-tanks near the N.E. and S.W. angles of the village, and various shrines appropriate for the particular sect to which the villagers belonged—the principal one being placed at the west end of the Râjapatha, with its entrance facing the rising sun. Minor deities had their temples on the outskirts of the village, outside or inside the wall or fence, which had four large gates facing the two main streets, and smaller ones at the angle of the village. It contained from twelve to over three hundred houses. In the given plan each of the eight inside blocks had two rows of houses; the narrower outside blocks only one.

[1] Râm Râz, "Essay on the Architecture of the Hindus," p. 42.

The plan (fig. 2) called *Nandyâvarta* (the abode of happiness) was named after the mystic figure upon which it was based (fig. 3). It was intended to accommodate a mixed population of different social grades, or belonging to different religious

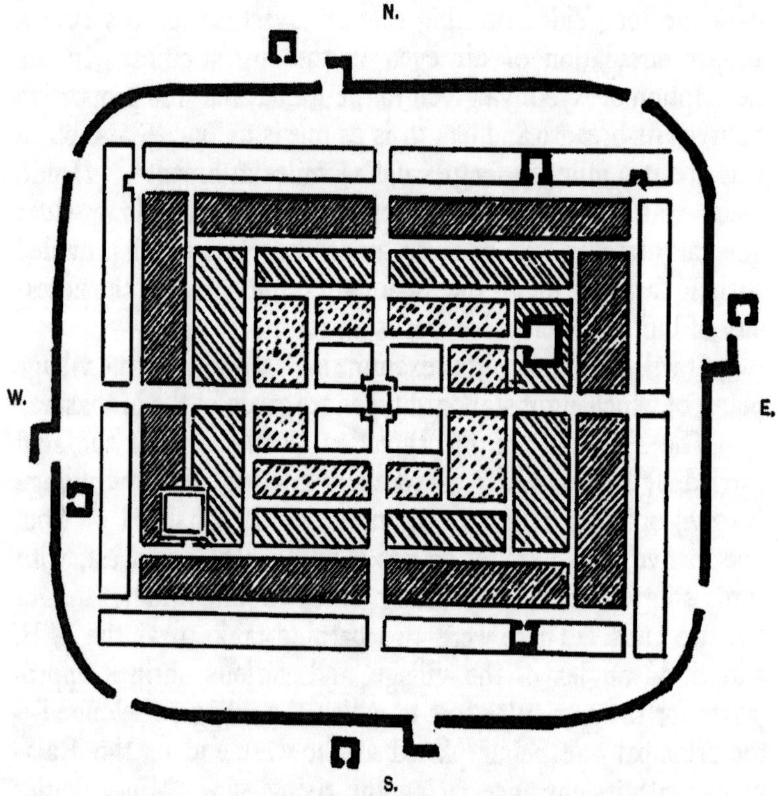

FIG. 2.—Village Plan called *Nandyâvarta* (corrected from Râm Râz, Pl. XLIV).

sects, *e.g.* Brahmans of four different schools, in which case the village had the affix *-mangalam*, or people of the four *varnas*, when the affix was *-puram*.[1] The arrangement of the different

[1] *Mangalam* means auspicious, and *puram* a fort. The implication seems to be that the Brahman village was protected by its own virtue, while the lay community defended itself by force of arms.

social grades is shown by the relative depth of shading in the plan; the highest class, in the centre of the village, occupying the four blocks which are left unshaded.

The outer blocks of houses, to which Râm Râz makes no reference, were probably the bazars placed near the gates of the town or village, both for convenience and for the purpose of collecting tolls. In the Umagga Jataka there are frequent references to the four bazars placed at the north, south, east, and west, and serving their respective quarters in the King's city. The two main streets, as always, formed the cosmic cross. In the centre of the village, at the meeting of the crossways, was, says the Mânasâra, the auspicious place for the assembly-hall, or for a temple of Brahmâ, which had four entrances.

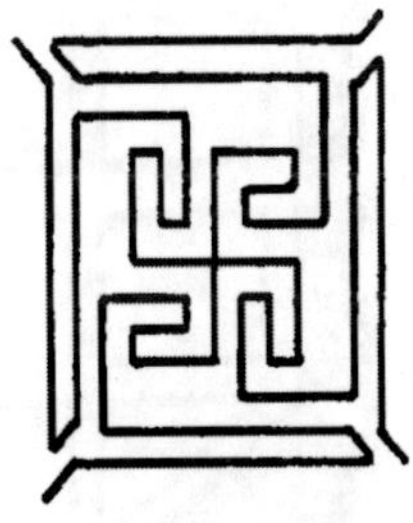

FIG. 3.—The Symbolic Figure Nandyâvarta.

The Nandyâvarta type of village contained a great number of shrines dedicated to various deities, for the location of which the Mânasâra gives minute directions.[1] This part of the subject will be considered more fully in another chapter.

The plan called *Padmâka* (fig. 4), after the lotus leaf, is interesting as showing how sedulously Indian town-planners avoided the inauspicious lay-out in which the main streets run upon diagonal lines in the direction of the intermediate points of the compass, the objections to which are not merely sentimental.[2] A plan with streets radiating in all directions from the centre of the village, like the spokes of a wheel, would be the first to suggest itself to an Indian designer, on account of its symbolism. He avoided it for very practical

1 Râm Râz, "Essay on the Architecture of the Hindus," pp. 45-6.

2 When the European experts who have planned the new Delhi are better acquainted with Indian conditions, they will, I hope, eliminate the features in their preliminary scheme which will make the lay-out of the imperial city inauspicious in Indian eyes.

reasons. First, that it was bad for purposes of defence, as it gave an enemy many opportunities of establishing himself in the centre of the village by a sudden raid. Secondly, that it tended to congestion of traffic, and an uncomfortable plan of house and

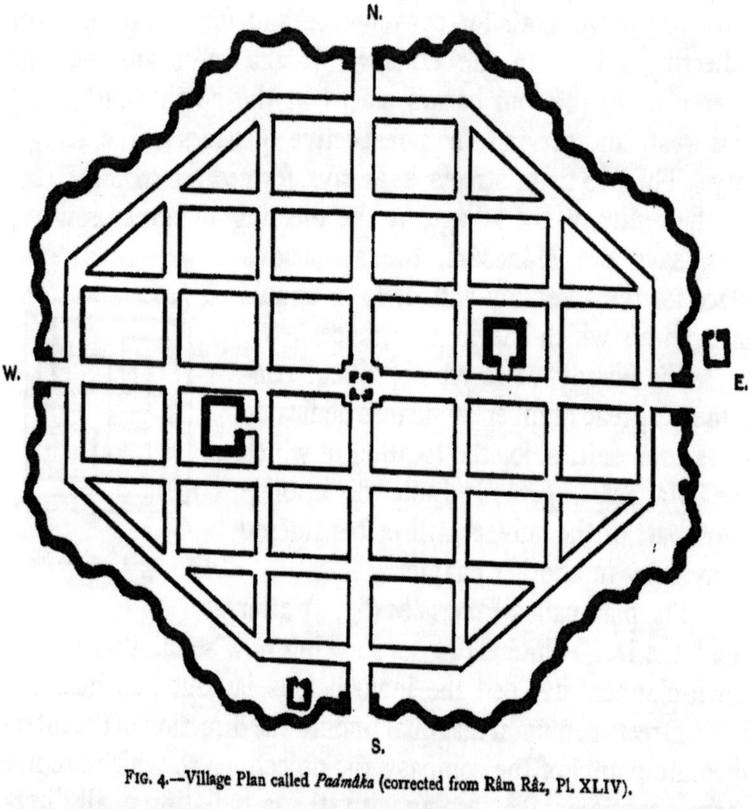

FIG. 4.—Village Plan called *Padmâka* (corrected from Râm Râz, Pl. XLIV).

garden, especially in the middle of the village. Thirdly, that the streets would mostly run in the wrong direction for the sun.

Another interesting village plan was based upon the *Swastika*, the mystic sign derived from the "magic square," which, as stated above, represented the four quarters of the world and of the universe. The magic of the swastika lay in the fact that in the Aryan military camp it was a formation used for defending the four gateways; it was also the Indo-Aryan religious compass, indicating the apparent movement of the sun across the heavens, which movement still forms part of Hindu

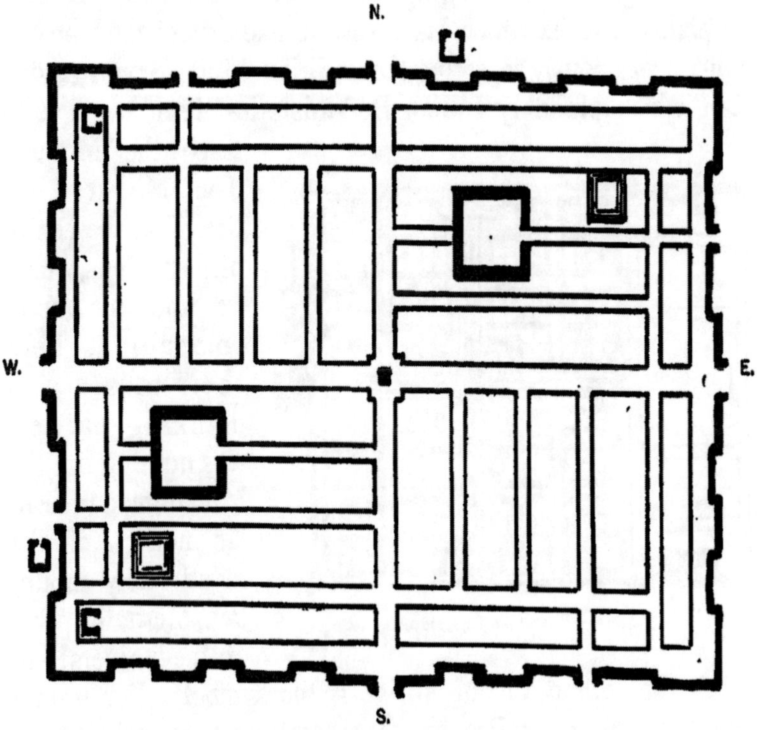

FIG. 5.—Village Plan called *Swastika* (corrected from Râm Râz, Pl. XLV).

religious ritual in the performance of *pradakshinâ*, or the circumambulation of a shrine, keeping the right side towards it. Philosophically the sign represents the principle of evolution; the reverse sign, associated with black magic and representing involution, was adopted by certain schools of Hindu philosophy. In this plan the direction of the blocks of houses in each quarter of the village indicated the movement from left to right.

A comparison of the planning of the Tâj gardens (fig. 6) with these ancient Indian village plans will make it clear that when Babar began to lay out his fourfold field-plot at Agra he was not, as he evidently thought (and as Anglo-Indians of the present day believe), bringing fresh ideas to revive the parched-up plains of India which his ancestors had devastated; he was only unconsciously repeating the traditional Indo-Aryan garden plan, which probably Indian Buddhists had been the first to teach the Moguls. The "Mount of Felicity" in the centre of his gardens, where he and his boon companions held their music and drinking parties, was nothing but the Muhammadan secular notion of the mystic holy mountain, Meru, the pivot of the universe, of which the Indian Vishnu shrine is the symbol. For untold centuries before the Prophet of Mecca was born it had been the high place upon which the Indian village council tree was planted. One may even admit the possibility that the irrigated garden plan might have been a more ancient idea than the other; that the Indo-Aryan village took the lay-out of the garden plot as the basis of its organisation. But more probably the village scheme was originally the plan of the military camp of the Aryan tribes when they first established themselves in the valley of the Indus.

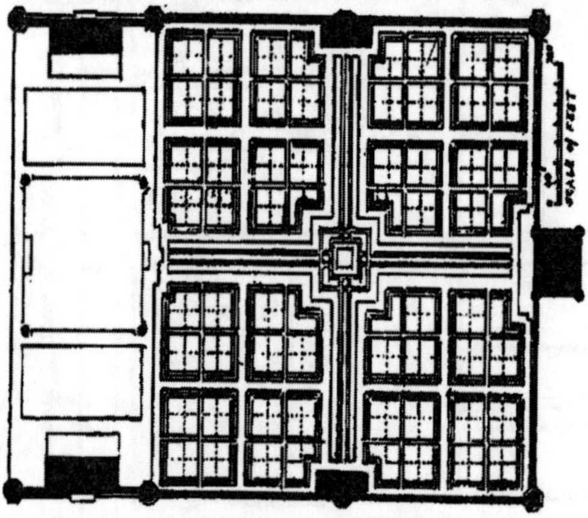

FIG. 6.—Plan of the Tâj Gardens.

PLATE I

A

B

INDIAN COTTAGES (*circa* 250 B.C.)

(*From the Bharhut reliefs*)

CHAPTER II

BUILDING BYE-LAWS—VILLAGE DWELLINGS—THE ASSEMBLY-HALL—THE ADMINISTRATION OF VILLAGES AND TOWNS—CONSTITUTIONAL GOVERNMENT IN ANCIENT INDIA—VILLAGE WALLS AND GATEWAYS

AMONG the building bye-laws laid down in the Mânasâra are the following: "Schools and buildings for religious study should be erected at the angular points of villages," *i.e.* they should be in the quietest places, out of the main traffic and near the least-used entrances of the village. A *dharamsâla* for travellers and pilgrims, with water and other accommodation, ought to be built at the S.E. approach to the village.

"Private houses or mansions may consist of from one to nine stories; but this is to be determined by the rank of the person for whom they are built. The lower classes must never construct their houses of more than a single storey."

"As far as practicable the height of buildings in the same street should correspond. Buildings of the same number of stories should correspond in height."

"The front, middle, and back doors of a house should be on the same level, and in a straight line with each other. The outer door should be placed not exactly in the middle of the façade, but a little to one side. The usual rule is that in a house ten paces in length, the entrance should be between five on the right and four on the left. The same rule should be observed in the gates of temples. A *vedikâ*,[1] or raised seat, should be constructed on each side of the door."

The quaint representations of buildings given in the Bharhut and Sânchî sculptures will give some idea of the aspect of Indian villages and towns in the third century B.C.; but one must not suppose that the sculptures of two stûpas in places not very far apart exhausted all the types of building then current in India. At the same time Asoka's vigorous propaganda of Buddhism, having Pâtaliputra as its centre, certainly had the effect of spreading the culture of the Magadha country over a great part of India, and the Buddhist Emperor's extraordinary building activity must have created a great demand for Bengali master-builders, and thus have established the reputation which they had even in Akbar's time.[2] There is unmistakable evidence of their handiwork in many parts of ancient India.

The commonest type of village dwelling shown in the Bharhut Sculptures (Pl. I) is, like those of the present day, a very simple structure and apparently built of sun-baked clay. We can gather from the descriptions in the Râmâyana of the hut built for Râma in his forest exile that the typical Indian cottage was then divided into four rooms, like the quarters of the whole village. The entrance, with double doors in the middle, as shown in Pl. I, A, opened into the quadrangle formed by a block of three or four single cottages, owned by different members of one family, in which the cattle which was their joint property took shelter by night. When there were only three cottages, the fourth side of the quadrangle was closed by a wall with a door or gateway in it. In the illustration (A) a woman stands in the quadrangle holding a basket into which a

[1] Vedikâ meant, originally, ground prepared for Vedic sacrifices with the sacred *kusha* grass, or the altar of sacrifice itself. Hence a seat for the gods or for honoured guests.

[2] The Aîn-i-Akbari, describing Akbar's buildings at Agra, refers to "the beautiful designs of Bengal and Gujerat."

PLATE II

A. THATCHED COTTAGE, FRONT VIEW

B. THATCHED COTTAGE, SIDE VIEW

C. INTERIOR OF THATCHED ROOF, SHOWING BAMBU CONSTRUCTION

D. ENLARGED DETAIL, SHOWING BAMBUS AND MATTING UNDER THE THATCH

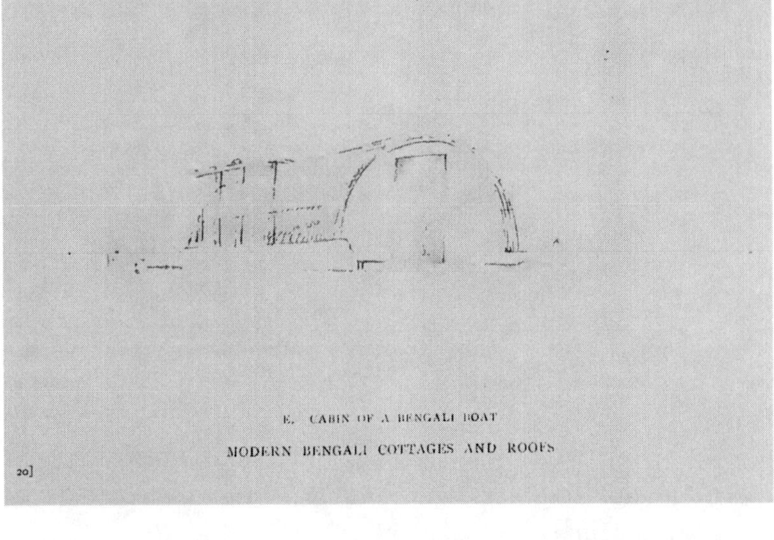

E. CABIN OF A BENGALI BOAT

MODERN BENGALI COTTAGES AND ROOFS

grain-seller is emptying a measureful. Outside, his assistant is waiting with his load of two baskets slung on a pole. There is a small window in the centre of the gable wall, and a larger one beneath it. The rooms of the front cottage, on either side of the doorway, are also lighted by windows in the centre.

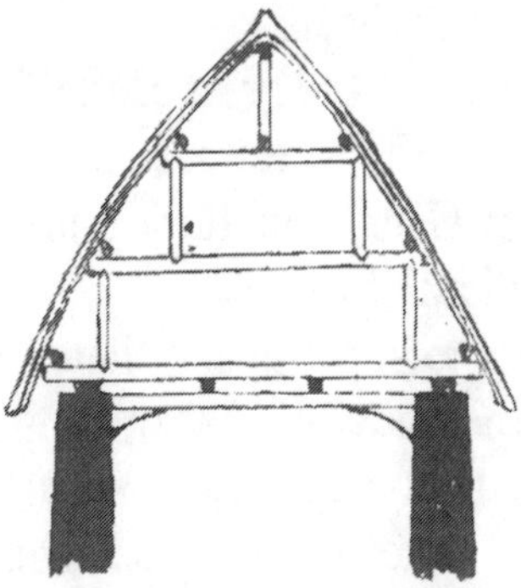

FIG. 7.—Seven-raftered Bambu Roof of Modern Thatched Bengali Cottage.

The roofs of the cottages at Bharhut are barrel-shaped, with semicircular gables, as in Pl. I, B, or built with pointed gables as in fig. A of the same plate. The exact material used to cover them is not quite clear, but similar forms of roof and the methods of construction applicable to them survive in the Bengali thatched cottage of the present day (Pl. II, and figs. 7 and 8).

It is necessary to explain that the peculiar double curvature given to these Bengali roofs and the drawing-out of the eaves at the four corners of the cottage are not mere freaks of the unpractical Oriental builder, but thoroughly scientific inventions designed for throwing off heavy rain. A thatched roof of the straight-lined European type could hardly be made water-tight for a long time in the torrential monsoon rains of the lower Ganges valley. The same reason applies to the more permanent roofs of brick and plaster, designed on similar lines, used in the old temples and mosques of Bengal.

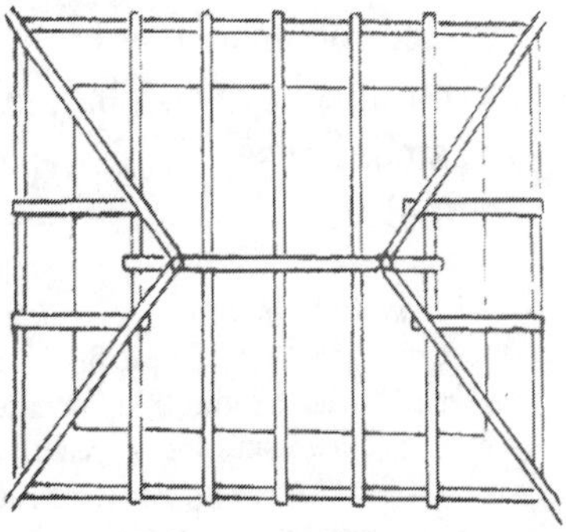

FIG. 8.—Plan of Fig. 7.

The progressive European, rather than learn anything from the Hindu builder, endures patiently the leaky roofs which the British engineer puts over his head in the plains of Bengal. It is enough for him that they are British, or as near British as the ignorant Hindu can make them.[1]

The derivation of the vaulted roofs of the great Buddhist chapter-houses, the stone vaults of Akbar's Rajput master-builders, and those of the mosques at Gaur, from these Indian village prototypes is quite easy to follow.[2]

I think, however, it is a great error to suppose that thatched or wooden roofs were universal in the India of Asoka's time, merely because the sculptures of Bharhut, Sânchî, and Amarâvatî give no indication of any other. Professor Rhys Davids tells us that the old Pâli writings describe great houses with a flat roof called the *uparî-pâsâdatala*, "where the owner sat, usually under a pavilion, which answered the purpose at once of a drawing-room, an office, and a dining-hall."[3] Such houses—with the entrance through a large gateway, to the right and left of which were storehouses leading into an inner courtyard surrounded by living-apartments—correspond exactly with the terraced-roof mansions of modern Rajputana; and there is every reason to believe that in localities where wood was scarce, brick and stone houses of this type were built in Asoka's time as they are to-day.

[1] It would be interesting to know how much is spent annually by the Public Works Department and by municipalities in Bengal in repairing roofs of official buildings "designed" after the regulation departmental patterns which the Bengali builder has to copy; and the annual average rainfall inside the roofs of these buildings would be the most curious of meteorological records, as I have had occasion to observe.

[2] See below, p. 91. Compare the sketch of the interior of a five-raftered Bengali thatched roof (Pl. II) with the vaulting of the Sonâ Masjid, Gaur ("Indian Architecture," Plate XLIII, A); and the plan of the seven-raftered roof, fig. 8, with that of the stone-vaulted roof of the Buland Darwâza, Fatehpur-Sîkrî ("Indian Architecture," p. 166, fig. 39), or with the roof of Ibrahîm's tomb at Bijâpûr, *ibid.* Pl. LXXXVII.

[3] "Buddhist India," pp. 68-9.

PLATE III

A. "THE PALACE OF THE GODS," BHARHUT SCULPTURES

B. A MODERN HOUSE, RAJPUTANA

ANCIENT AND MODERN HOUSES IN RAJPUTANA

Three-storied houses or palaces are frequently represented in Asokan sculpture. The general arrangement of the " Palace of the Gods " (Pl. III, A), which may be taken for a crude representation of a typical Indian mansion about 250 B.C., does not differ much from that of a well-to-do family house in modern Rajputana. There are the familiar *chhajas* (verandah roofs used as cornices), to protect the walls from rain and the burning heat of the midday sun, which are so conspicuous a feature in modern Indian buildings. The lower storey has open verandahs with the vedikâ, where the men of the household can sit to transact business or converse with their friends. The first floor has balconies with Bengali arches and screened openings, where doubtless the ladies sat as they do in the India of to-day. The upper storey, or attic, corresponds to the modern Rajput open-terraced roof, with its domed pavilions, or *chhattris*, only here the chhattri apparently covers the whole roof. It is probable that houses of this type were built in the third century B.C., not only in towns, but in the larger villages, whose inhabitants belonged to the higher classes of Indo-Aryan society.

Besides domestic and religious buildings, the Indian village, as before mentioned, had sometimes its Assembly-hall or Mote-house, where the village council met, as well as school buildings and rest-houses for travellers and pilgrims. These were generally pillared pavilions, which were the prototypes of the Dîwân-i-Âm, or public audience-hall, of the Mogul Emperors. A double-storied pavilion of this kind from the Bharhut sculptures is shown in Pl. IV, A. In this case the building is a religious one, but it must be remembered that all Indian religious buildings had their secular or domestic prototypes. A royal audience-pavilion of about the seventh century A.D., from a fresco at Ajantâ (Pl. IV, B), with a chhaja[1] and flat roof,

[1] The stone or wooden chhaja is derived from the bambu-and-mat or thatched lean-to roof of a verandah.

closely resembles the Mogul palace buildings of the sixteenth and seventeenth centuries.

Though the ancient Indo-Aryan village was essentially a self-governing community, managing its own domestic concerns and only paying to a central authority the customary *vali*, or tribute, due to it, the principle of co-operation for the purpose of carrying out larger public works which were beyond the means of single villages was always recognised. Not only were the village artisans liable to be called upon for the King's service in war or peace, but the villages united of their own accord to build assembly-halls, pilgrims' rest-houses, and irrigation works, to lay out and plant public parks, and to keep in order the main roads of the district.[1]

The wonderful organisation of Chandragupta's empire, of which Megasthenes gives us glimpses, was not the creation of the Mauryan statesmen, but the centralisation of the social and economic activities of the self-governing Indo-Aryan village communities. Pâtaliputra itself was only an aggregation of Indian villages joined together by spacious parks (the sacred groves) and stately avenues. The administration of the city by a board of thirty commissioners,[2] divided into six committees of five members each, was only an enlargement of the elected *panchâyat*, or Council of Five, assisted by a staff of permanent officials—the headman, accountant, watchman, banker, master-craftsman, schoolmaster, story-teller, and musicians—by which every Indo-Aryan village managed its own affairs. An inscription of the tenth century A.D., lately discovered in Southern India, prescribes the qualifications of voters and the mode of election for a municipal commission, similar to that of Chandragupta's city, consisting of thirty members—one for each ward of the town.[3]

[1] Rhys Davids, "Buddhist India," p. 49.

[2] See Vincent Smith's "Early History of India," pp. 125-7.

[3] See *infra*, pp. 172-4.

PLATE IV

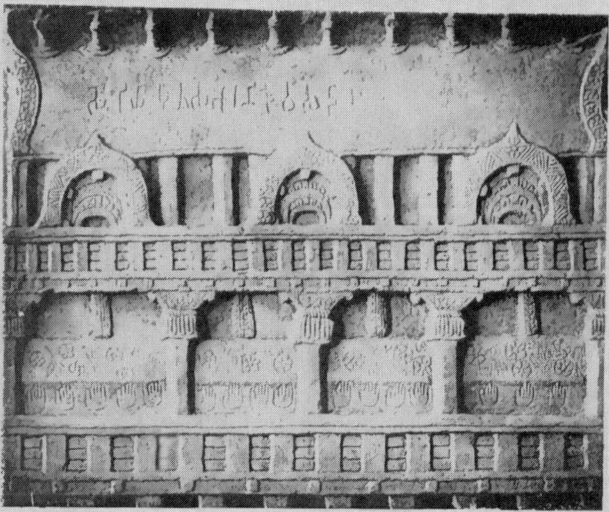

A. DOUBLE-STORIED PAVILION, BHARHUT SCULPTURES

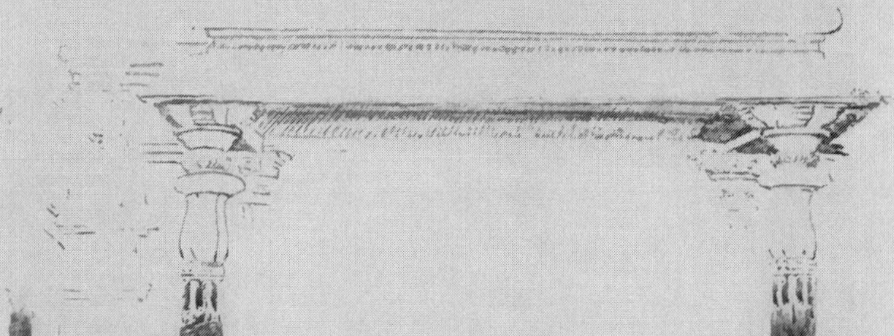

B. WOODEN PAVILION, FROM A FRESCO-PAINTING AT AJANTĀ

PILLARED PAVILIONS IN ANCIENT INDIA

24]

The King's Road, which ran from Pâtaliputra to the north-west frontier of India, was the main highway of commerce, linking together the hundreds of single villages planned on the principles of the Silpa-sâstras, which lay between the seat of the central government and the farthest confines of the empire. It was not the work of Chandragupta's government, but of the Indo-Aryan village communities. And there can hardly be any doubt that the construction of the great irrigation works of Chandragupta's time, and all the regulations for using them and keeping them in order, were natural developments of the traditional organisation of these communities, and not any new departure in the economic life of India.

For imperial administrative and political purposes villages in ancient and medieval India were grouped together in tens, twenties, hundreds, and thousands, each group acknowledging a Râja—the over-lord or chief of a tribe—whose duty it was to protect the village lands and the public roads under his control from robbers and to defend them from other enemies, in return for which each village or group of villages paid him a certain *vali*, or tribute. But the principle of mutual obligation between the rulers and ruled was recognised to such an extent that in case the officers of the over-lord who were responsible for public safety failed to detect and punish offenders, the overlord himself was expected to make good from his treasury any loss which individuals or the community might suffer. Whether this obligation was generally fulfilled by the central authority is another matter—the fact that this was one of the implications in *noblesse oblige* shows that the democratic principle of government was fully understood in ancient India.

The duty of loyal devotion to the supreme authority, which is always strongly insisted upon in the sacred literature of India, was something quite different to the Western notion of the divine right of kings. The principle of constitutional government for which the nations of Europe struggled throughout the Middle Ages until the present day was the essence of Indo-Aryan policy. The King was the Vicegerent of Vishnu on earth in so far and as long as he remained the constituted Defender of the Faith—of the laws, customs, and religion of Aryan civilisation.

The English schoolboy is taught to believe that all Oriental monarchs were like Darius of Persia, and that the Greeks were the sole defenders of liberty against Oriental despotism. The Indo-Aryans were not only lovers of freedom, like their Western brethren, but they asserted the principle of constitutional monarchy in their Magna Chartas and Acts of Parliament much more strongly than the subjects of European sovereigns succeeded in doing until quite modern times. "Holy sages," says Manu, the great Indo-Aryan law-giver, "consider as a fit dispenser of criminal justice that king who invariably speaks truth, who duly considers all cases, who understands the sacred books, who knows the distinctions of virtue, pleasure, and riches. Such a king, if he justly inflict legal punishments, greatly increases these three means of happiness; but punishment itself shall destroy a king who is crafty, voluptuous, and wrathful. . . . Punishment shall overtake his castles, his territories, his peopled land, with all fixed and movable things that exist on it; even the gods and the sages who lose their oblations will be afflicted and ascend to the sky." [1]

For purposes of military defence the capital towns and villages commanding strategic points were fortified. The Ummagga Jâtaka throws a sidelight on the relationship between Indian villages and their Râjas from the military point of view. In this legend of the Buddha's former births the Râja's first order before starting off on a warlike expedition was:

[1] "Institutes of Hindu Law," translated by S. G. Grady, chap. vii. sect. 26-9.

PLATE V

NORTHERN GATEWAY OF THE SÂNCHÎ STÛPA

"Go and build villages on the line of march!" When the Bôsat, his minister, had finished his preparations he said to the Râja, "'Great King! wait not a moment on the road, but advance immediately. I have already built villages for you at intervals of seven yodunas, established halting-places, and filled the hundreds of villages that are on the way with clothes and ornament, food and drink. I have kept elephants, horses and vehicles ready for you in those villages. When you go from one village to another leave behind in each successive village the unserviceable beasts and vehicles and take others in place of them.'"[1]

The shrines and other religious buildings of the ancient Indian village will be dealt with in subsequent chapters. The wall or stockade which enclosed the village must now be described. According to the importance of the village and the locality to which it belonged we may consider it to have been built of clay, wood, bricks, or stone, or a combination of these materials. Outside it was defended by a thicket of thorny shrubs and one or more moats, filled with water or sand; inside a broad path was kept, both for defensive purposes in case of hostile attacks, and, like the procession path of the Buddhist temple or stûpa, for the circumambulatory rite of the villagers—laymen as well as priests.

Of stone-built walls, such as an ancient Indian fortified village or town possessed, there is an extant example older than the sixth century B.C. in the hill-fortress of Giribbaja, near the modern Rajgir, said to have been planned by a master-builder called Mahâ Govinda.[2] Those represented in ancient Indian sculpture are sometimes of brick, but more usually of wood. The latter description are known by archæologists as "Buddhist's rails"—the label given to them by Fergusson which

[1] "Ummagga Jâtaka," translated by Yatawara, p. 187.

[2] Rhys Davids, "Buddhist India," p. 37.

inverts the whole sequence of their derivation. The rail surrounding a Buddhist or Jain stûpa, and placed there to protect it from the influence of evil spirits, was not derived directly from Buddhist or Jain ritual. The rite of pradakshinâ, which Buddhist and Jain pilgrims performed within the rails of their stûpas, was the ancient Vedic rite practised by all Indo-Aryans within the walls of their villages, and the rail was merely a symbolical adaptation to religious purposes of the heavy timber fence constructed by the hereditary village carpenters and joiners which protected the whole community from its enemies in the flesh.

Even the religious significance which attached itself to the rail in connection with Jain and Buddhist stûpas was of much greater antiquity than either Jainism or Buddhism, for this was the identical fence—the vedikâ—which enclosed the sacrificial area prepared with the sacred kusha-grass in Vedic sacrifices.

Similarly, the *torans*, or gateways, of Bharhut and Sânchi (Pl. V)[1] are reproductions of the four gateways of an Indian village or town when they were constructed of timber. Pl. VI shows one from the Amarâvatî sculptures, with part of the railing. The subject of the sculpture is Prince Siddhartha quitting his native town at the time of the Great Renunciation, the Prince being represented symbolically as a Bodhisattva, or Buddha that is to be, by a horse without a rider attended by heavenly beings, one of whom holds the royal umbrella over his head. Here the toran is a plain, businesslike structure, without any of the elaborate sculpture which adorned the gateways of Jain and Buddhist stûpas after the Mauryan epoch.

[1] The present gateways of Sânchî are later than the stûpa itself, which was one of those built by Asoka in the third century B.C. They were probably added about a century later, and the sculpture represents the transition from the severe simplicity of the art of Hînayâna Buddhism to the great elaboration of the Mahâyâna school. The town gateway shown in Pl. VI gives a good idea of the original Asokan torans of Bharhut and Sânchî.

PLATE VI

TOWN GATEWAY IN ANCIENT INDIA

It is evidently part of the defences of the town or fortress-palace of King Suddhodana. Above the toran, or torans (for it must have been doubled to carry the superstructure), is built a guard-house, with the usual barrel-vaulted roof and framed balustrade, made in the same way as the wooden walls of the town. This gateway is clearly the wooden prototype of the guard-houses of later Hindu and Muhammadan fortresses, with their ***naubat-khâna***, or music-gallery, where the royal drummers announced the King's going and coming at any state function, and sounded the alarm in case of attack.

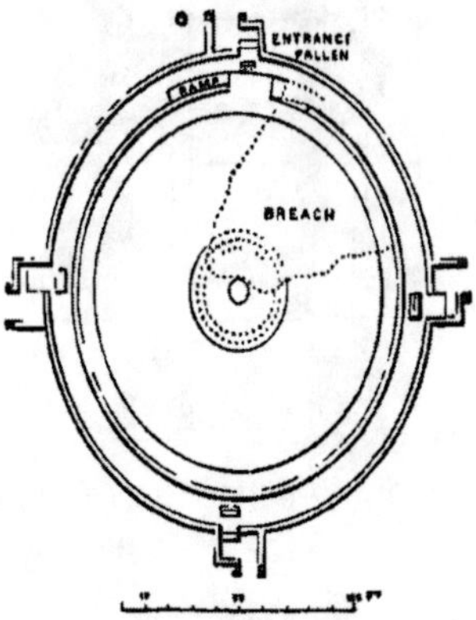

FIG. 9.—Plan of the Great Sânchî Stûpa (from Fergusson's "History").

But the origin of the toran may be taken farther back than the time of Buddha to the gateway of the Vedic Indian village. Here its practical use would also be for defence, and as a watch-tower upon which the village sentinels could easily clamber to survey the surrounding country and to give the alarm in case of a sudden raid upon their crops or cattle. There was magic in the swastika, which is introduced into the gateways of Bharhut and Sânchî (see plan, fig. 9), because it was a practical device for strengthening the defence of the village entrances. The symbolical meaning, as an indication of the path of the sun across the heavens, and the propitious direction for the priest or pious pilgrim to circumambulate, grew into it gradually with the evolution of Aryan religious ritual.

The construction of the wooden rail, and of the stone imitation of it, is shown in fig. 10. It may be observed that the form into which the horizontal bars is shaped is exactly that which is used in the traditional timber houses of Norway. It is, in fact, the simplest method for ensuring good horizontal joints in the walls of wooden houses.

Brick and stone walls in an ancient Indian village or town were constructed either on the principle of the "embattled fret" (fig. 11), which follows closely the outline of the timber railing, or in a wavy line like the edge of a lotus leaf, or "like the wreath of waves rising in the milky ocean."[1] The latter type can be seen in the village plan called Padmâka, described in the Mânasâra (fig. 4). It was probably built of mud or brick, but might have been simply a bambu fence bent round a line of upright posts.

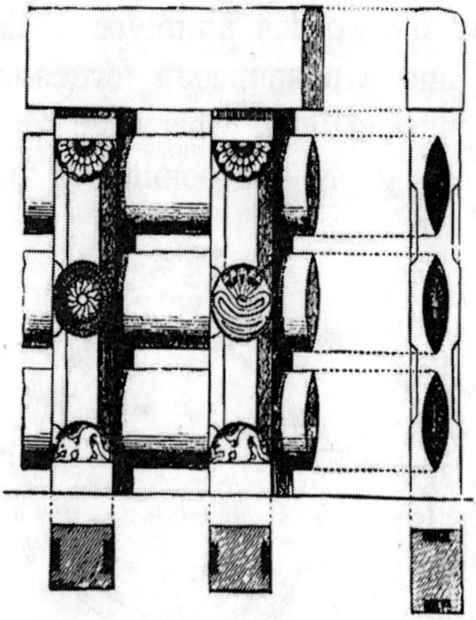

FIG. 10.—Rail of Stûpa No. 2 at Sânchî (from Fergusson's "History").

Pl. VII, B, from the Amarâvatî sculptures, shows a town gateway built of brick, with a wooden guard-house over it of the same description as that given in Pl. VI. This is the prototype of later Indian fortress-gateways like that of the Purana Kila at Delhi (Pl. VII, c), and the Hâthî Pôl of Akbar's Fort at Agra.

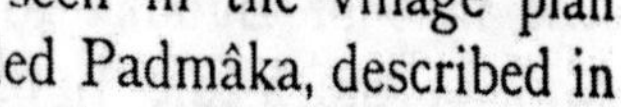

FIG. 11.—Plan of Brick or Stone Wall.

The origin of another important feature in later Indian architecture is also stated in

[1] Ummagga Jâtaka, p. 98. It may be noticed that the whiteness of houses and walls is often referred to in Sanskrit and Pâli literature, showing that the practice of plastering brick, stone, and clay walls with fine polished chunam was common in ancient India. The plaster was a protection against damp in the rainy season and kept the walls cool in the hot season.

PLATE VII

FORTRESS WALLS AND GATES

the gateways of the ancient Indo-Aryan village—the gopuram or gateway of Indian temples: both those which Fergusson classifies as "Indo-Aryan"—a type which now belongs to Northern India—and those which he labelled "Dravidian." The former, Pl. VIII, A, with the naubat-khâna over it, roofed in Bengali fashion, is clearly related to the town gateway of ancient India built of brick or stone with a wooden superstructure, as in Pl. VI.

A careful study of the façade of the great hall or *mandapam* of the temple of Virûpâksha at Pattadakal (Pl. VIII, B), one of the earliest of the so-called Dravidian type now extinct, will show a similar relationship between it and the fortified town walls of ancient India. The treatment of the walls, which are divided at regular intervals into pilastered bays each containing the shrine of a deity, is structurally based upon the "embattled fret," like the brick and stone walls which surrounded an Indo-Aryan fortified village or town: the walls are crowned with an entablature which is a close adaptation in stone of the ancient superstructure with the vaulted roof, which gave shelter to its Kshatriya defenders. Even the sun-windows of the traditional Bengali design are reproduced as decorative features on the stone chhaja. Over the entrance-porch, which may be taken as the type of an ancient Indian town gateway in localities where stone was the usual building material, the naubat-khâna appears as usual, only employed here for purely ornamental purposes.

In the Râmâyana the word gopuram is used in the sense of a town gateway, and the meaning of it, "cow fort," or shelter, also gives a clue to its secular origin in the daily life of an Indian village. The medieval temple gopurams are not cattle-shelters; but it is easy to imagine that in the ancient Aryan village communities the gate through which the cattle went to their pastures would be called the "cow-gate," and that in case of a hostile raid they would be first driven to the "cow-fort" for safety. And as the routine of daily life became recognised as the *dharma* of Aryan religion, the forms and names of secular things sanctified by immemorial usage in the Aryan family were woven into the ritual of the pious Hindu. In India, religion is never regarded as external to secular life, but as its consecration and illumination.

PLATE VIII

A. GATEWAY OF A MODERN BENARES TEMPLE

B. GATEWAY OF TEMPLE AT PATTADAKAL (EIGHTH CENTURY)

ANCIENT AND MODERN TEMPLE GATEWAYS

CHAPTER III

FERGUSSON'S CLASSIFICATIONS OF STYLE—DIVINE WORSHIP IN ANCIENT INDIA—THE VILLAGE SHRINE IN ASOKA'S TIME—THE INSPIRATION OF INDO-ARYAN ART

BEFORE proceeding to analyse further the structure and symbolism of Indian temple-architecture, it is absolutely necessary for the student to make a clean sweep of all the labels and systems of classification by which Western archæologists have agreed to mystify the subject. The reasons for rejecting them will, I hope, become clear later on. The "styles" of Fergusson, whether they are labelled Buddhist, Jaina, or Hindu, or "Indo-Aryan," "Chalukyan," or "Dravidian," are classifications all more or less false as history and misleading as indications of derivation. Fergusson's great pioneer work was fatally biassed by the fundamental misconception that the history of Indian sculpture, which is the history of Indian temple-building, from the third century A.D. was "written in decay,"[1] and by his total failure to read the symbolic language of Indian art. His theory that the distribution of the Hindu temples with the typical *sikhara*, or curvilinear spire, may be taken to indicate the limits of "the Dasyu province"[2] is grotesque; and to treat Buddhism, Jainism, and Hinduism as separate religious factions indicating so many different epochs of Indian architecture is not less opposed to all historical evidence.

The history of Indian civilisation is the history of its village

[1] "History of Indian Architecture" (2nd edit. 1910), Introduction, p. 36.

[2] Introduction, p. 14.

communities, which embraced within their pale many schools of thought differing in philosophical theories, yet all having their common root in the life of the village and in the Vedic philosophy, which remained the motive power of its social and intellectual progress even when teachers arose, like the Buddha, who disputed the efficacy of sacrificial rites and the divine authority which the Brahmans attributed to the Vedas.

The Indian village always remained the political unit of the state throughout the centuries when dynasty after dynasty succeeded one another in building empires upon that foundation, until the foundation itself was recklessly broken up to make a new one after modern Western models. Its wonderful organisation was the true secret of India's recuperative power when one horde followed another in ravaging the land, or when the continued failure of the monsoon rains brought desolation and famine. The working of the secular bureaucratic machinery, which has been substituted for a system of self-government probably the most perfect the world has ever known and consecrated by the religious sentiment of the Indian people, may justly excite the astonishment of the world. It is an amazing experiment based upon the same ignorance of Indian history which inspired the writings of Fergusson and his followers, but it has still to justify itself.

Just as the root of Indian religion is to be found in the daily life of the people, rather than in dogmas or religious feasts and ceremonies, so the derivations of Indian temple-architecture must be looked for in the simple shrines of the Indian village, where Indian life continues to find its fullest and most characteristic expression, rather than in the splendid monuments by which royal devotees sought to establish the supremacy of their own particular cult; though the sculptures of Asoka's monuments disclose some of the characteristics of Indian village shrines in the third century B.C.

The three different degrees of divine worship recognised in modern Hinduism—that of the *Ishta-deva*, or the special aspect of the Divine appropriate to the individual, the *Ego*; the *Grihya-deva*, or the guardian deity of the household; and the *Gramya-deva*, the patron deity of the village—represent the threefold religious responsibility of the Hindu—his duty to God, the family, and the state—the village standing for the whole body politic.

There were three analogous stages in the evolution of Aryan religion and of Indian religious building. First, the personal religion of the Aryan, which was a direct appeal to the Deity, and needed no shrines except those which God Himself provided; next, his position as the head of a household in which he was the family priest; and, thirdly, his joint responsibility in the performance of tribal sacrifices. In early Vedic literature there is no trace of the relic or symbol worship represented in Asokan sculpture, nor evidence of shrines or temples being dedicated to the worship of any deity; but it would be rash to assume from this negative evidence that all Vedic Aryans lived in a spiritual plane so much higher than the rest of humanity that they could dispense entirely with temples and symbols made by human hands. All that can be said definitely is that the philosophy of the pure Aryan religion, though it recognised many different manifestations of divine power in nature, was essentially monotheistic, and as much opposed to image worship as the Puritanism of Christianity and of Islam. It is this aspect of Aryan religion which is represented in the Buddhist sculpture of Asoka's time.

In pre-Buddhistic times the Kshatriyas, or fighting Aryans, recognised no priestly intermediary between themselves and the Deity. The Kshatriya head of a household was the sole exponent of the religious traditions of his race, and the Brahmans, who were a special class versed in sacrificial lore, held an inferior social position; they were perhaps originally only the attendants at tribal sacrifices who chanted the Vedic hymns and were charged with minor duties, such as the care of sacrificial vessels. But in course of time the increasing complication of sacrificial rites and the supreme importance of a correct performance of them increased the influence of the Brahman in the Kshatriya household, and made him the family priest. But the Aryan religion remained an exclusive one, the rites of which were jealously guarded as tribal secrets. There was no missionary propaganda among the early Aryan invaders of India, but elaborate precautions were taken to prevent the religion of the Aryan household and tribe being degraded by contact with non-Aryan allies, whose gross idolatry was anathema to the Vedic seers, and whose ignorance of Vedic ritual might spoil the efficacy of tribal sacrifices and bring dire disaster upon the whole community.

It is obvious, however, that as the Aryans gradually settled down to agricultural pursuits on the plains of India and organised themselves into peaceful village communities of which they formed the aristocracy, this intellectual and spiritual exclusiveness could not long be maintained. Social intercourse and intermarriage with non-Aryans would bring pagan rites into the Aryan household, and the federation of many different tribes under the leadership of a warrior of great renown as their Râja, or king, would likewise widen the boundaries of the Aryan body politic. It must have occurred to many Aryan thinkers, even before the time of Buddha, that the narrow exclusive policy which confined the light of pure religion to an aristocratic caste would inevitably fail to preserve intact the precious spiritual inheritance of the Aryan race. The propaganda of Asoka was, therefore, not to create an entirely new starting-point for Aryan religion, but to use the doctrines of the Kshatriya prince, Sākiya Muni, as a means of placing it upon a wider social and spiritual basis—that of the *Sangha*, or community, instead of the household or tribe. Thus the simple shrine which served for the religious rites of the Indo-Aryan village grew into the cathedral church of the Buddhist Sangha.

There are many representations of village shrines in Asokan sculptures. Pl. IX, A, shows a typical one from Bharhut, which proves that the Indian village shrine of the third century B.C. already contained all the constructive elements of the medieval Hindu temple. The main building was only a square or circular cell—such as might have served for the hut of a hermit, or yogi—covered by a dome, doubtless constructed with a wooden or bambu framework. 'It contained sacred symbols which were the objects of worship. This cell corresponds to the *garbha-griha*, or holy of holies, of a medieval Hindu temple. In front of it was a verandah covered by the usual Indian chhaja, which served as a shelter for the two guardians of the shrine, human or divine, who are shown standing in front of it. This is the primitive form of the *antarâla*, or inner chamber, of the later Hindu temple (fig. 12). In front of this, again, is the hall for the worshippers, the *mandapam* of the Hindu Silpa-sâstras, covered by the typical Bengali roof.

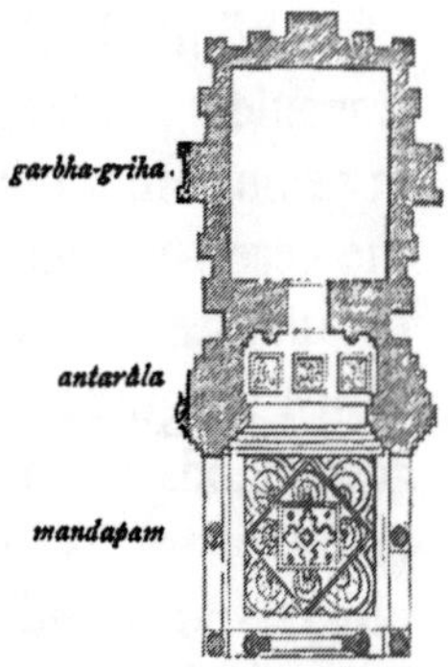

FIG. 12.—Typical Plan of a Hindu Temple.

The symbolic meaning of the railing enclosing the shrine, which is the prototype of the plinth of a Hindu temple, has been already explained. It is the rail of the ancient Vedic sacrifices, which showed that the place was holy ground. As in the rail and toran of the stûpa, the secular origin of such a village shrine and of each division of the Buddhist and Hindu temple can be easily traced. The familiar name *kuti*, or house, given to such a shrine is sufficient indication. It was originally the hut or cell of some holy man, a hermit, yogi, or rishi of great fame in the village, in which his staff, water-vessel, and begging-bowl would be venerated as memorials after his death. The sanctity of the man would cling to his hut, but the name given to it in the Asokan sculptures originally meant nothing more than that it was the house of a particular hermit or yogi. As, however, hero-worship gradually developed into definite religious cults such as Buddhism and Jainism, the house of the saint came to be regarded literally as the House of God.

Ordinarily the hut, with its verandah in front or all round it, would become one of the village shrines, the verandah sheltering some other religious devotee, perhaps a *chela*, or disciple of the deceased, who took charge of it. But when such a shrine became famous as a place of pilgrimage, a hall, or *mandapam*, which Fergusson calls a porch, was placed in front of it for the accommodation of the worshippers. The simplest form of the mandapam was an open pavilion supported by four or more pillars and roofed, according to the character of the local building materials, with bambu and thatch in Bengali fashion, or by a more permanent structure of timber carpentering, covered perhaps by skins, or by clay and plaster, or otherwise by flat slabs of stone arranged in successive tiers one over the other, as shown in fig. 13.

In all cases the model for the temple mandapam was that of the village assembly-hall, or mote-house, which was at the same time the local council-chamber, court-house, music-hall, theatre, and school. It was here that the village council gathered to discuss local affairs, to settle disputes, and decide upon the punishment of offenders against the traditional laws of the community. It was here that the villagers gathered in the evening to listen to the recitation of the national Aryan

PLATE IX

A. FROM THE BHARHUT SCULPTURES

B. DÛRGÂ SHRINE, MÂMALLAPURAM

C. FROM THE BHARHUT SCULPTURES

D. FROM THE BHARHUT SCULPTURES

VILLAGE SHRINES IN ANCIENT INDIA

epics, the Râmâyana and the Mahâbhârata; to take part in musical festivals, and to listen to the tales of the village *kathak*, or story-teller. It was here, also, that by listening to the learned disputations between the pandits of the village, or of wandering ascetics versed in the spiritual lore of the Aryan sages, that the Indian peasant, illiterate only in the narrowest technical sense, acquired that familiarity with abstruse philo-

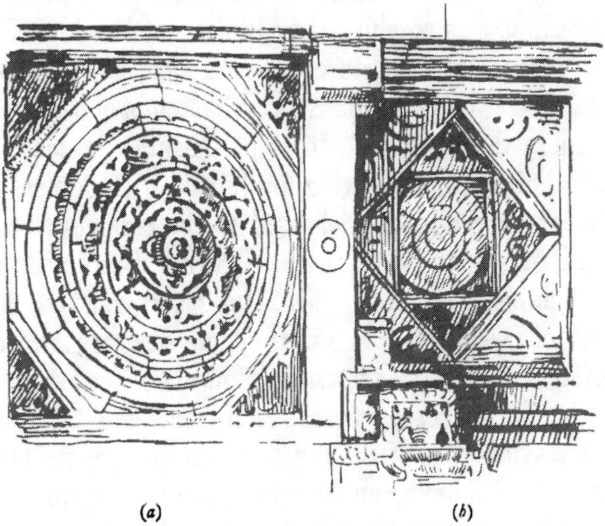

(*a*) (*b*)

FIG. 13.—Construction of the Domes of a Temple *Mandapam*: (*a*) with concentric rings, (*b*) with slabs laid diagonally.

sophical speculations which sometimes astonishes the European who tries to penetrate beneath the surface of Indian life. All this fine traditional culture is being entirely swept away in British India and in "progressive" native states by systems of education devised in the offices of Anglo-Indian cities, as far removed from real Indian life as Manchester and Birmingham, which destroy the spirituality of Indian life, turn the village craftsmen into city clerks, and uproot the whole foundation of Indian civilisation, based upon a far more perfect conception of law and order than that which they seek to establish.

The Mânasâra, as summarised by Râm Râz, contains several directions regarding the placing of village shrines, but the question arises as to whether it is permissible to assume that this part of Hindu craft-tradition is as ancient as the Buddhist sculptures of Bharhut and Sânchî. Râm Râz infers that it cannot be, because among these directions are some which place "the objects worshipped by Jainas and Bauddhas" outside the village. But I venture to think that he is mistaken in assuming that there is any sectarian contempt or disparagement implied in this passage. It simply records the fact that the principal object of veneration for Jains and Buddhists was the stûpa which originally belonged to the cremation or burial ground, outside the village pale. The provision made for Jain and Buddhist worship in this Silpa-sâstra, and the fact that shrines of Durgâ are placed in the same category, are sufficient proof that there is no sectarian feeling in the injunction.

One of Fergusson's most fatal errors was his conclusion that the symbolism of Buddhist art was more ancient than that of orthodox Brahmanism, instead of being, as we shall presently see, entirely derived from it. Brahmâ, Vishnu, and Siva are philosophical concepts which have their root in the earliest religious ideas of the Aryan race, and the blunder of dating the history of Hindu temples from about the seventh century A.D.,[1] instead of from the earliest origins of Indian religious building, has put archæological research on the wrong track ever since it was accepted as a truism on Fergusson's authority.

Primâ facie, it is wholly improbable that the philosophical speculations connected with the three positions of the sun in the heavens which are fundamental to all Indo-Aryan religious belief should have remained without concrete artistic symbols

[1] Fergusson, vol. ii. p. 89.

for so many centuries. The fact that the earliest have not hitherto been discovered is only an instance of how a false premiss may obscure the mental vision of experts; but when the fine work of the Indian master-builder in the nineteenth and twentieth centuries has entirely escaped the notice of Anglo-Indians, it is natural to expect that they should often lose their way in more remote fields of observation.

"No one," says Fergusson, "can accuse the pure Aryans of building temples at all, or of worshipping images of Siva or Vishnu."[1] He ignores such passages in the Mahâbhârata as that in Bhishma Vadha Parva, sect. cxiii.[2]: "The idols of the Kuru King in his temples tremble and dance and weep." The Saivism and Vaishnavism which run through the whole of the Hindu epics Fergusson treats as modern corruptions of the "pure Aryan faith" as expounded in the Vedas, and explains away the evidence which conflicts with his statements as falsifications of the Hindu sacred texts made by the wily Brahman of medieval times. But the architectural theories which he brought forward as evidence break down at every point on close examination. I hold no brief for Hindu theologians. All schools of theology write history from a theological rather than a scientific standpoint; but when one considers how Hindu religious traditions were handed down from one generation to another, the probabilities of any extensive deliberate falsification seem to be very remote. It is easy to falsify a written statement of which only a few copies are made, but that a national oral tradition, the precision of which was scientifically maintained by a most elaborate mnemonic system in which every word and syllable was counted, could be deliberately falsified by a few unscrupulous priests is less credible than the assumption that amateur archæologists sometimes make fatal mistakes.

1 "Indian Architecture" (revised edition), vol. i. p. 42.

2 Roy's translation.

When the Mânasâra Silpa-sâstra gives directions for the placing of Brahmâ, Vishnu, and Siva shrines in the Indian village, and defines their relations to those of Buddhist and Jaina stûpas, there is no reason why it should not be accepted as a tradition as old as any in the history of Indian building, provided that there is no positive evidence to the contrary to be found in ancient monuments. But it is necessary to remember that the Silpa-sâstras are technical, and not sectarian works, and that the terms used must therefore be considered in their technical sense only. It is just at this point that archæologists of Fergusson's school have gone astray.

A "Brahmâ" shrine which the Mânasâra directs to be placed at the meeting of the four crossways in the centre of the village (see fig. 4) is a cell, square in plan, with its walls fronting the four cardinal points, and an entrance on each side. The sectarian worship to which it is devoted may be Buddhist, Jain, Vaishnavaite, or Saivaite; in itself it is only a cosmic symbol which is common to all sects.

A "Vishnu" shrine, according to the Mânasâra, has one entrance, always facing the east, except when dedicated to the Narasinha (Man-lion) incarnation of Vishnu, in which case it was to be built outside the village, with its entrance turned away from it. In this exception there may be some old tradition of a Brahman or Kshatriya hero's success in warding off a great danger to the whole Indo-Aryan community. The special characteristic of a "Vishnu" shrine is the curvilinear spire, or *sikhara*—a symbol of Vishnu's pillar, standard, or of his holy Mountain—which Fergusson took as the typical feature of his "Indo-Aryan "style," though he left the origin of it unexplained.

The key to this question lies in the symbolism, which can be most conveniently reserved for a separate chapter. Here it is only necessary to mention one fact which goes far to show that the "Vishnu" shrine is as ancient as any other—viz. that miniature shrines of this type are constantly being dug up at Sarnath and other ancient Buddhist sites, side by side with the miniature stûpas which were the special symbols of the Buddhists and Jains. For reasons which are given below it is necessary to reject Professor Macdonell's theory[1] of the derivation of the sikhara from the stûpa, to which I subscribed previously.[2] The constructive principle was the same in both, but the symbolism of the stûpa was different.

The most noteworthy example of a "Vishnu" shrine, and one of the earliest now existing, is the famous Buddhist temple of Bodh-Gayâ, built in honour of the Bodhi tree (Vishnu's tree), and of Buddha as the Upholder of the Universe. Not many years ago the possession of the shrine was the subject of a great controversy in which the Government of Bengal opposed the claims of the Mahant of a neighbouring Vaishnavaite monastery to its custody. The official experts seem to have misapprehended the historical aspects of the case, and, as so frequently happens when history is misread, led the Government into a false position with regard to the religious traditions of India.

As a "Vishnu" shrine may be Buddhist, so it may also be Saivaite, for Siva to Saivaites is Brahmâ, Vishnu, and Siva. It is the image for which the shrine is built which determines the form of the latter. There is some internal evidence as to the antiquity of the Mânasâra traditions in this statement, for image-worship was not generally recognised by philosophical Hinduism until the rise of the Mahâyâna school of Buddhism about the beginning of the Christian era. But shrines for Brahmâ, Vishnu, and Siva were certainly built before this time.

A "Siva" shrine, in the technical sense, has one entrance

[1] "Journal of the Royal Society of Arts," Mar. 5, 1909.

[2] "Indian Architecture: Its Psychology, Structure, and History," 1913, p. 98.

facing west, or towards the setting sun, and the roof is of what Fergusson calls the Dravidian type—*i.e.* it is crowned by a dome, evidently derived from the stûpa, but in all buildings now extant reduced to a solidly built symbol. The coincidence that "Vishnu" shrines are chiefly confined to Northern India, and those of the "Siva" type to the south, has nothing to do with "Dasyu provinces,"[1] or with any ethnological question. It is explained by the fact that the schools of Hindu theology which take Vishnu for their *Ishta-deva*[2] are in the great majority in the north, while those which are the exponents of Saiva philosophy, taking Siva as their *Ishta-deva*, predominate largely in the south. Fergusson's conjecture that Saivism is "an aboriginal superstition assimilated by the Brahmans"[3] is pure nonsense.

The derivation of the Hindu temple from the *rathas*, or cars, of Aryan warriors, on account of the poetic imagery used in the Râmâyana and Mahâbhârata, and the attempts made by medieval builders to give literary imagination concrete form by placing stone wheels on the sides of the vimâna, as in the Sûrya temple at Kanârak, has, *pace* Dr. Coomaraswamy and other writers, no historical foundation. It is a clear case of putting the cart before the horse. The temple car on which the sacred image was carried in procession could not have been introduced into the temple ritual before the image itself became part of it—*i.e.* before the first centuries before and after the Christian era—and all the constructive types, as well as the symbolism connected with them, if Indian temple building had been developed before that time. There is no instance of vimânas being made like rathas, or cars, before the tenth century.

[1] Fergusson's "History of Architecture" (new edit.), Introduction, p. 14.

[2] See *ante*, p. 35.

[3] "History of Architecture" (new edit.), Introduction, p. 42.

It is equally fallacious to assume, as Dr. Coomaraswamy has also done,[1] that Indo-Aryans borrowed most of their architectural ideas from the non-Aryan tribes which became subject to them. There is absolutely no historical evidence that this was the case, but *per contra* there is strong reason for believing that all the higher culture of the ancient Indian village communities, including their organisation, arts and crafts, was directly due to Aryan inspiration, or to the practical adaptation of Aryan philosophical speculations to the concerns of daily life. I do not mean that the Aryans found India an artistic desert or peopled by primitive savages. The more or less civilised tribes whose immigrations preceded theirs may possibly have acquired their culture, directly or indirectly, from earlier Aryan sources; they may have represented an earlier stratum of Aryan civilisation. This would explain why the Aryans of Vedic India found it comparatively easy to adapt themselves to their Indian environment, without establishing impassable social barriers between themselves and their dark-skinned neighbours; for the exclusiveness of the caste system did not exist in the sixth century B.C. or for many centuries after the time of Buddha. Indian civilisation is, like Hindu sacrificial vessels, an amalgam of many metals; but the fire which fused them and separated the dross was the Aryan genius —the philosophy of the Vedas. If it has once more to go into the melting-pot, those who tear up its foundations should at least study its history carefully from its own standpoint, and equip themselves with sure knowledge of the materials they are using to form the new India, otherwise they are mere empirics in statecraft, playing with forces which they do not understand and which they are unable to control.

[1] "Arts and Crafts of India and Ceylon," p. 107.

CHAPTER IV

THE STÛPA AND ITS SYMBOLISM

THE previous chapters will enable the reader to put in its proper place in Indian architectural history, and in the life of ancient India, the interesting structure which I will now proceed to discuss, the stûpa or funeral monument, which Fergusson took for his starting-point. The stûpa itself, being originally only a tomb or cenotaph, never came within the enclosure of an Indian village except as a symbol; it belonged to the cemetery or cremation-ground outside. It was only when it had been consecrated as a religious symbol, like so many other structural elements in Indian building, that it became, like the village shrine, associated with life as well as death and was used to mark places made sacred by the events in the life of the saint whom it commemorated, and also as an ideograph in a hieratic language employed decoratively in Buddhist-Hindu art in the same way as Arabic and other script was afterwards used by Muhammadan craftsmen.

The stûpa did not originate with Buddhism, nor was it solely associated with that aspect of Indo-Aryan religious thought, though the effect of Asoka's ardent propaganda of the cult of Sâkiya Muni made the Buddhist stûpa much more common than any other. The Jains, and probably all other sects in Asoka's time, had their stûpas. The former place the earliest of the 24 *Tîrthankaras*, or saints, commemorated by their stûpas, as far back as the Vedic Rishis; and doubtless the oldest stûpas were not symbols of a religious cult, but memorials of the dead associated with the practice of burial instead of cremation. It may be observed that even in the present day the body of a Brahman who has taken the vow of a *Sannyâsin* and retired from the world to devote himself to a religious life is not cremated after death but thrown into a sacred river—the idea being that it has been made so pure by spiritual exercises that the purificatory rite of cremation is superfluous. Another exception to the rule of cremation is that of a Hindu victim to small-pox, in which case Sitala, the dread goddess who has possessed the body, is supposed to claim it from Agni, the god of fire. Probably the imminent risk of infection for relatives whose duty it was to prepare a corpse for the funeral pile was the motive of this custom.

It seems likely that the earliest Aryan immigrants into India also disposed of their dead by burial, marking the grave with the tumulus, which afterwards developed into the structural stûpa, and that they only adopted cremation after they had settled down to life under tropical conditions, for obvious sanitary reasons. Certainly in Asoka's time the stûpa was generally, like the modern chattri, only a cenotaph, or reliquary.

As the purpose of this work is architectural rather than archæological, it is unnecessary to repeat the detailed descriptions of the existing remains of early Buddhist and Jain stûpas, dating from about the fifth century B.C., which are given by Fergusson and other writers. The plan (fig. 9) and the section of the great Sânchî stûpa (fig. 14) will indicate the usual form and construction, and Pl. X the appearance of one of them from the outside, as shown in the Amarâvatî sculptures. The latter, however, representing the development of Indo-Aryan religion in the second or third century A.D., belongs to the Mahâyâna school of Buddhism, but the form and structure of the stûpa and enclosing rail remains practically the same as in Asoka's time. The chaitya of the Kârlê Chapter-house, Pl. XIX, indicates better the austerity of early Buddhist ritual, and, making allowance for the fact that the rails are only carved in relief on the face of the stûpa instead of enclosing it, one can realise from it the exact appearance of one of the 84,000 stûpas which Asoka is said to have built.

Fergusson and other archæologists have failed to remark that the stûpa was not a special product of Buddhist and Jain religious ritual and dogma; as it existed in Asoka's time it embodied the symbolism and ritual of all Aryan religion directly derived from the Vedas.

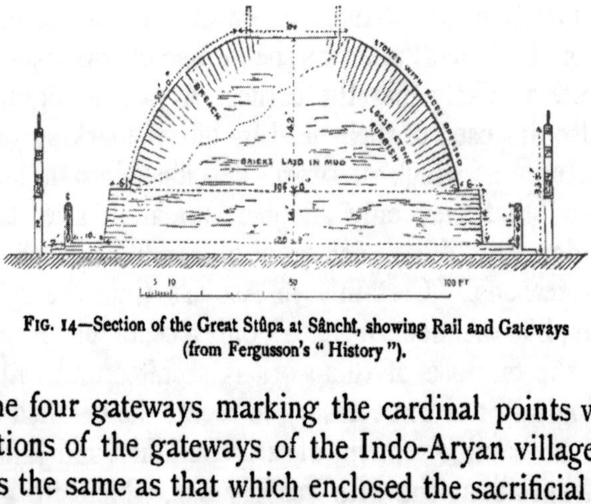

Fig. 14—Section of the Great Stûpa at Sânchî, showing Rail and Gateways (from Fergusson's "History").

The four gateways marking the cardinal points were reproductions of the gateways of the Indo-Aryan village. The rail was the same as that which enclosed the sacrificial area in the Vedic sacrifices. The Buddha, as an inspired Kshatriya teacher, disputed the Brahman interpretation of the Vedas and the efficacy of Brahmanical sacrifices; but his followers, whatever their varna or colour might be, worshipped him with the immemorial rites which belonged to all who came within the pale of the Indo-Aryan village community.

The three bars of the rail meant the three positions of the sun at its rising, at its zenith, and at its setting—and hence a spiritual defence, for these were the three times of daily prayer—

PLATE X

A STŪPA (FROM THE AMARĀVATĪ SCULPTURES)

48]

only the Buddhists called them Buddha, Sangha, and Dharma, instead of Brahmâ, Vishnu, and Siva, according to the orthodox Brahman formula. Four bars to the Brahman meant the four Vedas, the depository of the sacred traditions of the Aryan race; the Buddhists explained them as the four events in the life of the Blessed One—the Nativity, the Enlightenment, the First Sermon at Benares, and His Death, or Pari-Nirvana. The splendid open lotus flowers carved upon the rail (Pl. XIII, A) were symbols and votive offerings which had the same meaning for all schools of Aryan philosophy and religion. The rite of pradakshinâ, the circumambulation of the stûpa, which the pilgrims performed, was the ancient Aryan rite which was repeated every day round the enclosure of every Indian village. And in Asoka's time all the beautiful imagery of Aryan poetry which first found expression in the Vedic hymns was woven into the fabric of the stûpa. It was no longer a funereal mound, but planned like the Indian village on the lines of the cosmic order which the Divine Artificer Himself had drawn. The dome was the symbol of the sky, the blue lotus flower enveloping the earth with its inverted petals. The group of five columns which rose from the base of the dome at the point opposite the four gateways marked the arms of the cosmic cross, like the main streets of an Aryan village, and represented the five cosmic jewels, earth, air, fire, water, and ether. The reliquary, at the crown of the dome, was the Vedic altar of burnt sacrifice; the rail pattern upon it reproducing in a decorative form the actual rail which enclosed the sacrificial area, and also the village shrine. The umbrella over the reliquary, originally part of the royal insignia of the Kshatriya Prince Siddhartha,

[1] The Vedic connotation of this symbolism is to be found in the five posts of sacrifice, *i.e.* the four marking out the sacrificial area and the central stake or altar, or the four corner pillars which upheld the universe with Vishnu's pillar or tree in the centre. Or again, the four corner posts of the village enclosure with the council tree in the centre.

was transformed into the pyramidal Tee (fig. 15), which was only the Buddhist and Jain equivalent symbol for the mystic tree of Vishnu, the cosmic tree, the tree of wisdom, and the trysting tree of the village; for all Indian art derives ultimately from the life of the Aryan village.

Fergusson's ignorance of the symbolism of Indian art led him to interpret the sculptures of Buddhist stûpas as representations of "tree and serpent worship." Monsieur A. Foucher's brilliant analysis of the sculptures of the Sânchî gateway disposes of this fallacy, which has been the source of much misunderstanding of Indian art and religion. He shows that these sculptures, instead of representing the primitive animistic cult of wild aboriginal followers of the Buddha, really embody the esoteric teaching of Hînayâna Buddhism, which was based upon the true spirit of Vedic Aryan philosophy in refusing to permit the representation of the Deity in human form. Hero-worship was a popular sentiment which could not be ignored by Aryan religious teachers; it went down to the very foundations of Aryan religion, for the Kshatriya chieftain was the spiritual leader of his tribe before the Brahman hierarchy became a political power and developed the philosophical teaching of the Vedas; and, even then, the fighting Kshatriya often overcame the Brahman with his own weapons in philosophic encounters. Both the Buddha and Krishna, the hero of the Mahâbhârata, were Kshatriyas. It was not to be expected that the abstruse speculations of Aryan philosophy could be made intelligible to the whole Indo-Aryan community, composed of so many different intellectual and racial elements;

FIG. 15.—The Tee of a Stûpa.

PLATE XI

NORTH

D

WEST

C

EAST

A

B

SOUTH]

THE SYMBOLS OF THE FOUR GATES

but a popular sentiment like that of hero-worship could be spiritualised and prevented from sinking into gross superstition and idolatry. That was the motive of the ritual represented by the hieratic sculptures of the Asokan stûpas. Hînayâna Buddhism forbade the worship of the great Teacher as a divinity: it permitted the veneration of the symbols which represented the events of His life on earth and the principles of His teaching. It would not tolerate the superstition of Brahmanical sacrificial rites, but it allowed the Vedic altar to be used as a table for the symbols of the Buddhist Law, as a mound upon which to plant the Bodhi tree (fig. 16), or as a casket for the relics of saints.

That is exactly what is represented in the sculptures of Bharhut and Sânchî. As a symbol of the Nativity the Buddhist sculptor used the figure of Ushas, the Vedic Dawn-maiden, otherwise Lakshmi or Sri, the Goddess of Good Fortune, Abundance, and Fertility (Pl. XI, fig. A). She rises from the cosmic ocean standing upon Brahmâ's lotus flower, and two elephants, symbols of the rain-cloud, pour lustrations over her. Seven different kinds of trees, with Vedic altars as thrones of the gods placed in front of them (Pl. XI, fig. B), symbolised the Second Event in the Buddhist sacred cycle, the Illumination under the Bodhi Tree, which was said to have taken place in seven different lives of the Tathâgata, and represented, as Professor Rhys Davids has explained, the attainment of Nirvana, the zenith of spiritual consciousness. The Third Event was the preaching of the first Sermon at Benares, the turning of the Wheel of the Law.

FIG. 16.—Bodhi Tree with Vedic Railing.

It is easy to understand why the wheel appealed to the understanding of every Indian as an appropriate symbol of the whole teaching of Buddha, which was not a dogma of religion but a rule of life. The wheel was not only an ancient Vedic symbol of the sun, as representing the cosmic soul-force, but every Aryan in performing the rite of pradakshinâ round his native village—starting from the eastern gate and following the path of the sun along the Road of Auspiciousness to its zenith at the southern gate, its setting at the western gate, its descent into the nether world until it reached its nadir at the northern gate, whither the sons of King Sagara[1] pursued the sacrificial horse which had escaped from their charge, and, finally, returning to his starting-point in the east—was symbolically turning the wheel of the divine law and meditating upon the mystery of life and death.

The Fourth Event, represented by a sculpture of the stûpa (Plate XI, fig. D), was the Death of the Buddha, and the completion of the cycle of rebirths in his Pari-Nirvana, Reincarnation was symbolised by the serpent, which periodically sheds its skin and appears with a new body to resume the turning of the wheel of life.

The Buddhist Law was only the spiritual staff which should help the Aryan villager over the obstacles and pitfalls of the way of life. It was not any dogmatic solution of the riddle of the universe, but a practical way of salvation which appealed strongly to the deep religious instinct of a people oppressed by the burden of the extravagant ritual of Brahmanical sacrifices. The inspiration of Buddha would hardly have touched the imagination of all classes so deeply had his teaching cut across the most cherished religious convictions of India. The almost instant and universal success of Asoka's missionary efforts must

[1] King Sagara prepared a horse-sacrifice, but the horse was stolen by the sage Kapila. The king's sixty thousand sons who had charge of it searched for it high and low, and at length discovered it in the regions below the earth, grazing by the side of the sage, who was wrapt in meditation. When attacked, Kapila burnt them all to ashes by the fire which flashed from his third eye—the eye of spiritual consciousness. A descendant of Sagara, by turning the waters of the Ganges on to their ashes, obtained the admission of their souls into heaven.

be attributed to the political genius of the Buddhist leaders in adapting their propaganda to the traditional religious observances of Indian daily life. The thought of the nativity of Buddha as the sunrise, or dawn of a new spiritual life for every human being, quietly took the place of the original Brahmâ concept, the Vedic Creator who opened the petals of the world-lotus. The Sangha, or the congregation of the faithful, meeting under the village council tree, was equivalent to Vishnu, the sun at noon—the Preserver whose mystic tree or pillar upheld the universe. Siva, symbolised by the sun at its setting and when below the horizon, who was the Dissolver of life and apotheosis of the Vedic philosophy of the cosmos, became Dharma—the Buddhist law of daily life—superseding the Brahman law of sacrificial rites, and pointing the way to Pari-Nirvana when the Ego, released from the chain of human existences, was merged in the cosmic ocean. Nirvana and Pari-Nirvana were the two ends of the upright arm of the cosmic cross, the pole or axis of the universe, which was Vishnu's pillar, or churning-stick, or Siva's *lingam.* It was worshipped by Buddhists as a mystic fiery pillar.

The poets and philosophers of Vedic India pictured the night sky spanned by the Milky Way, with the seven bright planets of the Great Bear glittering athwart it, as Vishnu-Nârâyana sleeping on the seven-headed Serpent of Eternity, whose coils encircled the universe. These planets had once been the seven great Rishis who taught the Aryans divine wisdom. Buddhist India adopted the same symbolism with a different connotation. The seven great Rishis were the seven Buddhas. The serpent was the cycle of countless existences through which they had at last attained to Pari-Nirvana. These were narrated in the jâtakas, as told by village story-tellers on starlight nights under the mystic tree of Vishnu. The kathaks, or professional story-tellers, were probably the most successful propagandists of Buddhism among the uncultured non-Aryan masses; for it is easy to believe that these delightful old-world tales appealed more strongly to popular imagination than the abstract philosophy of the Vedas, especially as the doctrine taught by them relieved the people from the intolerable sacrificial ritual of the Brahmans.

The Brahman philosopher taught his disciples as they went the daily round of the village to think of the four gates as the four Vedas.[1] The Buddhist teacher struck a more human note when he substituted the Four Events in the life of the Aryan hero, the Enlightened One; and at the same time he respected the esoteric teaching of Vedic philosophy by inventing a form of aniconic symbolism which met the natural desire of the artist to visualise his spiritual thoughts. When this symbolism is rightly understood, it is easy to read the sculptures of Bharhut and Sânchî as a narrative of the life of Sâkiya Muni and his previous existences on earth, and also as an exposition of the teaching of the Hînayâna school of Buddhism. The sculptures of Amarâvatî represent a later development of Buddhist philosophy when the prohibition of anthropomorphic symbolism was removed from Indo-Aryan religious ritual by the propagation of the tenets of the Mahâyâna school.

[1] Originally three, corresponding to the three bars of the Vedic sacrificial rail which appears in the Asokan stûpas. A fourth Veda—the Atharva—was subsequently recognised, and at Amarâvatî the sculpture frequently represents four bars in the rail.

CHAPTER V

SYMBOLISM

THE LOTUS-LEAF ARCH, OR SUN-WINDOW—PILLARS, CAPITALS, AND BASES—THE VISHNU STANDARD AND PILLAR—THE HOLY MOUNT—THE SYMBOL OF DEATH

IT has been explained already that the Asokan arched window (fig. 17), commonly called "horseshoe" by Western writers—a form also applied to vaults and domes—was derived from the use of bent bambu, as in Bengali thatched roofs. The exquisite

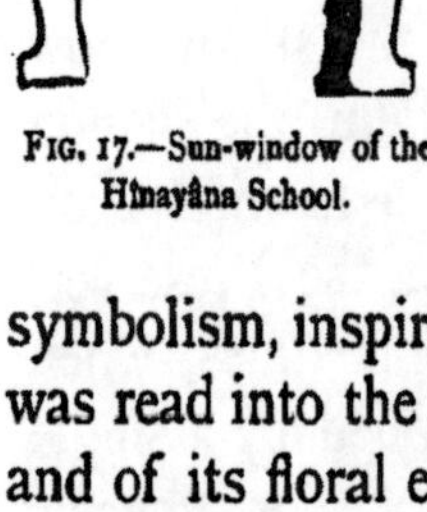

FIG. 17.—Sun-window of the Hînayâna School.

FIG. 18.—Sun-window of the Mahâyâna School.

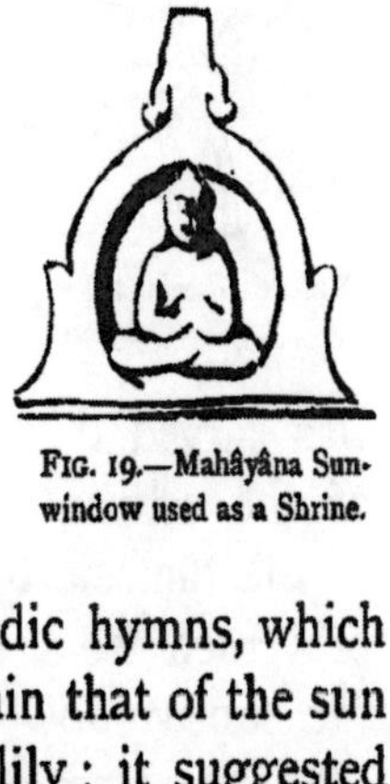

FIG. 19.—Mahâyâna Sun-window used as a Shrine.

symbolism, inspired by the poetry of the Vedic hymns, which was read into the structural use of it, was again that of the sun and of its floral emblem the lotus or water-lily; it suggested the sun on the horizon in a cloudless sky rising or setting over sea, lake, or river. As a theological symbol, therefore, it stood for Brahmâ, or Buddha, or Siva, and when image-worship gradually crept into Indo-Aryan ritual the arch became the aureole of a seated figure of the divinity, the form of which was associated in the mind of the devout with the lotus leaf. The outside line of the arched opening, following the curve of a village thatched roof, took the shape of a conventionalised leaf of the sacred pîpal—the Bodhi tree (fig. 20).

These sun-windows, as they may be called, in the oldest Indian buildings had no sculptured ornament, but in carved representations of them as symbols the ends of the purlins which supported the rafters of the roof were shown, and also, as a rule, the wooden screen or lattice which filled them. Later on, at Ajantâ and elsewhere, an elaboration of the symbolism was brought in (fig. 18). The outer edge on each side started at the springing from the mouth of a *makara*, a fish-dragon, which suggested the water or cosmic ocean from which the sun rose, and into which it sank at eventide: it was an emblem of the clouds or vapours which sometimes veiled, but never impaired, the glory of the sun.[1] At the pointed crown of the sun-window was carved the head of another dragon—Râhu, the demon of the eclipse—philosophically regarded as a manifestation of the tâmasic quality of Siva which Vishnu, the Preserver, prevented from destroying the universe. Sometimes, when the sun-window was only a symbol, it was filled by a single head representing Siva, either in his sâttvic or tâmasic

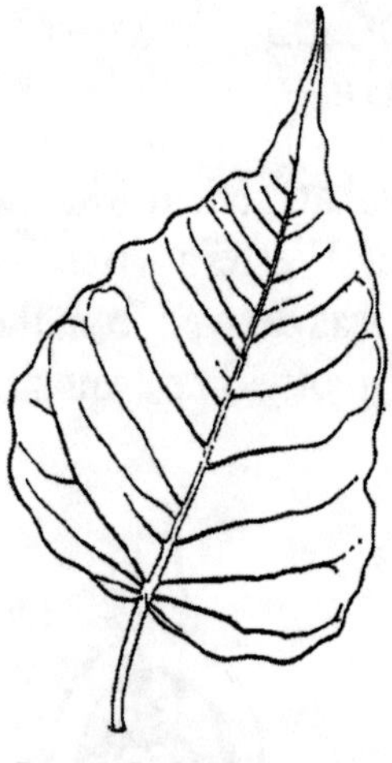

FIG. 20.—Leaf of the Pîpal Tree (*Ficus religiosa*).

[1] The *makara* was also the symbol of Kâma-deva, the God of Love, whose eyes, like those of a fish, never closed, but were for ever gazing at the object of his desire: the antithesis of the blind god of Europe. To the Indian mind, closed eyelids, or the shutting out of sensual vision, suggest meditation and the opening of the third eye of spiritual consciousness.

PLATE XII

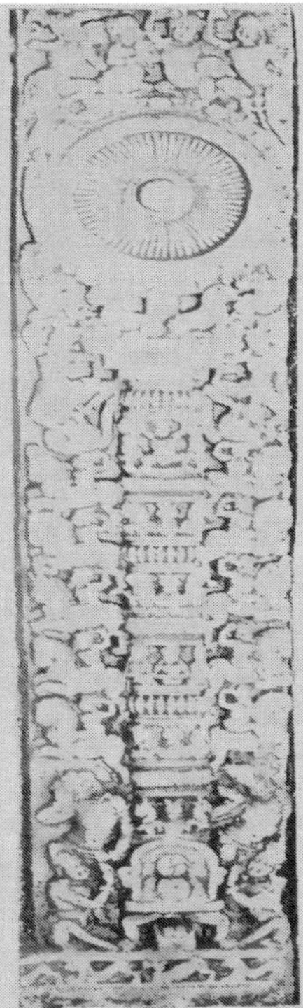

A. DHWAJA-STAMBHA FROM THE AMARÂVATI SCULPTURES

B. HORSEWOMAN CARRYING VISHNU STANDARD (BHARHUT SCULPTURES)

C. THE IRON PILLAR, DELHI

VISHNU PILLARS AND STANDARDS (DHWAJA-STAMBHAS)

aspect, as Avalokitêshvara—the Lord who looks down from above.

The consecration of structural forms, originally derived from purely utilitarian uses, through this religious idealism was obviously the reason why the Vedic rail and the sun-window were retained as decorative motifs in the traditional canons of the Indian building craft long after their structural significance was lost sight of. They were ideographs of an art-language which, though incomprehensible by those outside the Indo-Aryan pale, was perfectly understood by the people whose religious sentiments it expressed.

We will now see how this religious symbolism also determined the decorative treatment of another essential structural feature in Indian building—the column, pier, or pillar. In Asokan and later Indian sculpture there are two kinds represented: one is the *dhwaja-stambha* (flag-pole), or the *lât*, used to mark sacred places, to carry inscriptions and symbols, and as lamp-standards; the other is the structural form applied to the support of buildings, and subsequently, as in the classical "orders" of Europe, to their embellishment. The first kind is represented by the single pillars upon which Asoka inscribed his edicts, and by the pairs which, like the Boaz and Jachin of the Temple of Jerusalem, stood in front of the entrance to Buddhist and Jain stûpas and temples. They were originally the tribal ensigns or the standards of royalty, which were planted outside the entrance to the sacrificial area at the great horse-sacrifices in Vedic times.

A quaint sculpture at Bharhut (fig. B, Pl. XII) shows a female, probably Sri, or Lakhsmi, carrying Vishnu's standard surmounted by the mythical sun-bird Garuda.

The Buddhist, Jain, and Brahmanical temple-pillar also derives its symbolic decorative treatment from the ancient Aryan sacrificial ritual in which gilded posts, "octagonal and smoothly planed" and decorated with pennons, served to mark out the holy ground. Râm Râz gives interesting details taken from the Mânasâra Silpa-sâstra as to the ritualistic significance of different forms of pillars. A square-shafted one was associated with Brahmâ worship; an octagonal one with that of Vishnu; the circular or sixteen-sided one with Rudra-Siva as the Destroyer.[1] Translating this ascription into Buddhist terminology, it may be said that the square pillar stood for Buddha, an octagonal one for the Sangha, and a circular or sixteen-sided one for Dharma. A cylindrical pillar without capital or base was dedicated to Chandra, the moon.

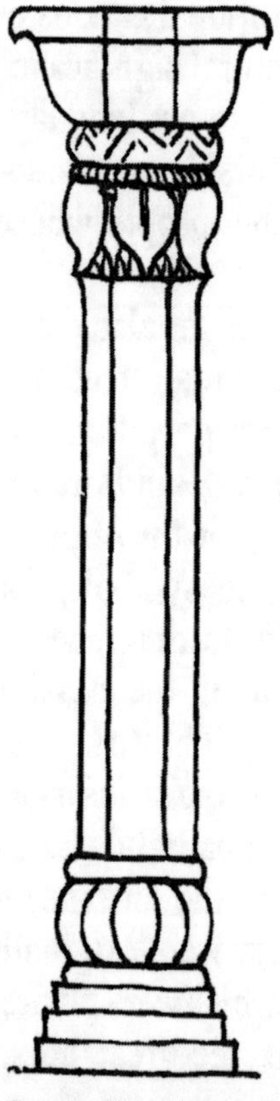

FIG. 21.—Vishnu Pillar from the Bharhut Sculptures.

In pillars or piers intended for structural support and built up of three or more pieces, the capital, shaft, and base are all primarily structural forms, and the decoration should not impair, but rather emphasise, the structural functions of each part. This principle was fully recognised by Indian craftsmen in applying their religious symbolism to the forms of structural supports. Fig. 21 shows the type of capital and base which appears in Asokan buildings; the structural and decorative elements in it, derived from the lotus flower and fruit, and from the sacrificial waterpot, prevailed in various combinations throughout the classic period of Indian architecture.

In all Indo-Aryan religious ritual, from the earliest Vedic

[1] To symbolise the Trimûrti, or the Three Aspects of the One, all three forms are combined in one pillar, as in the great temple of Elephanta.

times, the fruit of *Nelumbium speciosum*, the sacred lotus of Egypt (fig. 22) has always been regarded as a symbol of the throne and footstool of the gods; especially that of Brahmâ, the Creator, or the rising sun. The rosy petals enveloping it, which opened at the first flush of morning light, were the robes of Ushas, the Dawn Maiden, who flung open the doors of the sky. This idea and the form of the fruit itself were skilfully adapted by the craftsmen of wood and stone to the supports of temples and other buildings. The profiles of the capital were modelled so as to suggest the fruit; the petals turned down on

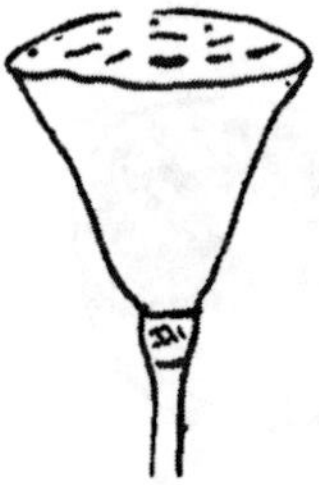

FIG. 22.—Fruit of the Sacred Lotus, *Nelumbium.*

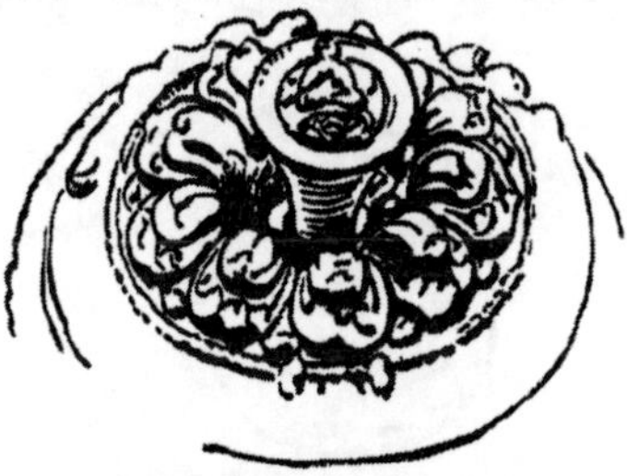

FIG. 23.—Top of a Nepalese Box in Repoussé Brass, showing Lotus Flower with Turned-down Petals, and Fruit used as a Handle.

to the shaft of the pillar formed the member to which Fergusson, not understanding the symbolism, gave the meaningless label "bell-shaped." In Asokan sculpture the lotus flower is very frequently represented with the petals turned down, so as to disclose the fruit or seed-vessel, which has a special symbolic significance as the *hiranya-garbha*, or womb of the universe.

Now, the fruit of the blue lotus, or, more strictly speaking, water-lily (*Nymphæa*), dedicated to the midday sun, and also that of the white *Nymphæa* (the flower of the moonlight sky),

[1] In the Mahânirvâna Tantra the mystic lotus flower of Brahmâ, which contains "the peaceful circle of earth," is said to have its four petals turned downwards. "The thousand-petalled lotus of knowledge" on the top of the holy Mount Meru, which is the dwelling-place of Para-Brahmâ, is similarly described.

opening by night, had a different shape (fig. 24) and a somewhat different symbolic implication. It was the jar which contained the *amrita*, or elixir of immortality, the nectar of the gods; and thus its form was adapted not only to sacrificial vessels, but to the ordinary Indian domestic water-pot, the lota. The shape of it was as admirably adapted for making a firm base to a pillar or column (fig. 21) as the form of the *Nelumbium* fruit was suitable for the structural purpose of the capital.

The section of the water-lily fruit given in fig. 24 shows how its symbolic use was associated with form as well as colour, for within it is the mystic wheel containing the seeds of life,

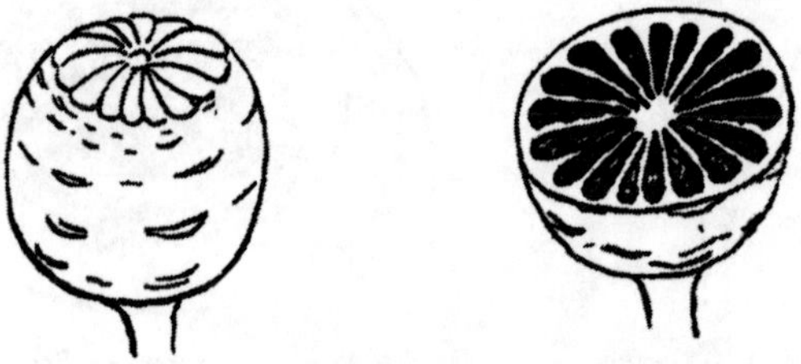

FIG. 24.—Fruit of Water-lily (*Nymphaea*) and Section showing the Mystic Wheel.

which are scattered over the waters in which it grows like stars floating in the cosmic ocean. A fresco at Ajântâ[1] seems to suggest that wooden poles of garden pavilions were actually inserted into metal lotas firmly fixed in a stone, brick, or wooden base—a practice which might have arisen from the use of domestic water-vessels in street decorations for fixing up and keeping fresh young plantain and palm trees. The following passage in the Ummagga Jâtaka, describing the preparations made for a royal procession, is interesting in this connection: "He also strewed the ground with white sand and flowers of various kinds, and put brimming jars of water on either side

[1] See Griffiths, "Ajanta," vol. i. pl. 17.

A. FROM THE SÂNCHI SCULPTURES

B. FROM THE BHARHUT SCULPTURES

C. FROM A FRESCO PAINTING AT AJANTÂ

THE SACRED LOTUS AND THE WATER-LILY

of the roadway with cocoa-nut flowers and ornamental plantain trees."[1]

Another motif which is used both structurally and decoratively in Indian art is a combination of the fruits of *Nelumbium* and *Nymphæa.* This was applied to the domestic water-vessel, as in fig. 25, and also to the capitals of pillars for producing the form used at Elephanta and Ajantâ, called by Fergusson "cushion-shaped" (fig. 26). It may be noted that an exaggeration of the torus to which the petals of *Nelumbium* are attached would produce a similar shape.

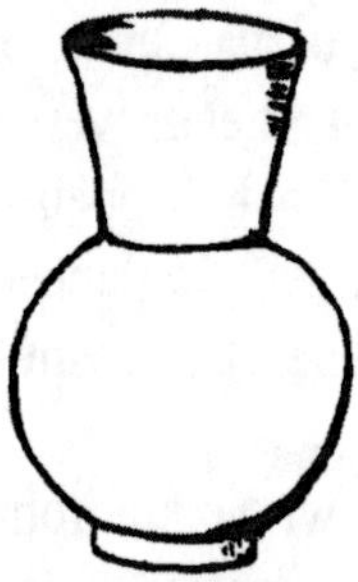

FIG. 25.—Indian Water-vessel.

The most important architectural adaptations of the water-lily motif were Vishnu's standard, and the Vishnu shrine, with its sikhara, or spire, described at p. 63. Vishnu's standard, or pillar—otherwise the holy Mount Meru, the pivot of the universe—was represented by the stalk of the blue water-lily, its ensign being the fruit containing the mystic wheel, and its bright fluttering pennons the petals of the flower. It was often surmounted by some heraldic animal, by the wheel itself, or by Vishnu's eagle, Garuda, or by figures of the Devas, the Shining Ones who dwell aloft. The simplest form of it is that shown in fig. 21, and in Pl. XII, B and C. A very elaborate composite design is one of a pair of *dhwaja-stambhas* represented in the Amarâvatî sculptures placed on either side of the entrance to the stûpa's procession path. It is reproduced in Pl. XII, fig. A. At the foot is an empty throne, with two figures in adoration on

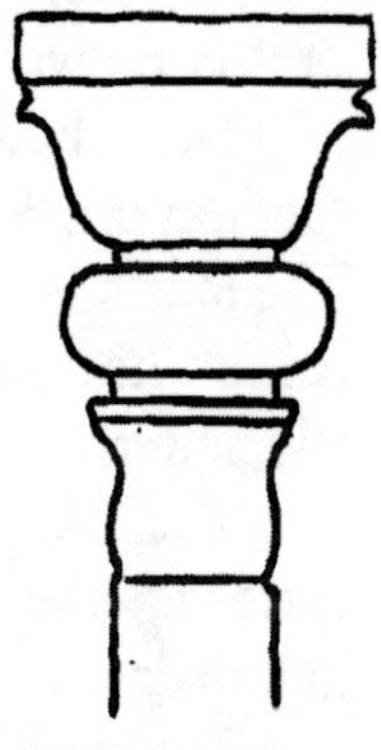

FIG. 26.—Capital of Temple Pillar.

[1] P. 134, Yatawara's translation.

either side of it. Behind the throne is the standard, the shaft built up of six fruits of the blue or white water-lily combined with mythical animals and figures. Five pairs of mounted figures, three pairs on lions and two on horseback, are ranged on either side of the shaft. They are probably the ten Visva-devas, or the ten chief powers controlling the forces of the universe. Above these deities, on either side of the shaft, a half-opened water-lily growing from it affords foothold to a female dancer, who, like the dancing Siva, probably symbolises the cosmic rhythm.[1]

The explanation of the symbolism of the whole stambha is no doubt that given in the Mahânirvâna Tantra of the Seven Upper Spheres, described as a revelation of Siva. First, rising above the seven nether spheres of Pâtala, the under-world, is the Brahmâ Lotus, with its four petals turned downwards, the fruit of which is "the beautiful circle of earth."

Over this is the blessed lotus, Bhîma the Terrible, with six petals and an inner circle having four openings. The fruit of it is Bhuvaloka, the region of the air.

Next above it is the rare flower of ten petals, Mahâpadma, the heavenly lotus, containing within its fruit the fire element. The fourth is the transparent lotus of the Ether, with sixteen petals: its fruit is the abode of Vâyu—Wind-force (*vajra*, electric power).

The fifth lotus is also transparent, with sixteen petals enclosing the fruit which is Jnâna-loka, the abode of pure knowledge.

The sixth is Gajna-padma, very rare, with two petals round

[1] Incidentally the connection of these two water-lilies with this stambha proves that the melon-shaped forms which help to compose it, technically known as *amalakas* (from *amala*, pure), are really the fruit of *Nymphæa*, which was also taken for Lakshmi's jar holding the amrita of immortality. The importance of this fact for elucidating the symbolism of the sikhara of Vishnu's shrine will be seen below (p. 63). The amalaka and Lakshmi's jar are used generally as interchangeable symbols, as they are in this stambha.

as the full moon. Within its fruit is the *Chîtamâni*, the jewel of Thought, and here Siva dwells in bodily form as Brahmâ, with the divine swan Hamsa, a mystic word which being transposed becomes Saham—I AM HE.

Crowning all is the vast lotus with a thousand shining turned-down petals, which contains the germs of thousand thousands of worlds yet unborn. It is the abode of PARA-BRAHMÂ, and there is the formless and motionless one, MAHÂ-KÂLÎ. "As the lightning is born from the cloud, and disappears within the cloud, so Brahmâ and all the gods take birth from KÂLÎ, and will disappear in KÂLÎ who is the giver of NIRVANA."

Now, the sikhara, or spire of Vishnu's shrine, which has been the subject of so much erratic archæological conjecture, is only an application of the water-lily symbol to the roofing of the cell which contained the deity's image in any of its sectarian forms—Buddhist, Jain, Vaishnavaite, Saivaite, etc. It is a square cell covered by the "four-petalled lotus with turned-down petals" and surmounted by the amalaka, the fruit of the blue nymphæa which is Vishnu's ensign. Obviously it becomes absurd to classify Vishnu's shrines as "Indo-Aryan" and Siva shrines as "Dravidian," when both have a common origin as symbols of Indo-Aryan religion. The coincidence that the area of the distribution of Siva shrines in India followed closely that of the Dravidian languages is totally irrelevant as an explanation of architectural style. Both Vishnu and Siva shrines are "Indo-Aryan." This being the case, the whole of Fergusson's elaborate classification must be abandoned as being unscientific and based upon historical fallacies. The technical questions relating to the sikhara and the pyramidal roofs of Siva shrines will be dealt with in another chapter.

The antithesis of the lotus and water-lily, which were always symbols of creation or life, was the white trumpet-shaped flower of the deadly datura plant, sacred to Siva.

The flower and fruit in combination were used as the decorative motif of the cross-brackets (fig. 26A) placed as a super-capital above the lotus-flower capital. Thus the temple pillar stood, like the flowering tree climbing round the cedar or pine, as a symbol of life and death. The datura is also the

FIG. 26A.—Cross-brackets used as Super-capital of Temple Pillar.

motif of the brackets supporting balconies and chhajas in Indian houses (Pl. III, B).

When the symbolic and structural significance of the Indian "orders of architecture" is understood it is easy to trace the derivation of medieval forms and combinations, and their later Muhammadan modifications, from their Asokan prototypes, for the tradition remained unbroken throughout the Mogul period and has continued to the present day.

PLATE XIV

TEMPLE AT AIHOLE (*circa* A.D. 600)

CHAPTER VI

THE *CHAITYA-GRIHA*, OR BUDDHIST CHAPTER-HOUSE—THE *RAISON D'ÊTRE* OF ROCK-CUT TEMPLES AND MONASTERIES—THE KÂRLÊ ROCK-CUT CHAITYA-HOUSE—THE BIRTH OF GOTHIC ART IN EUROPE

OF all the buildings of the Mauryan epoch that which is most distinctly Buddhist is the *Chaitya-griha*, or House of the Chaitya, which was the assembly-hall or chapter-house of the Order.[1] The religious observances enjoined upon members of the Order are distinguished from those of the Jains and of orthodox Brahmans by being congregational instead of individualistic, and thus Buddhist builders had to provide shelter for a much larger number of worshippers than would ordinarily gather together at Jain or Brahman shrines, except when the latter attracted large crowds of pilgrims. Though the religious tenets of the Jains and Buddhists had much in common, the social organisation of Buddhism differed from that of the former in recognising a distinction between laymen who merely accepted the teaching of the Master and members of the Sangha who devoted themselves entirely to a religious life. The necessity of providing accommodation for both classes, meeting together at stated times, in Buddhist places of worship, dictated the structural arrangements of the chaitya-griha. The Jains

[1] Fergusson, rather loosely, uses the word *chaitya*, which was the symbol or altar worshipped there, for the house itself. There was probably some technical distinction between a chaitya and a stûpa, but etymologically the two words have the same meaning —*i.e.* a tumulus, or heap.

in their temple-building usually followed the structural tradition of the Brahmanical sects.

The chapter-house was not a building taken over more or less complete, as were both the Christian church and the Muhammadan mosque, from an alien faith, nor was it "designed" in the modern architectural sense to meet the needs of Buddhist ritual. The elements of its structure grew together by a natural creative process. The chaitya itself, often enclosed in a simple circular shrine covered by a dome, as in Pl. IX, A, was both the object of adoration and the pivot of the design. The little Buddhist congregation of a Bengali village, when they met at the holy spot to listen to the dialogues of the Master and to walk round the chaitya-shrine, "turning the wheel of the Law," according to the ancient Vedic rite, needed some shelter. So they put over the shrine a simple bambu pavilion with a mat roof, like the covering of a Bengali boat-cabin (*chhai*) (Pl. II, fig. E), or bullock-cart; or sometimes a more substantial building of clay or brick, roofed like one of their own cottages. The plan of such a building (fig. 27) was that of a long room, generally semicircular or apsidal at the end occupied by the chaitya, with entrances at the opposite one. This allowed space for the congregation to sit in front of the chaitya shrine when listening to recitations of the word of the Law, and to walk in procession round it.

FIG. 27.—Plan of a Village Chaitya-house.

At Têr, the ancient Tagara, in the Waldrug district of Hyderabad, there is a building of a similar type, one of the oldest structural chaitya-houses now existing, which was discovered by Mr. H. Cousens in 1901. It is built of brick and plaster, with a roof exactly like that of the village huts sculptured at Bharhut (Pl. I). The entrance faces east: a single window over the doorway was intended to throw a strong con-

PLATE XV

VISHNU PILLAR AT AIHOLE

46]

centrated light upon the chaitya at the farther end. The hall, or *mandapam*, shown in front of the chapter-house in the illustration (fig. 28), was most probably intended for the lay members who attended the service, or it may have been used as the assembly hall of the village.

Generally, we may assume, the lay members listened and circumambulated outside the chaitya-pavilion, or hall; but in the more important chapter-houses the devotions of the lay members were provided for by verandahs on the long sides of the hall. Plate IX, c, shows one of this type, in which, however, there is no stûpa-like altar, but a simple table or throne covered by an umbrella. The verandahs are covered by lean-to roofs or chhajas, which support balconies, intended for a music-gallery, with the usual wooden rail surrounding them.

FIG. 28.—Ancient Buddhist Chaitya-house at Têr (from Fergusson's "History").

The finest of the very few structural chaitya-grihas yet discovered is one which Fergusson and his followers, to the confusion of their readers, put into his Dravidian compartment, though he points out its resemblance in plan to the ancient Buddhist chaitya-hall at Sânchî. This is a stone building, probably of the sixth or seventh century A.D., situated at Aihole in the Bijâpûr district of the Bombay Presidency. Although so many centuries later than the buildings of the Mauryan epoch, it may be taken parenthetically out of its chronological sequence to explain the arrangement of the great rock-cut chaitya-halls which are to be described next.

It is somewhat remarkable that this temple belonged apparently to the Jain sect: it was an exception to the rule that the Jains in their temple-building kept to the orthodox Brahmanical types, as their individualistic ritual demanded. Possibly, however, their ancient ritual differed from modern practice, and resembled that of the Buddhists more closely than it does now. But, in any case, in this temple a hall of the Sangha is provided, as if for an order of devotees distinct from the lay community.[1] The plan drawn by Dr. Burgess (fig. 29) shows the chaitya-cell placed in a pillared hall, with a pradakshinâ procession-path round the shrine for those who had admittance to the chapter-house. Outside is another one for lay worshippers, in a verandah—the roof of which is supported by stone piers—surrounding the whole building. As shown in the illustration of it (Pl. XIV), the latter, including the verandah, is raised upon a high plinth, and the entrance to the hall is through a porch the roof of which is supported by a massive Vishnu pillar (Pl. XV). The roof over the chaitya shrine has fallen, and the loose rubble which has been piled round the ruins makes it difficult to determine whether it was a sikhara of the Vishnu type, or whether it was domed like a Siva shrine. The latter might be expected over a chaitya, and it is significant that it is known locally as a Dûrgâ temple, a fact which makes a domed "Siva" roof, derived from the stûpa, almost a certainty.

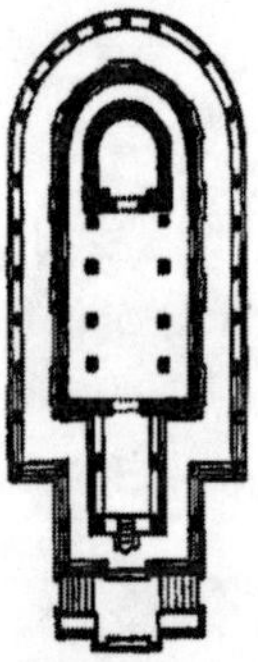

FIG. 29.—Plan of Temple at Aihole (from Fergusson's "History"). (Scale 50 feet to 1 inch.)

This Aihole temple is, or was, distinguished by its extraordinarily fine sculpture, as will be seen from Plates XIV and XV. The two superb high reliefs of flying Devas in the last

[1] The Sangha, like other Buddhist institutions, was only an adaptation of the organisation of the Aryan clans to the rule of life propounded by Sâkiya Muni: it was an Order within the larger Order of the Aryan community.

PLATE XVI

SCULPTURES AT AIHOLE

plate, which shows the condition in which they were discovered, have since probably been destroyed; for the photographs taken by Dr. Burgess in 1874, and published in his Report of the Archæological Survey of Western India for that year, show them already in a shockingly mutilated state. Such is the treatment of great works of art which archæological historians contemptuously dismiss as "Puranic."

Before proceeding to describe the great rock-cut chaitya-halls, some splendid examples of which belong to the first three centuries before the Christian era, a few preliminary observations regarding the practice which obtained in India, more than in any other country in the world, of excavating places in the living rock adapted both for religious and secular uses seem to be necessary. A cave temple or monastery suggests to the Western mind something essentially ascetic and barbaric, as our word "grotesque" implies. In India it represents a refinement of luxury for the users, an exceptional trial of skill for the craftsmen, and a special act of devotion and consecration on the part of the individual or the community for whom the work is performed. The reason why cave-dwellings remained in use in India long after the art of building had reached a high degree of perfection was partly climatic and partly geological; it was partly also due to the intuitive instinct that close to the bosom of Mother Earth, wherever the *genius loci* invited to prayer and meditation, was the best place for her children in adoring their Creator.

In India, instead of building, as in temperate climates, so as to admit sunlight right into the interior of houses, man instinctively tries his utmost to diminish the glare and heat. A dwelling carved out of the living rock, when it is designed with due regard to lighting and ventilation, is not only an ideal retreat for the student and religious recluse, but it affords better protection from the torrential rains of the monsoon and from the exhausting heat of the dry season than any building which the utmost skill of the carpenter, bricklayer, and stonemason could construct. It was not, therefore, the ascetic side of Indian religion which finds expression in the wonderful cave temples and monasteries, but rather the same spirit of *bhakti*, or the feeling that God demanded the best man could offer Him, both in a spiritual and material sense, which ever moves the mind of India.

The earliest rock-cut meeting-houses of the Buddhist order belonging to Asoka's time are generally small and, like the stûpas, of the plainest description, though some of them exhibit a high proficiency in technique. In the beginning the ritual of Buddhism was of the severest Puritan form, and did not countenance any elaboration either of structure or of symbolism, though all the artistic resources of Asoka's empire were at its disposal.

Fig. 30 represents the Asokan type of chaitya-house with plain octagonal pillars sloping inwards, as if to resist the outward thrust of the roof, though in this case they are not structural pillars, but cut in the solid rock; it is one of the earliest of the Ajantâ series, and is evidently a close reproduction of a wooden building. For further details of these early Hînayâna buildings the reader must refer to Fergusson and other writers; they are of great archæological interest, but the structure of them can be studied in similar works of a later date.

It was not until about a century after the death of the great Emperor who is canonised as a saint in the Buddhist calendar that Buddhism began to adapt the elaboration of the ancient Vedic ritual and the symbolism of Indo-Aryan art to the structure and adornment of its chaityas, chaitya-houses, and monasteries. By that time the teaching of the doctrines of Buddha was being affected by the development of new schools of Indo-Aryan philosophy, and Hînayâna Buddhism in the

PLATE XVII

ENTRANCE TO THE KARLI CHAITYA-HOUSE

north of India was being transformed into the school of the Mahâyâna, or Greater Vehicle.

The magnificent chaitya-house at Kârlê, carved in the rocks of the Western Ghats between Bombay and Poona, though not the most ancient, is typical of the best architectural work of the Hînayâna School in India. Fergusson dated it tentatively about the first century B.C. The main work of excavation may, however, have been begun even as early as Asoka's

FIG. 30.—Interior of Hînayâna Chaitya-house at Ajantâ.

time; but some of the figure sculpture which belongs to the Mahâyâna School must have been added several centuries later. The description given above of the structural chaitya-houses will make it easy to understand the planning of it (fig. 31). In front of the entrance were the traditional pair of Vishnu standards (*dhwaja-stambhas*), usually placed in front of stûpas of great sanctity or the temples of Buddhism, Jainism, and Brahmanism. Only the left one, a sixteen-sided pillar (Pl. XVII), is now standing, the place of the other one being covered by a later Dûrgâ shrine. It is interesting to notice that the symbolical tradition is still maintained in this comparatively modern Hindu building, for, as the Silpa-sâstras record,[1] the sixteen-sided pillar is technically known as *Rudra-kantha*—*i.e.* it is consecrated to Siva in Brahman hagiology, or Dharma in the equivalent Buddhist meaning ; Dûrgâ being the *sakti* or female energy of Siva in his tâmasic aspect as Rudra. The modern shrine is therefore the correct symbol for the right-hand pillar,

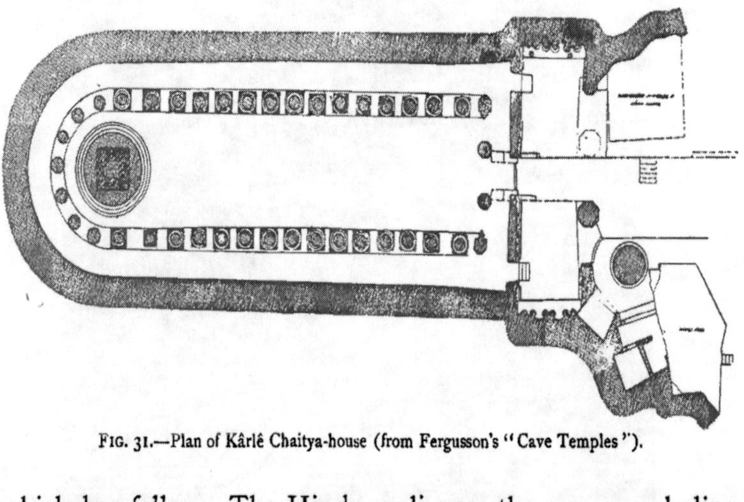

FIG. 31.—Plan of Kârlê Chaitya-house (from Fergusson's "Cave Temples").

which has fallen. The Hindu mali uses the same symbolism when he plants a pair of trees, as male and female, beside the well of his orchard or garden, and celebrates their wedding with sacred rites.

The capital of this Vishnu standard is not, as Fergusson supposed, a Persepolitan idea imported into India by the craftsmen of Asoka's court, but the traditional Indian rendering of ancient Vedic symbolism. It is the *amalaka*, the fruit of Vishnu's blue water-lily, and of the pure white flower of Siva,

[1] See above, p. 58.

PLATE XVIII

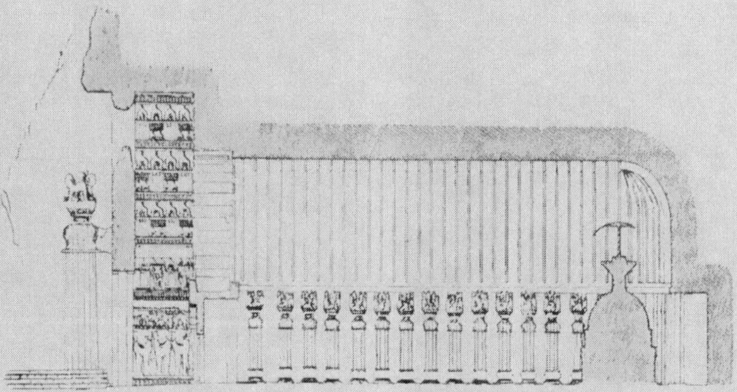

LONGITUDINAL SECTION, KARLÉ CHAITYA-HOUSE

FAÇADE OF THE KARLÉ CHAITYA-HOUSE

placed within the four legs of a Vedic altar of sacrifice; one part of the sixteen-petalled flower is turned down upon the shaft, as in the pillars of the Bharhut sculptures (fig. 21), and the other grows upwards to support the altar on which the four lion-guardians of the doors of the sky are placed. The entrance to the chaitya-house was through a porch with three entrances, over which was the *naubat-khâna*, or music-gallery, similar to that shown in the Bharhut relief (Pl. IX, c). This is now in a very ruinous condition,[1] and only the mortice-holes of wooden attachments to it now remain.

The façade of the entrance, which was screened from outside view by this porch and gallery, is illustrated in Pl. XVIII. The central doorway, opening into the nave, or hall of the Sangha, was the entrance for members of the order; the left entrance was for the laymen, so that they might circumambulate the chaitya and pass out by the exit on the right-hand side without disturbing the congregation.

This combination of three doorways in all the chaitya-houses and in other sacred edifices where the bodhi tree was the object of adoration, was a purely practical arrangement for the convenience of worshippers.

Plate IX, D, shows the Asokan prototype of the twelve-pillared mandapam (*baradari*), used as a shrine for the sacred tree. The three doorways in each side of it could have been used in the same way, the inner circuit being reserved for the elect of the order and the outer one for laymen. Some Buddhist stûpas are provided with a double rail round the pradakshinâ path for the same purpose. In Brahmanical shrines, also, the impure low castes could thus be separated from the twice-born. The ritualistic significance which attached itself to this combination of doorways was, no doubt, the reason why

[1] I do not know whether, like many ancient monuments, this has been lately restored by the Archæological Survey of India.

it persisted with a symbolical meaning only, when the original practical purpose had ceased to exist, as it does in modern Bengali temples.

The great lotus-leaf arch, or sun-window, over the main entrance served to light up the chaitya with the most impressive effect; but, like other constituents of the structural design of the chaitya-house, it was not merely placed there with the self-conscious motive of formal academic composition, which modern authorities declare to be the whole art of architecture; the light had to be focussed upon the chaitya, for the latter was the sacred object upon which the devoted labour of the craftsmen was concentrated. Incidentally the window which illuminated the altar was used to provide the best possible ventilation for the whole chaitya-house. The ends of the purlins which would have supported the wooden or bambu rafters of an Asokan house or cottage (Pl. I, B) roofed in this way, but here piously carved for decorative effect only, appear on the inner edge of the arched window; the outer edge is the pîpal leaf, as before explained. Part of the opening is filled with a framework of wood, resembling the torans of a village gateway. A framed lattice of this kind is almost invariably shown in the sculptured sun-windows used as symbolic decoration, except when they serve as shrines for deities. The whole façade above the entrances is decorated with these symbols, combined with the Vedic sacrificial rail. Most, if not all, of the figure sculpture was added in the later Buddhist or Mahâyâna period.

The extreme dimensions of the interior are about 124 feet by 43½ feet. The great nave, or hall of the Sangha, is shown in Pl. XIX. It is 25½ feet wide, and separated from the pradakshinâ path of the laymen by fifteen sculptured pillars on either side, with capitals similar to the two which flank the main entrance, but otherwise differing slightly in symbolism. Their shafts are octagonal, or, in the technical terms of the

PLATE XIX

INTERIOR OF THE KARLĒ CHAITYA-HOUSE

Silpa-sâstras, they are "Vishnu-necked."[1] The bases are Lakshmi's jars of plenty. Instead of the lions which crown the capitals of the pillars outside, each Vedic altar here is a throne for two pairs of Devas mounted upon kneeling elephants (Pl. XX). They are remarkable for proving what a high degree of excellence Indian sculpture had reached before the enervating Græco-Roman influence manifested itself in Indian Buddhist architecture. There is not much in the whole range of Gandhâran art to be placed in the same class with this and some of the Sânchî sculptures for spontaneity and freedom in design, fine expression, and bold technique.

The seven octagonal pillars behind the chaitya are plain, without caps or bases. The chaitya itself is also without any sculptured decoration, but it must be remembered that fresco painting on a ground of fine white plaster, together with painted banners hanging from the wooden ribs fitted in the roof, gave a rich glow of colour to the whole of the interior. The lower portion of the wooden tee, or pyramid of umbrellas (Vishnu's tree), placed upon the Vedic altar on the top of the chaitya, still remains. The underside of each umbrella was carved with a lotus flower; the symbolism of the tee being analogous to that of Vishnu's standard described above (pp. 62-3).

Obviously the vaulted roof, nearly semicircular in section but stilted at the springing, with its wooden ribs, were derived from the bambu-and-mat chhai of the Bengali village chaitya-house. Though there are striking resemblances with regard to planning and general arrangements between these great Buddhist temples and the Gothic cathedrals of Europe, it is impossible to draw any useful comparisons between them. The technical problems which confronted the Indian craftsmen in carving these chaitya-houses out of the living rock were totally different from those with which the Gothic builders had to deal:

[1] Or "Sangha-necked," as Buddhist craftsmen would have called them.

the fairy shafting of Gothic vaults and their widely spaced supports would have crumbled into dust under the immense weight which these mighty, close-set pillars of the Sangha were designed to uphold.

But the romantic spirit which informed the art of Indian Buddhist builders was the spirit of the Gothic cathedrals, and Gothic art was the gift of Indo-Aryans to their brother craftsmen in the West. In its pristine splendour the chapter-house of Kârlê must have been one of the grandest places of worship ever made by the hands of men.

It is easy to follow the journey of the Lotus of the Good Law from India into China, and thence into Korea and Japan; but how the art of Kârlê and Ajantâ passed into western Asia, and thence into Europe, to blossom again in the glorious cathedrals of France, is a fascinating chapter in the world's romance which remains to be written.

It must have been partly through the craftsmen who followed the Asiatic hordes which overran Europe continually for many centuries after the beginning of the Christian era, and partlythrough the contact of East and West in the long struggle of the Crusades. But this much is certain, that East met West very long ago in the fellowship of art, and when a great art impulse comes again in Europe and in Asia the meeting-ground will be the same.

And when that romance of real life is written, one chapter of it may tell how, after Charles Martel hammered the Moors on the battlefield of Tours and drove them from the fair fields of France, many of Abdur Rahman's craftsmen remained as captives or deserters to the winning side—for craftsmen were non-combatants, often unwillingly pressed into military service; and how, settling down in their new adopted country and working side by side with their brother-craftsmen of the Latin race, they helped to build those splendid abbeys which were

PLATE XX

VISHNU PILLARS, KARLÉ CHAITYA-HOUSE

the nurseries of Gothic art, bringing to the West the masonic secrets of the East, the traditions and the inspiration of the Indo-Aryan abbeys of Ajantâ and Ellora which were at that moment the grandest and most beautiful in the world. Thus the two branches of the Aryan race were joined together once more by spiritual and domestic ties for the advancement of the common cause of humanity.

For other chaitya-houses of the Hînayâna school of Buddhism at Bhâjâ, Bedsâ, Nâsik, Ajantâ and elsewhere the reader must refer to the descriptions given by Fergusson and Dr. Burgess. They are all planned on the same principle, and it is quite easy to follow the symbolism of their structure and decoration by means of the description of the Kârlê chaitya-house given above. The later chaitya-houses of the Mahâyâna school will be taken in their chronological sequence.

CHAPTER VII

THE VIHÂRA, OR MONASTERY—THE GAUTAMÎ-PUTRA MONASTERY, NÂSIK—MONASTERY AT BEDSÂ—MODELS OF MONASTERIES AT MÂMALLAPURAM

WE must now pass on to the *vihâras*, or monasteries adjoining, or sometimes included in, the chaitya-houses and other shrines to which the religious devotees of ancient India attached themselves. It is wrong to assume that either the chaitya-houses or the monasteries which belonged to them were exclusively Buddhist institutions, although the oldest materials for their architectural history are practically all Buddhist. The life of religious recluses dwelling together in forest âsramas is often described in ancient Sanskrit literature. The Silpa-sâstras give particular directions for the planning of villages intended for those who lived a monastic life; and just as the builders of Buddhist chaityas and chaitya-houses followed very closely, as we have seen, the ancient Indian tradition of structure and symbolism, so there cannot be much doubt that the dwellings of the Buddhist bhikkus in Asoka's time differed very little from those which had been used by devotees of other sects before the tenets of the great Kshatriya reformer were propagated by his zealous royal disciple.

An ordinary âsrama occupied by Buddhist bhikkus is quaintly shown in one of the Bharhut reliefs (Pl. XXI), which represents the Jetavana monastery of Srâvastî, which in Fa Hian's time, or the fifth century A.D., had grown into a great establishment with splendid buildings seven stories in height.

PLATE XXI

A

B

ANCIENT INDIAN MONASTERIES (*circa* 250 B.C.)

Here it is only the usual collection of simple shrines and primitive hermits' huts which had existed in India from time immemorial, but some pious benefactor is superintending the paving of the ground with bricks, a cartload of which is being unloaded in the foreground. One of the monks is bringing water to pour on the sacred tree, planted on a mound surrounded by the Vedic rail, which grows beside one of the shrines. The bhikku's water-vessel is the same as that used by a Brahman sannyâsin in the present day, and the bullock-cart is an exact rendering of the country vehicle for which modern invention has not yet found a practical substitute. This persistence of ancient types need not always be taken as a proof of the immobility of the Indian mind, but rather to indicate that certain fundamental problems of life were fully resolved in very early times by the pioneers of Indian civilisation, and cannot be radically altered without uprooting the whole foundation upon which that civilisation rests.

FIG. 32.—A Modern Indian Sâdhu.

The two-storied monastic dwelling shown in the same plate is also from the Bharhut reliefs. It resembles in general arrangement some Buddhist monasteries in Sikkim, which have a large prayer-wheel fixed in a verandah on the ground floor so that passers-by can turn it; the upper floor combining a shrine and living-accommodation for the monks who attend it.

An ordinary wandering friar in ancient India carried his hut with him in the shape of a palm-leaf umbrella (*chhattra*), as the sâdhu of the present day does (fig. 32). The umbrella placed over a Buddhist chaitya was a mark of royalty in a double sense, as belonging both to the insignia of the Kshatriya

Prince Siddhartha of Kapilavastu, and to that of the spiritual Lord, the Monk of Bodh-Gayâ.

A fixed *chhattri*, or shelter, for a yogi or bhikku in the absence of a tree, would be simply an umbrella supported on four sticks; but respect for the holy man frequently inspired individuals or the community to build permanent chhattris of fine carpentry, brickwork, or masonry; others were four-pillared pavilions covered by a dome, like the village shrine shown in Pl. IX, A. Akbar built such a yogi-seat of stone close to his palace at Fatehpur-Sîkrî. Yogis also went through their spiritual exercises in square cells made of matting, clay, brick, or stone, with a domed or vaulted roof. Their sleeping-cells are shown in ancient Indian sculptures as oblong huts with a single apartment roofed like the Bharhut cottages.

An ancient Indian monastery consisted simply of rows of such cells ranged round or in front of the shrine, which might be a solid stûpa, or a cell containing an image dedicated to the particular cult to which the monks belonged. In the early Hînayâna monasteries the chaitya was only sculptured in low relief on the wall of the quadrangle, which was the hall of the Sangha, opposite the doorway.

None of the early structural monasteries now remain. Among the oldest and most interesting of the rock-cut examples are those situated among the hills which form the watershed of the upper Godaveri River, at Nâsik, an ancient seat of Indo-Aryan learning mentioned by Ptolemy. The Gautamî-putra Monastery, now known archæologically as "Cave III," belonged to the Hînayâna school, like the great chaitya-house of Kârlê, with which some of the Nâsik monasteries are contemporary. The plan of it (fig. 33) shows the oblong sleeping-cells of the monks; there are none of the square yogi seats which appear in later Buddhist monasteries after the Brahmanical doctrine of Yoga had filtered into Buddhism through the teaching of

PLATE XXII

FAÇADE OF THE GAUTAMÎ-PUTRA MONASTERY (SECOND CENTURY A.D.)

Nâgârjuna. The simple ritual of the Hînayâna school only demanded a stone bench which ran round three sides of the hall (41 feet broad by 46 deep) in front of the cells, upon which the monks sat to listen to the word of the Blessed One. The position of the chaitya, sculptured in low relief, is shown in the plan by the projection on the walls of the cells which face the central doorway.

The entrance to the hall was through a verandah (Pl. XXII) fronted by six pillars of the Sangha with capitals almost identical in their sculpture with those at Kârlê, except that some of the Devas on the Vedic altars ride upon bulls and lions instead of elephants. The bull was the sacrificial animal, the symbol of procreation, the *vâhan*, or vehicle of Siva, and thus the guardian of the western quarter, or the gate of the setting sun. The lion stood for the blazing heat of the sun high in the heavens which dried up the deadly mists of the plains: it was thus the vehicle of Dûrgâ, the Inaccessible, Destroyer of demons—who was Siva's bride and represented Nature-force, the counterpart of the Great Spirit who is the Lord of Death. The lion as a sun-emblem was the guardian of all four quarters, and became the *vâhan*, or throne symbol, of the Buddha to signify his world-wide dominion and the glory of his spiritual conquests. The elephant was Indra's rain-cloud and guardian of the south, whence came the rushing monsoon winds carrying Lakshmi's

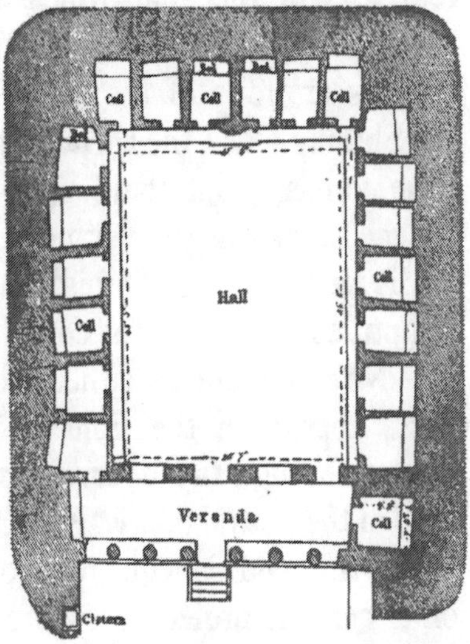

FIG. 33.—Plan of Gautamî-putra Monastery, Nâsik.

nectar-jar upon their wings. The horse, guarding the northern quarter, was the noble steed upon which the Aryan warriors rode to victory in India from their ancient home in the north. This early Buddhist sculpture is purely and intensely Indo-Aryan: it is the joyous nature-symbolism of the Vedas carved in wood and stone.

There is a slight difference between the Vedic altars of the Gautamî-putra capitals and those at Kârlê: in most of them the four legs of the altar which enclose the water-lily fruit, or *amalaka*, are carved into dwarf figures, the *pisâchas*—little demons or trolls of the nether-world who are the servants of the Shining Ones, the Devas of the higher spheres. The pillars have no bases, but stand upon another stone bench provided for the monks in the verandah. In front of the pillars is a Vedic rail, supported by pisâchas on a colossal scale. Another sculptured rail forms the entablature supported by the capitals.

No sun-windows, either as decorative symbols or for giving light, appear on the front of this monastery. The hall is lighted through two doorways and two oblong windows. The head of the central doorway is sculptured with a toran like those at Bharhut and Sânchî, and two guardian deities (*dwâra-pâlas*) on either side protect it. Over the door are placed the three symbols of the Illumination (the bodhi tree), the Preaching of the Law (the wheel), and of Pari-Nirvâna (the stûpa).

Fergusson's critical judgment upon the sculpture of the Gautamî-putra Monastery is very wide of the mark. He compares it with that of the adjoining Nahapâna monastery, which may be somewhat earlier in date, and praises the "graceful bell-shaped Persian capitals" of the latter to the disparagement of the "pudding-forms" of the other. Here he was betrayed into the misconception which with other modern writers has become an obsession, that all that was finest in Indian art always came straight from western Asia, and that the history of Hindu sculpture is "written in decay." None of the sculpture at Kârlê and very little that belongs to the Mauryan epoch in India had any connection with Persia in the sense intended by Fergusson and other archæologists. These capitals are Vedic-Indian, or Indo-Aryan, and only Persian so far as Persian art was in early Vedic times itself inspired by Aryan culture. The superficial similarity between these and Persepolitan capitals was the result of the common origin of their symbolism, not to the presence of foreign craftsmen in the India of Asoka's time. The splendour of the Mauryan court may have attracted

FIG. 34.—Section of Rock-cut Vihara at Bedsâ (from a drawing by the Archæological Survey of India).

skilled craftsmen from Persepolis, but they worked in India under Indian inspiration just as the Gandharan craftsmen did some centuries later. They were but craftsmen learning the art language of India, not artists enriching it with their own creative ideas. The symbolism of this Hînayâna Buddhist art proves this to be the case, as Fergusson himself would have admitted if he had understood it.

An exceptional form of rock-cut vihâra is the early Buddhist one at Bedsâ, ascribed to the second century B.C., which has its cells placed round a chaitya-house having the usual barrel-vaulted roof and an apse round the chaitya. The plan and section are shown in figs. 34 and 35.

The Gandhara monasteries, described by M. Foucher, were generally rows of cells ranged in a square, the centre of which was occupied by the chaitya; but occasionally the cells were placed in a circle round the sacred symbol. The panch-ratna, or "five-jewelled" temple, from which the plan of the Taj Mahall was derived, was probably a small monastery with a verandah all round the cell containing the chaitya or image and a yogi's seat at each of the four corners—the nava-ratna or nine-jewelled temple being a similar one with two stories.

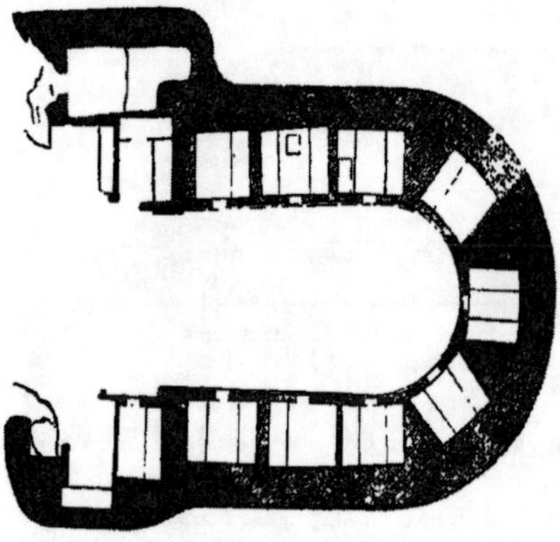

FIG. 35.—Plan of Vihara at Bedsâ (half to scale of Fig. 34).

The most characteristic of ancient Indian monasteries, often described in Indian Buddhist literature and by the Chinese pilgrims, Fa Hian and Hiuen Tsang, were the many-storied pyramidal ones. Perhaps there was in these lofty structures some reminiscence of the pyramidal ziggarats of Babylon, used for astronomical observations; but the use to which they were generally applied was of purely Indian origin. They were both monasteries and colleges, their arrangement being adapted for the graduation of the courses of study followed in these institutions, both Buddhist and Brahmanical. The Pâli books record that the spiritual training of members of the order was divided into six graduated courses. As soon as the first section of the prescribed texts was mastered, the monks were exempted from the common drudgery of their ordinary daily life. When they could expound two sections perfectly they were permitted to reside in an "upper furnished room." Those who were expert in three sections

PLATE XXIII

MONOLITHIC MODEL OF A FOUR-STORIED MONASTERY, MĀMALLAPURAM (*circa* A.D. 670)

were allowed a lower class of servants to wait upon them. Proficiency in four sections entitled the monks to the services of lay disciples, called "pure men" (*upasakas*). The reward for passing the fifth stage was an elephant-carriage. Finally, the monk who had complete knowledge of all six sections was qualified as an abbot and was allowed the dignity of an escort. No doubt the idea of this graduated curriculum was not exclusively Buddhist, but based upon the scholastic tradition of Vedic learning.

The design of these pyramidal monasteries was eminently adapted for the practical working of such a system. Indeed, if the prestige of the British Raj is not compromised by the borrowing of Indian ideas, it might be adapted (with the help of lifts, telephones, and imagination) to the uses of modern secular administration. It certainly would lend itself to the administrative principle that the highest official ranks should have the coolest places; and possibly it could be used as an architectural expedient for ensuring that full mental vigour in departmental heads which, in these degenerate days, can only be expected in Indian hill-stations.

Hiuen Tsang gives the following descriptions of the appearance of such structures at the celebrated Bengali University of Nâlanda, the modern Barâgâon, seven miles north of Râjagriha and not far from Pâtaliputra, Asoka's imperial city—the modern Patna. "The houses of the monks," he says, "were each four storeys in height. The pavilions [halls of the Sangha?] had pillars ornamented with dragons, and had beams resplendent with all the colours of the rainbow—rafters richly carved, columns ornamented with jade, painted red and richly chiselled, and balustrades [Vedic rails?] of carved openwork. The lintels of the doors were decorated with elegance and the roofs with glazed tiles of brilliant colours, which multiplied themselves by reflection and varied the effect at every moment in a thousand manners."

All those which the Chinese pilgrim described, and also those which Kanishka built in the Gandhara country, are now only heaps of ruins. Their upper stories were, no doubt, often built entirely of wood; and even more substantial ones of brick were pulled down as soon as they were deserted, to provide building material for neighbouring towns and villages. Fortunately, however, there exists a very fine model of such a building, one of the so-called Raths at Mâmallapuram, near Madras, carved out of a large granite boulder (Pl. XXIII). There is every reason to believe that it closely resembles the pyramidal monasteries of ancient India in the north as well as in the south.

The date of this Dharmarâja Rath,[1] as it is now called, has been ascertained with tolerable certainty as *circa* 670-700 A.D. It is a reproduction in miniature of a Saivaite monastery of four storeys; it is, in fact, an amplification of the plan of the Bharhut Bodhi tree shrine shown in Pl. IX, D, by the provision of accommodation for devotees permanently attaching themselves to it. The nine-spired temple at Buxar, in the Hughli district, and similar twenty-five-spired ones at Lâlgi and other places in Bengal, are designed on the same principle; only the Bengali roofs have a convex curvature, on account of the heavy rainfall of the locality, and the square cells are crowned with Vishnu sikharas instead of by Siva domes.

Though the interior of the Dharmarâja Rath is not shown in the model, it is easy by analogy to realise the plan of it. Making allowance for the difference of climate and material—the Bengali temples being built of brick—the ground plan of the Mâmallapuram model follows closely the northern prototype from which it was derived.[2] There was a square shrine

[1] Rath means, literally, the chariot of a warrior, or processional car of a sacred image.

[2] The particular Bengali temples mentioned are, of course, quite modern, but the type is a very ancient one, which the builders of Muhammadan Gaur adapted to their mosques.

(or, hall of the Sangha, if the building was occupied by Buddhists), surrounded on all sides by a verandah roofed with the curved Bengali chhaja. On the side of the entrance of the shrine the verandah breaks forward slightly, so as to form a porch. At each corner of the verandah there was a square cell, either for a living yogi or for a sculptured symbol of a deity. But one of the corners might have been used, as in a storied Bengali temple, for the staircase leading to the first floor; or this might have been placed in the thickness of the walls of the shrine, or hall of the Sangha.

The miniature sun-windows, with which Kârlê and Nâsik have made us familiar, are sculptured as ornaments at close

FIG. 36.—Gargoyles of the Dharmarâja Râth.

intervals along the whole length of the chhaja, and carved "Gothic" gargoyles throw off the rain from the pradakshinâ, or procession-path, on the next storey (fig. 36).

The half-finished sculptured pillars and pilasters in front of the verandah and porch present the ancient motif of Vishnu's pillar, with the amalaka capital, the architectural use of which we have already traced back to the time of Asoka. For the bases, instead of Lakshmi's nectar-jar, the sculptors have used the symbolic lion-guardians—Dûrgâ's emblems—which usually stand detached in front of the entrances, as they do at Elephanta. The reason for this innovation was that the dimensions of the rock were not sufficient for carving them in their traditional places on each side of the steps.

In the original, wherever it might have been, it is probable that the ground-floor of the monastery, here simulated in sculpture, was built of stone—all the upper floors being of brick and plaster, or wood, or a combination of these materials. The monastic cells which surrounded the shrine or hall of the Sangha, on the first floor, are shown in both types—*i.e.* there are four yogi cells at the corners and twelve oblong sleeping-compartments (three on each side), connected with them by lower covered corridors which may have been provided with benches. The Vedic rail which forms a plinth outside the whole range of cells, though still recognisable as such, has lost its triple bars. The ancient sun-windows are repeated as dormers in the roofs, but instead of the screen or lattice which they contain at Kârlê and Nâsik, they have become miniature shrines. The dome of the yogi cells has also become bell-shaped by the addition of outward curving eaves for throwing off the rain (fig. 37).

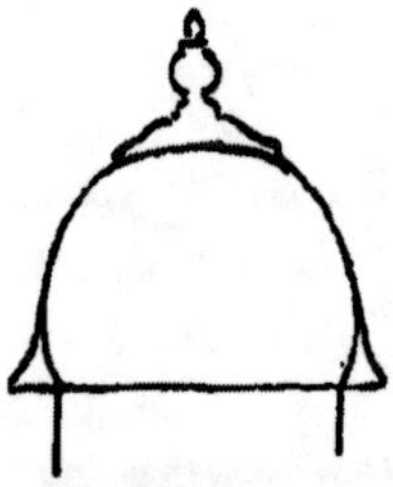

FIG. 37.—Diagram of Dome, showing Eaves added for throwing off Rain.

In front of the cells was the usual procession-path round the shrine or chaitya-hall, which probably had a pillared verandah outside like the temple at Aihole (Pl. XIV), in which a staircase leading to the next storey might have been placed. Fig. 38 shows the plan as I assume it to have been. It differs considerably from that suggested by Mr. Chisholm, which Fergusson adopted.

The plan of the second floor, or third storey, was similar, except that there was accommodation for eight monks only. The highest story provided for an equal number of yogi seats but only four sleeping-cells. The shrine here was octagonal, instead of square, and this slight difference from the usual northern plan (which Fergusson, curiously enough, overlooked) is the only distinction which justifies the name "Dravidian"

PLATE XXIV

MONOLITHIC MODEL OF A TWO-STORIED MONASTERY, MAMALLAPURAM (*circa* A.D. 670)

given to this kind of building. The Mânasâra, says Râm Râz, gives the technical name of a square shrine as *Nâgara*; an octagonal one as *Drâvidha*, and a circular one as *Vesara*.[1] But as the entire planning and every other structural and symbolic detail of these pyramidal monasteries were Indo-Aryan ideas, imported from the north, it would be entirely misleading to take a minor difference of this kind as a reason for classifying all Siva shrines as "Dravidian." The fact that Siva shrines are now mostly found in Southern India had nothing whatever to do with their architectural origin.

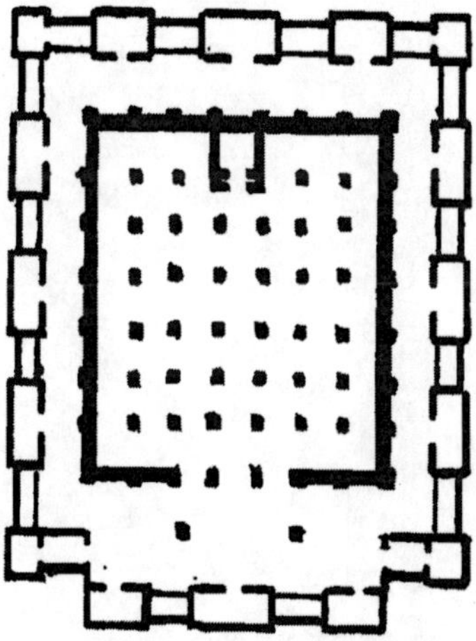

FIG. 38.—Conjectural Plan of First Floor of Dharmarâja Râth.

Another splendid specimen of seventh-century craftsmanship is a great monolithic model at Mâmallapuram, called now Bhîma's Rath, which reproduces on a smaller scale a two-storied Saivaite monastery. The dimensions of it in the granite rock are 48 feet in length, 25 feet in breadth, and about 26 feet in height. Like most of the raths at Mâmallapuram, it remained unfinished, and owing to the sculptors having gone too far in imitating the details of a structural building, the upper part of the rock split right through the roof, probably while they were working at it.

Plate XXIV will give a good idea of the noble design of the original building and of the extraordinary skill of the sculptors. The planning of it and general design were evidently the working out of a tradition which went back to the Buddhist two-storied halls of Asoka's time, as shown in the Bharhut reliefs (Pl. IV, A).

[1] Râm Râz, p. 49.

In this particular the Saivaites of the seventh century were probably borrowers or adaptors of Buddhist structural ideas, though Saivaite and Buddhist art as a whole comes from a common Indo-Aryan source. The ground plan (fig. 39) shows the hall, or temple, measuring in the model about 10 feet by 30 feet, which was probably intended to be open on the sides, like the Bharhut prototype.

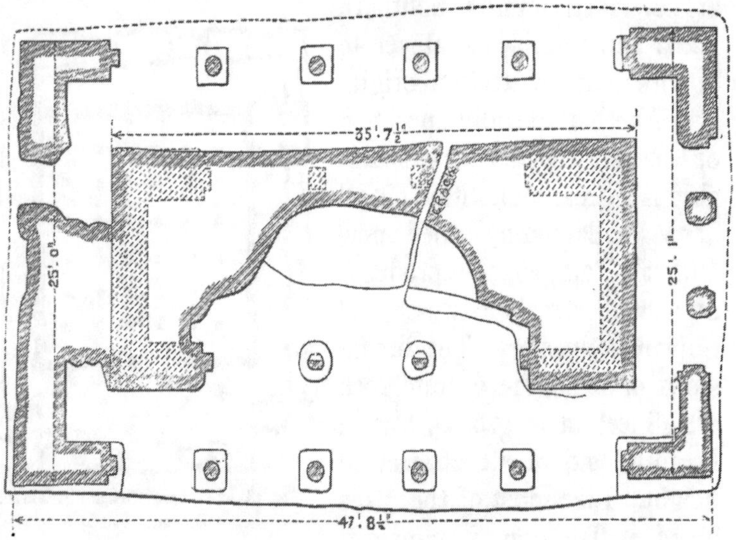

FIG. 39.—Plan of Bhîma's Rath (from Fergusson's "Cave Temples").

Excepting the roof, all the details—the pillars and pilasters; the chhajas; the rows of cells surrounding the procession-path on the first floor, etc.—are the same as in the four-storied pyramidal monastery last described. At each end of the great hall or temple in the upper storey a Siva shrine is sculptured under a richly carved gable, which in Europe would be said to be a masterpiece of Gothic craftsmanship. The brackets which support the arches under the barge-boards are identical with those which afterwards appeared in Akbar's buildings. Under the eaves, on each of the long sides of the building, are five other projecting shrines, three large and two small, placed opposite to the five monastic cells. They are flanked by pilasters of the same design as the pillars of the ground floor, and are covered by sun-window roofs in dormer fashion. The ridge of the roof was intended to be crowned by a row of eighteen *kalasas* (water-pot finials), but these were never finished, like many other details. In the original building most probably the whole of the upper storey, including the roof, would have been built of brick and plaster, like the fifteenth-century mosques of Gaur, the construction of which was derived from Bengali prototypes. In the Jahângîrî Mahall at Agra there is a similar vaulted roof built of stone slabs, and Indian builders were as capable in the seventh century as in the fifteenth of using stone for such a purpose. Even in Asoka's buildings the choice of the material depended upon the supply available in different localities. There were skilled carpenters where wood was plentiful, skilled bricklayers where bricks were used, and equally skilled masons where stone was most abundant.

CHAPTER VIII

VISHNU AND SIVA SHRINES—THE ALLEGORY OF THE DAWN-MAIDEN—THE BRAHMÂ SHRINE—ORIENTATION OF INDIAN TEMPLES

It has been made evident in the last chapter that in ancient Indian monasteries the groups of cells inhabited by the monks were always very small and of no structural importance. All the architectural interest of the monastery was centred on the shrine or shrines around which the monastic cells were grouped, and on the Sangha halls, or the pillared pavilions, which belonged to the former. We have seen what the sacred symbol, the chaitya, or stûpa, venerated by both the Jains and disciples of the Buddha, was like. It is necessary now to describe in greater detail the shrine of Vishnu, the ancient symbol of the holy Mount Meru, which was also adopted by Buddhists and Jains, just as many pagan symbols were adopted by early Christians with a different connotation.

Whatever century historians may assume to be the beginning of the period when the followers of orthodox Hinduism who took either Vishnu or Siva as their patron deity (*Ishta-dêva*) began to be sufficiently numerous and powerful in the State to take political and social precedence over other sects, it is certain that the philosophical and dogmatic differences typical of Vaishnavism and Saivism not only belonged to Buddhism, but prevailed in the earlier schools of Indo-Aryan thought. They were probably very much the same as those which in Greek philosophy distinguished the Epicureans from the Stoics.

To go back to the Indian village: if one divides the southern half of the pradakshinâ path, which followed the movement of the sun in the day, from the northern half, which represented its night's journey, and assumed that the villagers of the southern quarters belonged to one school of philosophy and those of the northern quarters to another; and, further, that the southerners maintained the supremacy of the cosmic powers which caused the sun to rise to its zenith at noon and brought happiness in this present life; while the northerners held to the ascetic ideal and looked forward to future bliss through being merged in the supreme Spirit which rules the universe, we shall have a sufficiently clear conception of the broad distinctions between Vaishnavism and Saivism.

There must have been, of course, in India—as at other times and in other places—many thinkers who held the middle course between the two extremes. The Buddha was one of those who succeeded in working out a philosophical formulary so generally acceptable that for a time his following absorbed the great majority of both extreme schools of thought. The architecture of Buddhism, therefore, for several centuries represented the architecture of India, not because it created any new architectural standards or ideals, but because the influence of Buddhism was supreme in the State. Buddhist architecture, like Buddhist philosophy, absorbed the traditions of Vedic India, but did not obliterate them.

After several centuries Buddhism itself split into two camps: the Hînayâna—the Little Vehicle—which was the orthodox agnostic school, and the Mahâyâna—the Great Vehicle—which accepted, among other things, the doctrine of Yoga. Then gradually the Brahmans, who under the peaceful sway of Buddhism had superseded the Kshatriya, or warrior class, as spiritual leaders of the people, succeeded in establishing, upon the basis of so much of the Buddha's teaching as they had accepted, more abstruse metaphysical and philosophical theses, so that both the Hînayâna and Mahâyâna schools merged into modern Hinduism in the same way as the earlier schools of Vedic India had merged into Buddhism. The Hînayâna, which was then the southern school of Buddhism, grew into the modern Saivaite school, which inherited the ascetic traditions of pre-Buddhist times; while the Vaishnavaites, who represent the reforming schools of northern India, absorbed the following of Mahâyânist philosophy. It must, however, be remembered that in modern times the two main sects, or groups of sects, have intermingled at so many points that the old distinctions have been largely superseded by others which individual Hindu teachers, like Sankarâcharya, Râmanûja and Chaitanya, have introduced.

The apparent anomaly, which has confused Fergusson and many others, is that a Vishnu shrine is not necessarily Vaishnavaite in the sectarian sense, but only one that is dedicated to the Vaishnava aspect of Brahmâ, Buddha, or Siva, as the case may be. Similarly, a Siva shrine may be Saivaite, Buddhist, or Vaishnavaite. Fergusson did not perceive that throughout all these sectarian changes there prevailed the great architectural tradition which was Indo-Aryan, and that these symbols represent philosophical concepts accepted by all the chief schools of Indo-Aryan religion.

The idea of the Vishnu mystic pillar, or holy mountain supporting the sky, is of very remote antiquity and common to Europe and Asia. The Christian church tower and steeple, and the Indian Vishnu sikhara are one and the same symbol with different implications. The Vedic philosophers took it as the symbol of the equilibrium of the two opposing cosmic forces, which they named Brahmâ and Siva, or evolution and involution. The three symbols together, the Trimûrti, are not separate "gods," but three Aspects of Ishwara, the first manifestation of the cosmic creative power proceeding from the Unknowable, Brahman. But the man in the Indian village, though not a polytheist, as is popularly believed,[1] would always think of a Vishnu shrine as the holy Mount Meru, or as Mount Mandara, Vishnu's abode in the Himâlayas.

Architecturally we are not concerned with the primitive Aryan rite of circumambulating a sacred hill or mountain with which the Vishnu shrine is connected, but certainly the Indian sikhara is of far greater antiquity than the sixth or seventh century, the date which Fergusson erroneously gave to the great Buddhist shrine of Bodh-Gayâ. What is perhaps the earliest and most interesting representation of it seems to have escaped the notice of orientalists altogether. It occurs in one of the bas-reliefs of Nineveh discovered by Layard, and described by him as the Palace of Sennacherib.

FIG. 40.—Vishnu Temples and Royal Tombs at Nineveh (Layard's "Nineveh," 2nd series, Pl. 16).

In this relief (fig. 40) the palace itself is evidently the group of flat-roofed buildings on the right. To the left of this are three domed buildings which I have no doubt are meant to be royal tombs; they are prototypes of the stûpa—Siva's symbol—which was the royal tomb of ancient India. The two conical buildings behind these are temples—shrines of the holy mountain which appears in the background. To make the symbolism clearer, the flowering tree, the Tree of Life, and the pine or cedar, the Tree of Eternity, are planted close to the tombs and on the slopes of the mountain.

[1] See Introduction, p. xxxv.

I must leave others to enlarge upon the inferences to be drawn from the appearance of Aryan Vishnu, and Siva symbols, or their prototypes, in the royal tombs of Nineveh in the eighth century B.C. The most significant point to be noticed is that the juxtaposition of Vishnu's sikhara and Siva's stûpa, or the symbols of Life and Death, is exactly what occurred so frequently in ancient and medieval India. Fergusson's description of the former as "Hindu and Indo-Aryan" and of the latter as "Buddhist and Dravidian" not only misled himself, but gave to others entirely false clues to the history and chronology of Indian art.

The earliest Indian Vishnu shrines yet discovered are the monolithic ones carved in miniature which have been dug up in great quantities on the site of Sarnath, the Deer Park where the Buddha preached the Law to his first disciples, and also at Bodh-Gayâ. They are found together with vast numbers of miniature stûpas, many of which are probably of greater age, as the stûpa was the most sacred emblem of the first disciples of the Buddha. But just as at the present day Hindus will often worship at Muhammadan shrines of great sanctity, so in early Buddhist times many who belonged to other schools of thought brought their pious offerings to the shrines of Sâkiya Muni. Then Buddhism seems to have gradually adopted the Vishnu symbol as a distinctive mark of the Mahâyâna school.

Fig. 41 is a typical specimen of the Vishnu symbols dug up at Sarnath: it has an image of Ganêsha carved upon it. It is crowned by the amalaka; the finial, water-pot, or *kalasha*, is missing in most cases. It was probably carved in a separate piece and perhaps in a different material. Like all Vishnu shrines, the sides of the sikhara are ornamented with sun-windows: Vishnu watches for the approach of his lovely bride Lakshmî, or Srî, who is Ushas, the Vedic Dawn-maiden.

The identity of Lakshmî with Ushas, I venture to assert,

is proved by the allegory of the Churning of the Ocean, an ancient Indo-Aryan myth, the meaning of which has long been a mystery to Oriental scholars. It is really a vivid picture of the dawn and sunrise in the Himâlayas, which were evidently the cradle of one branch of the Indo-Aryan family; with Kailâsa, the great snow-capped peak of Siva, and Mount Mandara, Vishnu's abode, in the background. The Devas, the powers of light, combine with the Asuras, the powers of darkness, to churn the cosmic ocean for the nectar of life and immortality. They use for a churning-stick Vishnu's mountain, Mandara, and for a rope the serpent Ananta, or Eternity (the Milky Way), which encircles the earth. After a long churning, fire and poisonous smoke (the first glow upon the mountains before dawn, and the gathering together of the mists and clouds in the valleys) obscure the sky, and the Devas are disheartened. Siva drinks the poison and becomes "blue-throated," *i.e.* the crimson glow on his snowy peak gradually turns to dazzling white and the mountain slopes below the snow-line become violet-blue. At the same time Lakshmî, the dawn, appears, seated on the Brahmâ lotus, bringing with her health, dance and song, happiness and prosperity, and the jar of nectar which Indra, the rain-god, pouring his refreshing

FIG. 41.—Miniature Vishnu Shrine found at Sarnath.

showers upon her, takes into his keeping. As she rises from the cosmic ocean and prepares to fling herself upon Vishnu's breast, the Devas shout triumphant hymns and the powers of darkness fling themselves down into the underworld where they dwell.

The whole site of Sarnath was covered with innumerable brick-built and monolithic stûpas of different dimensions, and it is probable that pairs of Vishnu and Siva symbols were often placed there by the same devotee. Perhaps some of the brick bases now remaining will prove to have belonged to Vishnu shrines, instead of stûpas, for the tall sikharas which crowned them were much easier to destroy than the more solid structure of the stûpa.

The structural importance and historical interest attaching to the great Vishnu shrine of Bodh-Gayâ are unique. Seeing that all the symbolism of Buddhist art was derived from the ancient Indo-Aryan tradition, the fitness of building a shrine to symbolise the Vaishnava aspect of the Blessed One at the spot where the Buddha had overcome the powers of Mâra, the Evil One, needs no further explanation. It was an immemorial tradition to mark the site of a famous Bodhi tree with a Vishnu shrine, and the place where the yogi who sat under it was cremated with a Siva shrine, or stûpa. Fergusson's chronological estimate of the building is an amusing attempt to reconcile the inconsistencies of his stylistic categories. He had to explain how the "Hindu" sikhara, typical of "a Dasyu province," came to be built on one of the most sacred sites of Buddhism. He surmounted the difficulty by calling the Vishnu sikhara a stûpa: in the "Cave Temples of India" he declared that it was "evidently of foreign design, as there is nothing of the same style in India, either before or after it." He adds that "anyone at all familiar with the architecture of the East would know that it was built by the Burmese in the

PLATE XXV

ARCHES IN THE SIKHARA OF THE BODH-GAYA TEMPLE

thirteenth or fourteenth century A.D." In the first edition of his "History of Indian and Eastern Architecture" he revised this estimate by attributing it to the sixth century A.D.

Dr. Burgess, in the revised edition of Fergusson's work,

FIG. 42.—The Temple of Bodh-Gayâ, Restored (from Cunningham's "Mahâbodhi").

published in 1910, observes that the date of the erection of the "chaitya" is still obscure. When all the misconceptions of Fergusson and his followers regarding the origin and symbolism of the stûpa and sikhara are cleared away, General Cunningham's contention that the Bodh-Gayâ temple was built in the reign of the Kushan King Huvishka, or in the first century B.C., may after all prove to be nearer the mark than any other conjectures. Moreover, there need be no hesitation in believing that the arches in the interior (Pl. XXV) belonged to the original structure and were not, as Fergusson supposed, placed there by the Burmese restorers in the thirteenth and fourteenth centuries.

When further progress is made in the study of Indian craftsmanship, it will, I am sure, be proved conclusively not only that Fergusson was again in error in laying down the axiom that Hindu builders never used the arch structurally before Muhammadan times, but that the Muhammadans in India were themselves the borrowers and derived the Indian forms of the pointed arch from the brick buildings of Hindu Gaur.[1]

I have mentioned above that pairs of temples with an antithetical or complementary significance, like the dhwaja-stambhas at the gateways of stûpas, were often built side by side in India, as they were near Sennacherib's palace at Nineveh. Mâmallapuram furnishes one instance (Pl. XXVI), which is interesting as it gives a clue to the derivation of the most usual method of constructing a sikhara, *i.e.* with stone ribs built up in short sections and tied together at regular intervals by through horizontal courses of masonry.

These two shrines are, like the other Raths at Mâmallapuram, monolithic models. The popular traditional names given to them, Arjûna's and Draupadi's Raths, should be very significant to Indians who study their own history, but convey nothing to Europeans who are misled by arbitrary archæological terms of Western origin. Arjûna was the hero of the Mahâbhârata who won victory for the Pândavas by the

[1] This question is discussed in greater detail in my previous work on Indian Architecture.

PLATE XXVI

MONOLITHIC MODELS OF SIVA AND DURGA SHRINES, MAMALLAPURAM (*circa* A.D. 670)

magic weapons he obtained from Mahâdeva himself, through the practice of austerities in the depths of the Himâlayan forests. Arjûna's Rath is, therefore, only a poetical synonym for a Siva temple; the adjoining one, Draupadi's Rath, named after the common wife of the five Pândava brothers, is dedicated to Pârvatî, Umâ, or Dûrgâ, which are all poetical names for Siva's nature-force or *sakti*, popularly called his wife.[1] Draupadi's Rath is not, therefore, a Vishnu shrine, but symbolises Pârvatî, the Creatrix, as she is represented in the famous sculpture of the Trimûrtî at Elephanta.[2]

It is, doubtless, an exact reproduction of an ancient Indian village shrine. The form of the roof was derived from primitive construction of bambu and thatch, but very skilfully adapted to the technique of brick and stone, and not, as amateur European craftsmen consider it, an unintelligent imitation. When the up-to-date building craft of Anglo-India equals the magnificent work of ancient and medieval India, or even that of living Indian master-builders, there may be some show of reason in the neglect and disparagement of the Indian building tradition.

Siva and Vishnu shrines occur in pairs at Pattadakal in the south-west of India (Pl. LIX); at Khajurâho in Central India; at Bhuvanêshwar in Orissa; and no doubt many other instances could be cited in every part of India had the great quantity of archæological material collected since Fergusson wrote not been arranged according to his unscientific categories. In every instance where these pairs are found, archæologists, Indian as well as European, have described the Vishnu shrine as northern, or Indo-Aryan, and the Siva shrine as southern, or Dravidian, regardless of the locality in which

[1] Compare the similar Dûrgâ shrine built outside the Kârlê chaitya-house (Pl. XVIII) as a substitute for one of the pair of dhwaja-stambhas.

[2] See below, p. 163.

they are placed and of the obvious fact that the craftsmanship of both belongs to the same school and often is of precisely the same date—the only distinction between the two temples as regards style being in the symbolism.

This symbolic distinction had an important bearing upon the respective constructive principles of Vishnu and Siva shrines. The distinction is also recognised in the sectarial marks painted on the foreheads of Vaishnavaites and Saivaites. As Vishnu, regarded as a nature-symbol, is the sun at its zenith and nadir, the Vaishnava schools of philosophy generally took for their sectarial marks various lines which stood for the upright arm of the cosmic cross,[1] and the sikharas of Vishnu shrines (whether Buddhist, Jain, Vaishnavaite or Saivaite) were built in soaring lines—the lines of the mountain peak—like the Gothic spire, its Western analogue. The rival schools of Saivaites draw horizontal lines upon their foreheads to indicate the philosophical concepts of Brahmâ and Siva, which were based upon the earliest Vedic symbolism of sunrise and sunset—or the horizontal arm of the cross. The roofs of Siva shrines, though they might emulate those of Vishnu in height, were therefore always built in horizontal courses, like the pyramids of Egypt.

There was also a composite form of construction, *i.e.* instead of building Vishnu and Siva shrines separately in pairs, both technical methods and both symbols were combined in one temple. This is the characteristic of the medieval school of temple-building in Western India, which Fergusson, for want of a better name, called "Chalukyan," from the dynasty which ruled over that part of India.

All over the north of India there are to be found innumerable fine examples of the simplest type of Vishnu

[1] See Moor's "Hindu Pantheon," Pl. I, for a complete series of Indian sectarial marks.

PLATE XXVII

A RUINED SIKHARA, SHOWING CONSTRUCTION

shrines, consisting of a cell—the holy of holies—and an antechamber; but without the splendid halls of worship (*mandapams*) which belong to the larger and more famous ones. It would take volumes to do justice to the intuitive sense of beauty and splendid craftsmanship which they display. A complete study of their structure would be a valuable addition to architectural knowledge, but would form a considerable monograph in itself. In some of them a cone of brickwork, suggestive of the structures shown in the Nineveh bas-relief (fig. 40), forms the core upon which the stone facing of the sikhara is built. Many are built entirely of exceedingly fine brickwork, with cut or moulded ornaments, finished with fine polished stucco.

Pl. XXXIV is a beautiful example of a brick sikhara, illustrating the composite style, called by Fergusson "Chalukyan," in which both the Vishnu and Siva principles of construction are combined in one sikhara. The amalaka, Vishnu's symbol, is used as an ornament in the horizontal courses of the brickwork, and the sikhara would be crowned with Siva's symbol, the stûpa dome, instead of by the amalaka. In the present instance the dome has fallen. Pl. XXXV, from another temple, shows the fine brickwork on a larger scale, with some of the white stucco which covered it.

Pl. XXXIII shows a fine stone-built Vishnu shrine, possibly of the eighth century, at Barwar Sagar, in the Jhansi district, Central Provinces. Here small porches are added in the north, south, and west sides, making it a *chaumukh* (four-faced), as in a Brahmâ shrine; but the principal entrance on the east, the sikhara, and the miniature sun-windows skilfully used as ornaments in combination with the amalaka, indicate that the Vaishnava aspect of the Trimûrtî is specially worshipped.

A ruined temple at Khajurâho (Pl. XXVII) shows very

clearly the usual method of constructing a ribbed sikhara when stone is the material. The core is made of rough coursed rubble, without mortar or cement, bound together at intervals by larger horizontal slabs of stone. The weight of the heavy amalaka which crowns the sikhara acts as a key-stone.

We will now proceed to analyse the structure and symbolism of a Siva shrine, of which Arjûna's Rath at Mâmallapuram is a typical example. To clear the ground of the misconceptions which Fergusson's analysis has created, it will be best to begin with two definite propositions. First, that the Siva shrine is a development of the stûpa. Secondly, that the stûpa, a symbol not only of the Jains, but of orthodox Brahmanism, before it was adopted by Buddhism, was the true prototype of the modern Siva lingam.

For the first proposition let us compare the two illustrations in Pl. XXVIII, which give the front view of Arjûna's Rath, and that of the chaitya in the chapter-house of Ajantâ numbered twenty-six. The side view of Arjûna's Rath in Pl. XXVI will be useful for reference. It is necessary to observe that though both are monolithic models and not structural shrines, there is a considerable difference in the treatment. The porch and the interior of the shrine, which are exactly reproduced in Arjûna's Rath, are only carved in relief upon the front of the Ajantâ chaitya, so that the image seems as if it were placed within the porch, whereas in reality it would be within the shrine under the dome. Now, the porches in the two models are almost exactly similar. The columns are of the same design, only in one they are more elaborately carved than in the other. The entablature above the chhaja supported by them both are alike in reproducing two rows of monastic cells, one above the other, and are evidently of common origin. The Buddhist image is seated upon a throne guarded by lions: Dûrgâ's lions guard the entrance of Siva's temple.

PLATE XXVIII

A

B

SHRINES AT AJANTA AND MAMALLAPURAM

The shrines behind the porch differ in shape of plan: in the Ajantâ model it is circular, or of the vesara type, according to the definition of the Silpa-sâstras,[1] while Siva's shrine is square, or of the nâgara type. The base of the chaitya is sculptured in two stories, each divided by pilasters into shrines filled with figures. The two lower stories of Arjûna's Rath are treated in exactly the same way. A minor difference is that the monastic cells do not continue all round the chaitya as they do in the shrine of Siva, and no yogi cells are shown in the former. Arjûna's Rath is a *nava-ratna* (nine-jewelled) temple, or one that has eight yogi cells with domes, besides the dome which covers the principal cell containing the sacred image. But the so-called "Dravidian" dome differs only from the northern dome in showing externally the eight ribs used in the construction of both,[2] and by having outward curving eaves added to throw the rain off the walls of the cell (see fig. 37). The dome of the chaitya is crowned by the Vedic altar and tee; the other, when completed, would have had the water-pot finial (*kalasha*).

FIG. 43.—Plan of the Internal Structure of Ancient Jain Stûpa, showing the "Eight-petalled Lotus."

There is then not the least difference between the two shrines as regards "style." Such differences as there are only arise from structural conditions—that one was a cubical

[1] See above, p. 89.

[2] Fig. 43 shows the structural arrangement of the interior of an ancient Jain stûpa near Mathurâ.

shrine, built in three stories; the other a cylindrical shrine built in one storey. One was crowned by a Brahmanical symbol which was also Buddhist; the other by a Buddhist symbol which was also Brahmanical.

There is no need to demonstrate the fact that the sculptured Mahâyâna chaitya of Ajantâ was a development of the Hînayâna chaitya of Kârlê (Pl. XIX); it must therefore be obvious that the Siva, or so-called Dravidian temple, is also derived from the chaitya or stûpa. Its prototype was the cubical tomb with a domed roof shown in the Nineveh sculpture (fig. 40); the chaitya of Hînayâna Buddhism was a variety of this prototype with a circular (lotus) plan instead of a square one.

This derivation throws new light both upon the history of the Saiva cult and upon the origin of the phallic symbol, the lingam, which now belongs to it. Siva, as the Lord of Death and Immortality, was always associated with the cremation or burial ground, and naturally one of his symbols would be the stûpa, which became a cenotaph in India, but was a tomb in its earlier derivations. In his Brahmâ aspect, as the Lord of Life, Siva had another symbol, the bull, which is carved beside Arjûna's Rath at Mâmallapuram (Pl. XXVIII). Among the Aryan community, whose wealth consisted largely of cattle, the bull had been the symbol of procreation from prehistoric times. It was also the sacrificial animal, and therefore connoted in its symbolism the ideas not only of life and death, but of the bliss of immortality[1] which Vedic India hoped to attain by means of sacrifices.

Now, there was an early phallic worship, common to the whole primitive world, but except for one or two casual allusions to it in the Upanishads, the Aryan philosophy of India was in no way identified with it. Oriental scholars, like

[1] Siva's bull is called *Nandi*,—bliss.

H. H. Wilson and Monier Williams, have been puzzled to account for the Saivaites using a symbol associated with the licentious orgies of Western paganism; for not only, as Monier Williams observed, is the relation between the sexes in India regarded as a sacred mystery and never held to be suggestive of indecent ideas, but Saivism is one of the most austere cults of all India and preaches asceticism as a religion. I believe the explanation is this: the original symbols of Saivism in ancient India were the bull and the stûpa—life, death and sacrifice. But the ideas connected with symbols are always interchanging, especially in the case of those which, like the bull and the stûpa, represent pairs of opposites. The oldest Saivaite lingams yet discovered[1] (apart from the stûpa itself) have no phallic suggestions of any kind. They consist of four carved heads, arranged crossways on a short pillar which is fixed in the centre of a square lustration salver, and evidently correspond to the Mahâyânist Brahmâ symbol of a stûpa with four shrines facing the four cardinal points (fig. 54). This was the first step in the transference of the Brahmâ, or procreative, attributes of the bull to the Saiva or tâmasic attributes of the stûpa—or rather, their combination in one and the same symbol. When it is considered that the low-caste priests who attend Saiva temples are generally illiterate, and on that account held in great contempt by the learned Brahman pandits who expound the philosophy of the Saiva cult, it is easy to understand how vulgar phallic notions became associated with the symbol. The influx of Scythian tribes into India probably tended towards the corruption of the popular aspects of Hinduism; but it was not until Muhammadan times, and as a concession to the hatred

[1] The Indian Museum, Calcutta, has many examples of them; they are probably contemporary with the rise of Mahâyâna Buddhism about the first century of the Christian era, when the aniconic symbols of Vedic India began to be anthropomorphosised.

of Islam for anthropomorphic symbolism, that the lingam in its present form was substituted for the four-headed Brahmâ image, like the splendid sculpture at Elephanta (Pl. LIV and fig. 55).

The symbolism of the stûpa is, however, still retained in the domes surmounting the high pyramidal roofs of Siva shrines; but as these no longer serve a structural purpose, they are built in solid masonry and brickwork, and only give in their external sculptured form the evidence of their structural origin.

While innumerable Vishnu and Siva shrines are thus dedicated to the last two persons of the Hindu Trimûrtî, it might seem as if Brahmâ, the Creator, remains without any structural symbol of worship. It is a fact that there are very few temples in India dedicated exclusively to Brahmâ, but every chaumukh shrine, or that which has four doors facing the cardinal points, covered by a Vishnu sikhara or a Siva dome, is a Brahmâ-Vishnu or Brahmâ-Siva temple, as the case may be. It is only the uninformed European who regards Brahmâ, Vishnu, and Siva as three "gods," instead of the three Aspects of the One.

An important point to which the attention of archæologists seems never to have been directed is that the orientation of an Indian temple invariably indicates the particular Aspect of the Nature-force (*Prakriti*), or Soul-force (*Purusha*), to which the temple is dedicated; for the worshipper must place himself or herself "in tune with the Infinite," just as an Indian singer always knows, either by intuition or by study, the time of day or night and season of the year at which the râga he sings must be sung. A Brahmâ temple has four entrances, facing the four cardinal points; a Vishnu temple one entrance, facing the rising sun; and a Siva temple one entrance, facing the setting sun. But the three Aspects are often combined in one temple. Thus the mandapam of a temple will symbolise Siva in its constructive principle; the shrine itself with four doors will symbolise Brahmâ; while the image and the sikhara which covers the shrine will symbolise Vishnu. The north and south aspects and the intermediate points also have their special dedications.

CHAPTER IX

THE EVOLUTION OF INDIAN FINE ART AND ITS INFLUENCE ON TEMPLE BUILDING—THE GANDHARAN SCHOOL—THE PHILOSOPHY OF INDIAN TEMPLE BUILDING — INDIAN ARCHES—THE TEMPLE OF MÂRTÂND

IN the preceding chapters I have endeavoured to trace the evolution of Indo-Aryan temple architecture from its foundation in the ancient village communities, and to show the true relationship between the branch of Indian religion, called in Europe "Buddhism," and the other two branches of the same tree, Vaishnavism and Saivism. The further development of Vishnu and Siva temples from simple village shrines into the great medieval cathedrals of India will be discussed in its proper chronological sequence. We must now go back to the last centuries before the Christian era, and mark the beginning of a new movement which was destined to have a profound influence upon the whole art of Asia, and even upon that of Europe.

We have seen in the great chaitya-house of Kârlê, in the monasteries of Nâsik, and later in the gateways of Sânchî, how the dislike of the Vedic philosophers for anthropomorphic symbols of the Deity acted upon the art of Hînayâna Buddhism. The Devas — the bright nature-gods of the early Rig-Veda—sit upon their altars on the mighty pillars of the Sangha to listen to the inspired teaching of the Buddha. Brahmâ, with his lovely handmaiden the Dawn—she whom gods and demons churned from the cosmic ocean and gave to men as Srî—is there. Indra upon his elephant, the rain-cloud; Dûrgâ upon her tawny lion, the scorching heat of the Indian plains—all the Vedic gods are there as witnesses of the Truth. But Buddha, the Blessed One Himself, is only represented by the precious relics placed within the Vedic altar upon the chaitya of the Pari-Nirvâna.

Suddenly, about the beginning of the Christian era, the chaitya becomes something more than a nature-symbol and a reliquary: it is transformed into a shrine for the Buddha as the Deity, and everywhere images of the Blessed One as the Preacher, or as the Great Yogi, appear within the chaitya-houses and monasteries of the Sangha. Are we to suppose that during the five centuries which had elapsed since the first preaching of the Law, all the followers of the Buddha had kept strictly to the spirit of Aryan philosophy, as expounded in the Deer Park at Sarnath, and even refrained from making for themselves graven or painted icons to keep in memory the personality of their beloved Master? As human nature is, this would be altogether incredible. There must have been numbers of pious Buddhists, outside the strict rules of the Sangha, who kept among their household gods His pictured and graven image, before which they would sit in silent adoration as they meditated daily upon His inspired precepts. All that we really know is that from the chaitya-houses and monasteries of the orthodox Sangha, upon which the finest artistry of the Aryan genius was lavished, such pictures and images were excluded.

It is easy to understand, also, that a close restriction of this kind upon the highest imagination of the painter and sculptor is sufficient in itself to account for the comparative barrenness of Indo-Aryan fine art during the centuries when the Western branch of the same family tree was producing such wonderful fruit in the temples of ancient Greece. In later times it had the same sterilising effect upon the Muhammadan art of Europe and Asia. But for this restriction early Aryan sculpture and painting might have grown to the same height in India as it did in Greece; for the ideal gods of Hellas were of the same æsthetic growth as the early hymns of the Rig-Veda, sung by the Aryans in their Eastern home to the nature-gods they worshipped. Here, however, the artistic genius of the Western Aryans stopped short. They never were inspired with a more profound metaphysic than the Homeric gods; for Greece lost her freedom, and her artists became the servants of foreign patrons less intellectual than their own countrymen before that consummation was reached. It was left to their brother-artists in the East to proceed from the primitive nature-gods of the Rig-Veda to the inspired conceptions of the Upanishads; but there never was at any time that irreconcilable antagonism between the ideals of Greece and of India which modern classical scholasticism fondly imagines—because the inspiration both of Greece and of India lies beyond its æsthetic comprehension.

The first great impulse of the new movement, within the jurisdiction of the Buddhist Sangha itself, was synchronous with a considerable readjustment of political conditions in Northern India. In the year 184 B.C. the Mauryan dynasty founded by Chandragupta became extinct, and a new one, known as the Sunga, was established upon the imperial throne of Pâtaliputra. Pushyamitra, the first of the line, was not a follower of the Buddha, but celebrated his accession and a decisive victory over Menander, a Baktrian monarch who, like Seleukos, was ambitious of repeating the conquests of Alexander, by the old Vedic rite of the great horse sacrifice.

But the dominions over which Pushyamitra ruled were of small extent compared with those of Asoka. After the death of the latter, the glory of the Mauryan empire was soon eclipsed by the rise of another dynasty, that of the Andhras, which at that time occupied the deltas of the Godâvarî and Krishnâ Rivers, but gradually extended their sway over the whole of the Dekhan; until in 27 B.C. they overthrew the successors of the Sungas, and established themselves as the leading power in Central and a great part of Northern India.

The Andhra kings seem to have been Buddhist; the gateways of Sânchî (Pl. V) and the carved railing of the Amarâvatî stûpa (Pl. X) were among the architectural works dedicated to that cult which were completed under their patronage between the second century B.C. and the end of the third century A.D., when the dynasty was superseded by others.

In the meantime the north-western part of Asoka's dominions had been occupied by invaders of Scythian or Iranian descent about the second century B.C., and by A.D. 45 a chieftain of the Kushans, one of their tribes, founded a dynasty under which Buddhism, the religion adopted by these clans probably as the result of Asoka's missionary enterprises, began to enter upon a new phase.

The impelling cause was only incidentally dynastic and racial. The new invaders, by their adoption of Buddhist culture, merely contributed one more racial subdivision to the Indo-Aryan synthesis. The Kushan king, Kanishkâ, emulated Asoka's zeal for the religion of his Indian subjects, and there is no reason to suppose that the Scythian invasions disturbed to any great extent the organisation of the Aryan village communities in north-western India.

The philosophy of Yoga, as expounded by Patanjali, seems to have been the basis of the teaching of the Buddhist monk, Nâgârjuna, who appeared in Kanishka's reign as the leader of a new school which eventually led to the secession of the northern Buddhists from the orthodox tradition of the Sangha. From about the beginning of the Christian era the northern or reformed schools were known as the Mahâyâna, or

Great Vehicle, to distinguish them from those of the Hînayâna, or Little Vehicle, which remained steadfast to the early teaching of Buddhist philosophy.

It is a common but erroneous view of the history of Indo-Aryan religion to regard this new movement as the herald of what Europeans describe as the triumph of Brahmanism, or of Hinduism over Buddhism. Brahmans were among the first disciples of the Buddha, and it was the Brahman acceptance of his teaching in the Deer Park at Sarnath which set the seal of victory upon the Enlightenment under the Bodhi tree. The new Brahmanical teaching which sprang up later within Buddhism itself, and eventually superseded the original doctrines of Buddha, was as far removed from the older orthodox Brahmanism of those who remained outside the Buddhist pale as it was from the Buddha's own teaching.

The philosophy of Yoga, of which Patanjali was the chief exponent, contained by implication the doctrine of Incarnation; for if the soul within the human body could be and was joined with the Divine through the spiritual exercises enjoined by Yoga, it followed that the Divinity Itself could also be manifested to the world in the person of the saints and seers who taught this spiritual wisdom. And as soon as Buddhist philosophy admitted the possibility of a personal God, it became inevitable that the Buddha should be venerated as a manifestation of the Supreme Deity, though he himself might not have asserted such a claim. Similarly Kṛishna, the hero of the Mahâbhârata, and the inspired author of the Bhagavad Gîta which contained the philosophy of the Vaishnavaite sect, was regarded as one of the incarnations of Vishnu.

The Kushan dynasty, under Kadphises I, established itself in North-west India *circa* 45 B.C., when the ferment of these new ideas was beginning to transform the primitive teachings of Hinduism. The western borders of the Kushan dominions were in contact with the Roman Empire, and included part of the old Græco-Baktrian Empire of Seleukus. As this new dynasty grew in power and affluence, numbers of Græco-Roman masons and carpenters, who were always travelling in search of employment, were attracted to the Kushan capital, Purushapûra—the modern Peshawar—to assist in building the monasteries, chaityas, and chaitya-houses which were required for the crowds of Buddhist monks who collected there. This feeble backward splash of Aryan culture which thus flowed over North-west India until the Kushan dynasty came to an end in the fourth century A.D., created that Gandharan school of building and sculpture the influence of which upon Indian art has been so strangely misinterpreted and exaggerated by Western scholars.

Whatever inspiration there was in this new court fashion, it was but a feeble reflection of the flame which the Aryan genius had lighted in India ten centuries before these Kushan kings came under its influence—a flame which continued to burn brightly for many centuries after the Kushan dynasty had passed away.

Hellas herself was under the heel of Rome; the light of her own inspiration was becoming dim, and her best artists devoted their talents to the service of Roman patricians. Among the best of the Gandharan craftsmen there were sometimes a few to compare with the second-best of the Greek sculptors and painters who adorned the villas of Pompeii and Herculaneum. But except for an occasional piece of fine academic craftsmanship, Gandharan sculpture is generally petty in ideas and feeble in execution, and nothing that was produced under the patronage of the Kushan kings approached in grandeur of conception the chaitya-house of Kârlê or the monasteries of Nâsik, or showed the warm vitality and unaffected beauty of the Sânchî gateways. So far from inspiring the ideals of Indo-Aryan art, it was not until the Gandharan master-masons had drunk in the inspiration of Indo-Aryan philosophy and religion that any of their sculpture became worthy of comparison with the best original art of India.

Indirectly, however, the inflow of this current from the West greatly assisted the new movement from within, which was already tending towards the removal of the restraint which had hindered the higher development of Indo-Aryan sculpture and painting from the earliest Vedic times. The Kushan kings were evidently liberal patrons of the fine arts, and, like the Great Moguls, were personally interested in sculpture and painting. Though of the Buddhist faith, they were indifferent to the rule of the Hînayâna school, which forbade any icon of the Master's personality in the service of the Sangha. The elders of the Buddhist Church in Gandhara, anxious to reconcile their royal patrons' dilettantism with the ritualistic traditions of their creed, withdrew the prohibition, but laid down strict rules, in the spirit of Vedic philosophy, to prevent vulgar idolatry. The image of the Blessed One was not to be fashioned, like those of the Olympian gods, as an ideal human ; nor was it to be worshipped until it had been consecrated with appropriate rites. The imager by spiritual insight must realise the Divinity which transfigured Him when He attained Nirvana under the Bodhi tree at Gayâ: he must transport himself by meditation to the Tusitâ heavens, where the Buddha now watched humanity with compassionate eyes, and show the divine glory revealed to him there.

The naïve endeavours of the unimaginative Western craftsman to adapt his materialistic art to these unfamiliar mystic ideas are to be seen in the early sculptures of the Gandhara school. The intellectual atmosphere of the Kushan court must have presented many analogies to that which exists in modern India: there were the similar endeavours to understand the Indian mind *de haut en bas*, the same aloofness from it, and the same honest, but hopeless, misconceptions. There is also a curious suggestion of modern commercialism in the average work of the Gandharan craftsmen. One can easily imagine them crying their wares in the manner of the Western shopkeeper: "Large stock of Olympian gods in latest fashion to suit every taste. Correct Baktrian images, as supplied to the Royal Court," etc.!

The profound critical error which Western writers have made is in supposing that these new court fashions, imported from the West, were any more inspiring to Indo-Aryan artists at the beginning of the Christian era than the "styles" of architecture, principles of anatomy and perspective now taught in Indian schools of art. As a historical chapter in Indian art the Gandharan school is only interesting for its gradual assimilations of Indian ideals. Except for a few technical mannerisms, Indo-Aryan art remained uninfluenced by it.

But the effect of the encouragement which it gave to Indian sculpture and painting was very vital. From the beginning of the Christian era Indian sculptors and painters began to vie with others in creating images showing the Deity in every aspect, as symbols of philosophic concepts, and to be used as aids to meditation. The stûpa became a shrine in which gold, silver, bronze, or stone images of Jain and Buddhist saints, of Vishnu or of Siva, were placed. The dedication of such icons as votive offerings became the duty of devout Hindus of every sect.

The same precautions were taken by the Brahmanical sects to prevent image worship being regarded as anything more than a help and preparation for those who were unable to grasp the abstruse conceptions of Vedic philosophy. The Vedic Rishis had said: "The vulgar look for their gods in water; men of wider knowledge in celestial bodies; the ignorant in wood, clay, or stone; but the wisest men in the Universal Self." Similarly the Mahâ-Nirvana Tantra, after giving elaborate rules for the consecration and worship of images, adds the warning: "Those who (in their ignorance) believe that Ishwara is (only) in images of clay, or stone, or metal, or wood, merely trouble themselves by their tapas. They can never attain liberation without knowledge. . . . Yoga is the union of the embodied soul with the Supreme Soul; Pûjâ is the union of the worshipper and the worshipped; but he who realises that all things are Brahman, for him there is neither Yoga nor Pûjâ." [1]

The traditions of the Silpa-sâstras, which classify the structure of vimânas, or shrines, by the type of image contained by them, no doubt go back to this time. The Mânasâra says that they are of three kinds. The first, called *st'hânaka*,[2] contains an image standing erect; the second, called *âsana*, contains a seated image; and the third, called *sâyana*, a recumbent one.[3]

The st'hânaka type would contain an image of Vishnu as the Pillar of the Universe, or of the Buddha in a similar aspect as the Teacher of the Law. The roof of it would be the sikhara. The âsana type would be represented by an image of Buddha or of Siva in a Yoga attitude, or seated on a throne—the roof of the cell being flat or domical, or a combination of the terraced roof and dome. Arjûna's Rath at Mâmallapuram (Pl. XXVI) is an illustration of it.

Bhîma's Rath at the same place (Pl. XXIV) is a monastic temple of the sâyana type: it is oblong in plan and covered by a vaulted roof with pointed arch or lotus-leaf gables. This was designed for a recumbent image, such as that of Vishnu-Nârâyana reposing in the cosmic serpent Ananta, or the analogous image of the Buddha in the sleep of Pari-Nirvana.

The Teli-ka Mandir, or Oilman's temple, at Gwalior

1 Translated by Arthur Avalon, pp. 348–9.

2 Standing firm, like the trunk of a tree.

3 Râm Râz, p. 49.

PLATE XXIX

THE TELI-KA MANDIR, GWALIOR

(Pl. XXIX), is another fine example of the sâyana type, but here the cell remains square, and only the double vaulted roof, gabled at the ends with sun-windows, shows that it was meant for an image of Vishnu-Nârâyana. Fergusson attributes it to about the tenth or eleventh centuries; but the data by which he calculated, in the absence of inscriptions, were in most cases very unreliable, and probably the temple, like that at Bodh-Gayâ, is a good many centuries earlier than his estimate.

The raising of sculpture from an accessory detail to the principal subject in design, or, in modern phraseology, from a decorative to a fine art, was an epoch-making event in Indian architecture. The sculptured images of the gods whom we see at Kârlê and Nâsik merely as onlookers, became the sacred symbols for which the shrines were built. The symbolism of the shrine, as regards plan and structure, had to be adapted to the particular type of image for which it was intended. And these considerations particularly affected the design of the roof. Indian temple builders never troubled themselves with pagan notions of beauty for beauty's sake. The skilful jugglery of lines and spaces which modern academicians teach as the art of building would have seemed to them childish play.

The great thinkers of India, who anticipated Western endeavours to establish religion upon a scientific basis, taught their master-builders to express in concrete architectural terms the theoretical principles of the cosmic forces, as the different schools of philosophy conceived them to be. Indo-Aryan builders were pure scientists—philosophers in brick and stone. Yet the fine intuition of the artist-craftsman clothed the science of natural religion with a grace and splendour of its own; and thus Indian art grew, like a tree or flower, conscious of its own beauty and rejoicing in it always—receiving it in wondering adoration as a gift from heaven, but never struggling to attain to it by the pedantic and coquettish arts of the Renaissance.

The builders of the Saiva schools aimed at expressing the power of knowledge, of abstract thought—the static force of the universe. And they did so first by the image of the Great Yogi sitting with mind and reason set upon the Eternal, like a lamp in a windless place "which flickereth not." The plain cubical cell, with a flat roof or dome, which contained

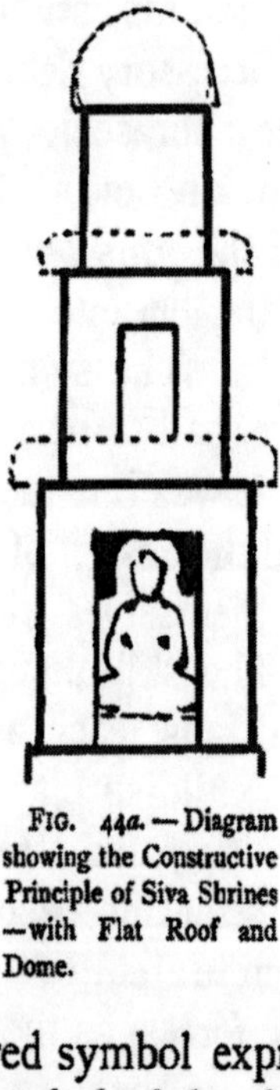

FIG. 44*a*.—Diagram showing the Constructive Principle of Siva Shrines—with Flat Roof and Dome.

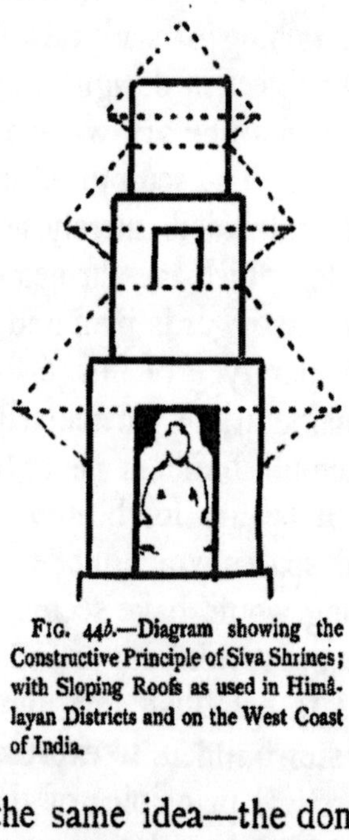

FIG. 44*b*.—Diagram showing the Constructive Principle of Siva Shrines; with Sloping Roofs as used in Himâlayan Districts and on the West Coast of India.

this sacred symbol expressed the same idea—the dome being only a symbol of the sky, or of the chhatra of royalty.

When they sought to give importance to the shrine by additional height, they simply raised the roof by putting cube upon cube like a pyramid, and crowning the topmost one with a dome (fig. 44*a*).

But in the Himâlayan districts, where the rainfall is very heavy, flat terraced roofs have obvious practical inconveniences; so here it was found expedient to adapt the sym-

PLATE XXX

JAIN TEMPLE AT MUDABIDRI

bolism to the sloping wooden roof of the locality as shown in fig. 44*b*, a type of temple building which passed into China with the Buddhist religion.[1] Similar roofs were used on the west coast of India, where similar meteorological conditions prevail (Pl. XXX). In Bengal the local form of roof with convex curvature was adapted for the same purpose. When will the practical British architect in India begin to learn wisdom from the Indian master-builder?

FIG. 45.—Sculptured Shrines, Ellora.

It will now become clearer why Indian builders before Muhammadan times used the arch, as a constructive principle, so seldom. The arch, as I have explained elsewhere,[2] symbolised the aura of the sacred image, and every possible variety of the arch was constantly used for constructing the shrines or niches in which images were placed (fig. 45). For larger structural purposes it was also used occasionally, as in the sikhara at Bodh-Gayâ (Pl. XXV); but the trabeate system of building was preferred because it suggested a philosophical

[1] The dotted lines in the diagrams indicate the roofing.

[2] "Indian Architecture: its Psychology, Structure, and History," Chap. VI.

idea. There was also the practical reason that when good timber and building stone of almost any dimensions were plentiful, the beam and bracket were generally more expedient than the arch, especially in a country liable to severe earthquakes.

When the Muhammadans destroyed the images contained in the niches and adapted the buildings for their own worship, the niche itself and the arches which formed it remained as sacred symbols; and thus from the more extended use of the Indian pointed arch for structural purposes a new era in architectural history was opened both in Europe and in India.

It was in the buildings of the Vaishnavaite schools that the arch was most frequently used constructively, for colossal standing figures of Vishnu, or of Buddha, covered by the sikhara instead of by a flat roof or dome, would tend to bring the arch into use—as was the case at Bodh-Gayâ. The intention of the builders of the Vaishnavaite schools—both those of Brahmanism and of Buddhism—was to symbolise the dynamic (*râjasic*) or active principle of nature—known to modern science as evolution. And for this they took the upright image of Vishnu or of Buddha as Upholder of the Universe, and for its shrine the ancient nature-symbol of the holy mount, which Vishnu upturned and used for a churning stick in the allegory of the cosmic dawn.[1]

Plate XXXI gives the section of a Vaishnava sikhara, but in this temple there is a combination of symbols, *i.e.* instead of building a pair of temples, one for the Vaishnava Aspect and another for the Saiva Aspect, a Siva lingam is placed in the Brahmâ shrine under a lotus dome crowned by Vishnu's sikhara, and Siva's bull occupies the centre of the pillared mandapam provided for the worshippers. Thus

[1] The equilateral triangle standing on its apex is a geometric Vishnu symbol; the reverse is a Siva symbol.

LONGITUDINAL SECTION.

SECTION OF A VISHNU TEMPLE

122]

one temple serves to symbolise the Three Aspects of the One. There may, however, be another explanation of the appearance of Siva's symbols in this temple—that it is a Vaishnavaite shrine appropriated for Saivaite worship. But in either case the Three Aspects are represented in the structure of the temple—Brahmâ in the cubical cell for the image, Vishnu in the sikhara, and Siva in the domes of the mandapams and of the shrine.

The application of this symbolism explains all the forms of roofs which covered the holy of holies in Indian temples. Even in Gandhara and in the adjoining districts influenced by Gandharan art the construction of roofs is never a meaningless reproduction of foreign forms, but a well-reasoned adaptation of them to Indian philosophic ideas. The remains of Gandharan buildings in Gandhara itself have only an archæological interest; but when Indian master-builders had assimilated and revitalised the emasculated Aryan tradition brought by the Græco-Roman craftsmen, Indo-Gandharan art became really great, both in sculpture and in building—as even modern departmental art may become when the lessons of history have been learnt by Anglo-India.

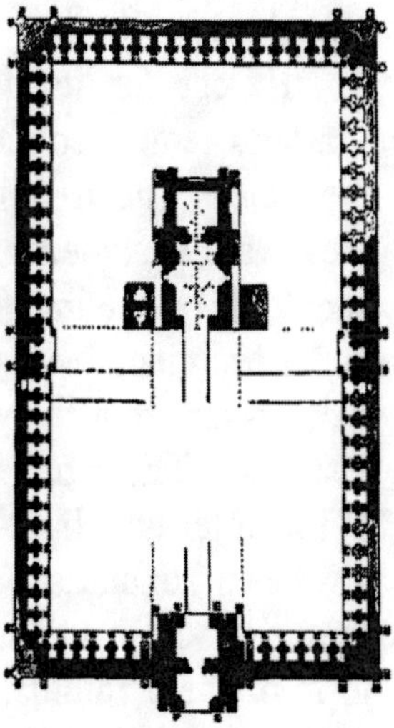

FIG. 46.—Plan of the Mârtând Temple (from Fergusson's "History"). (Scale, 100 ft. to 1 in.)

The finest building of the Indo-Gandharan school is unquestionably the ruined temple of Mârtând in Kashmir, built by King Lalitâditya-Muklâpîda between 725 and 760 A.D. There is not much left of it now, except part of the *garbha-griha* (the shrine) (Pl. XXXII), and the ruins of the quadrangular wall with monastic cells which enclosed it (fig. 46).

The Indian master-builders of the eighth century have only taken some of the foreign suggestions brought in by the Gandharan craftsmen, and used them with much better effect than the latter did. An exact parallel to this is to be found in the way in which modern Indian builders sometimes adapt —when they are allowed to work in their own way—Public Works "Gothic" and "Classic" designs, reanimating the dry bones of Western academic formularies with the inspiration of real art.[1]

Except for its quasi-classic pilasters the design of the Mârtând temple conforms strictly to the Hindu tradition of the time. The trefoil arches were not a foreign suggestion: they were designed as a frame for the aureoled head and shoulders of the image for which the shrine was built. Nor is the pediment over them anything more than a decorative motif taken from the wooden hipped roofs of the Himâlayan districts. The actual roof of the shrine was probably wooden. If the latter was built for a Vishnu image, it must have been a wooden adaptation of a brick or stone sikhara. If it was meant for a Siva image, it would have been the Himâlayan form of the pyramidal roof (fig. 44*b*), like that over the shrine of the Mudabidri temple (Pl. XXX).

[1] Several good illustrations of this are found in the Report on Modern Indian Building, published by the Government of India in 1913.

TEMPLE AT MÁRTÁND (EIGHTH CENTURY A.D.)

CHAPTER X

THE GUPTA EMPIRE—VIKRAMÂDITYA'S STATECRAFT—INDIAN COLONISATION—CHINESE ACCOUNTS OF INDIA IN THE FIFTH AND SEVENTH CENTURIES—HARSHA OF THANESAR AND HIS GOVERNMENT—THE FEAST OF THE INDIAN TRINITY AT PRAYÂGA

IN the beginning of the fourth century Pâtaliputra became again the seat of an empire under a new dynasty founded by the chieftain of one of the Indo-Aryan clans of Magadha, the Lichchhavi, which was closely allied to the Sâkiya clan, whose illustrious Prince Siddhartha was still venerated by all India as the Buddha. The name of the chieftain, Chandragupta, revived the glorious memories of the Mauryan line, and might well have inspired an ambitious youth to emulate the prowess of Asoka's grandfather.

It was not mere racial vanity, perhaps, but an ardent patriotic hope which made the head of the historic Indo-Aryan clan choose this proud name for his son. History was repeating itself in more ways than one. Alexander's famous raid in the fourth century B.C. had roused the clans to the necessity of combination for national defence. In the fourth century of the Christian era, Aryâvarta, the holy land of the Aryans, was again threatened by dangers both from within and without. The existence of a foreign dynasty on the north-west frontier was a constant menace to Aryan India, even though these foreigners partially adopted Aryan institutions and the Aryan religion. Fresh hordes of semi-civilised tribes were pressing towards the Indus Valley from the highlands of Central Asia. The Kushan power was weakening and seemed unlikely to keep them at bay for long.

The dangers from within were not less alarming. For centuries the overgrowth of monastic institutions and the popularity of the ascetic ideal, which not only orthodox Brahmans and Jains but the Buddhist Sangha preached and practised, had been slowly sapping the manhood of India and laying the country open to the barbarians of Asia. Indo-Aryan thinkers had for long realised the danger, and the doctrine of *karma-yoga*, attributed in the Bhagavad-Gîta to the hero of the Mahâbhârata, Krishna, was a clarion call to the Aryan people to face the realities of life and to defend their Dharma against the common foe.

It is very typical of the errors of the Western historian that this movement has always been described as the beginning of the revival of Brahmanism and of the decadence of Buddhism. Brahman thinkers, as the intellectual aristocracy of India, may have been the most active leaders in propagating this mission of the fourth century; they had been equally active in spreading the message of the Buddha over Asia. The Bhagavad-Gîta did not denounce the teaching of Buddhism; it only taught that the Dharma of the Aryan people was to be readjusted to meet the changing conditions of every age. It was the ancient doctrine of Yoga restated. Besides the Yoga of Spiritual Knowledge (*jnâna-yoga*) which the Buddhists preached as a means of self-realisation, there was the Yoga of Action (*karma-yoga*). Now was the time for action, not for contemplation. The balance of the cosmos could only be maintained by perfect equilibrium of its three forces—sâttvic, râjasic, and tâmasic. The force of goodness, or truth (*sattvam*), alone could not maintain its order. The Buddha had been the inspired teacher of sattvam; the truth

PLATE XXXIII

VISHNU SHRINE, BARWAR SAGAR, CENTRAL PROVINCES

of his doctrines was not in question. But it was the hero, Krishna, as the incarnation of Vishnu, the Preserver, who was to be the patron saint of the new era.

It was with such feelings that Chandragupta and the Lichchhavi clan set about the task of consolidating once more the material forces of Aryâvarta. In his short reign of five years, says Mr. Vincent Smith, "he extended his dominions along the Gangetic Valley as far as the junction of the Ganges and Jumna, where Allâhâbâd now stands; and ruled, during his brief tenure of the throne, a populous and fertile territory, which included Tirhût, Bihâr, Oudh, and certain adjoining districts."[1] In A.D. 326 Chandragupta died and his mantle fell upon his son Samudragupta, a young prince who had been thoroughly trained in the arts of war. And so successfully did he prosecute his father's mission that by the end of his reign, about 375, nine Râjas of the Gangetic plain, known as Aryâvarta, had become tributary to him. On the north, he ruled to the foot of the Himâlayas; on the south to the Narmada River; on the east to the Hooghly; and on the west to the Chambal River and the Jumna.[2] Moreover, by a tremendous raid through Southern India he had filled his treasury with the riches of Golconḍa and of the gold mines of Mysore.

It is extremely characteristic of Indian historical feeling that not only the martial exploits but even the name of this great warrior-king were completely forgotten by posterity; and the facts now recorded, as Mr. Vincent Smith says, are the most conspicuous illustration of the success gained by modern archæological research. Unfortunately the treatment of this material as historical evidence by Western writers has only added to the obscurity with which Indian history is still enshrouded.

[1] "Early History of India," p. 266.

[2] Vincent Smith, "Early History of India," p. 271.

The details of the war and the name of the warrior were forgotten; for such matters never impressed the mind of India. But the things which really mattered remained for ever graven on her heart. It was Samudragupta's son, Chandragupta II, still celebrated in Indian romance as the god-like hero Vikramâditya, who, like Asoka, completed his grandfather's task. Historians, deceived by their own categories, may describe Asoka as a "Buddhist," and Vikramâditya as a "Hindu"; but such distinctions are only delusive. India recognises both as ideal Hindu sovereigns: the one of the sâttvic type, and the other of the râjasic type.

Upon his accession, about A.D. 375, Vikramâditya's first undertaking was to push the boundaries of his empire right across to the Arabian Sea, through Malwâ and Gujerat, by the conquest of Surâshtra or Kâthiâwâr, where a dynasty known as the Saka had ruled since the beginning of the Christian era. It was probably as a consequence of this campaign that the Saka chieftains emigrated to Java, and, joining others of the same clan who had colonised the island in the previous centuries, began to build those wonderful monuments which are among the finest and most splendid creations of Indian art.[1]

This was not the first or only colonising enterprise of India. Ceylon had been brought under the influence of Aryan culture by Asoka's missionaries in the third century B.C.; and according to tradition a Hindu Prince of Indraprashta, with a large number of followers, had gone farther east as early as the fifth century B.C., and founded the great colony of Cambodia which flourished until the fifteenth century A.D. These great Indo-Aryan colonies furnish some of the most glorious chapters in the history of Indian architecture, but they cannot be included in the present volume. The key to the understanding

[1] For a detailed description of the Bôrôbudûr and Prambânam sculptures, see "Indian Sculpture and Painting," by the author.

PLATE XXXIV

VISHNU TEMPLE, PUJÀRIPATI, CENTRAL PROVINCES

of them, and of a great deal more in Asiatic art, is in the art of India itself.

Vikramâditya, finally, pushed back the Indian frontiers of the Kushan Empire to the banks of the Indus; and, having thus secured Aryâvarta from further incursions from the north-west, he performed the ancient Aryan rite of the great horse sacrifice, and set up dhwaja-stambhas of Vishnu to record his victories in various places. Among them was the famous Iron Pillar of Delhi[1] (Pl. XII, c), one of the most extraordinary achievements of the Indian craftsman; for it was not until the latter part of the nineteenth century that Europeans were able to forge iron columns of such dimensions, and even now the quality of metal which has preserved it from rusting for so many centuries seems to be a mystery to modern science.[2] It is a Vishnu pillar of the same type as those sculptured at Bharhut, the base, now buried underground, being Lakshmî's jar of plenty.

The great defender of the Aryan Dharma then began setting his house in order. He seems to have removed his capital to a more central position, which may have been Ayodhya, the famous city of Râma, as Mr. Vincent Smith suggests. Those who regard all Hindu monarchs as types of "oriental despotism," and believe that all that is best in Indian institutions is but a poor imitation of Western ideas, will expect to find that Vikramâditya's victories were followed by the assertion of autocratic government on the model of European empires. If that had been the case it is certain that the deeds of Vikramâditya would have fallen into the same oblivion as his father's. It was only because he fulfilled

[1] Mr. Vincent Smith says that its original position was probably at Mathurâ. It was removed to Delhi in A.D. 1052 ("Early History of India," p. 356).

[2] The secret of casting iron so that it will not rust was known to Indian craftsmen in Travancore some twenty years ago.

to the highest degree the Indo-Aryan ideal of constitutional sovereignty that his memory was cherished, like that of Akbar, as Vishnu's Vicegerent on earth.

What Vikramâditya did, as the champion of Indo-Aryan institutions, was to restore peace and order throughout his dominions, and revive the ancient traditions of popular self-government which was the original basis of Aryan civilisation where the true spirit of Aryan statecraft was ever able to assert itself. The Aryan clan to which the Guptas belonged was one of those which from time immemorial had been accustomed to self-government upon the principle of the Aryan village community. The head of each clan, the Râja, was the head of a confederation of villages—miniature republics as they have been aptly called. The Mahâ-Râja was the head of a confederation of clans, and Vikramâditya the suzerain of a larger confederation, over which he ruled, not as an autocrat, but as the upholder of the Dharma of the Aryan race. The grouping of clans which acknowledged his supremacy and paid the customary *vali* was not disturbed. The Râjas and Mahâ-Râjas recognised as loyal to Aryan institutions were not deposed: only those who were hated as Mhlechas, or enemies of the Dharma, were, as the records of the time say, "rooted out."

It was not therefore a Brahmanical revival, in the narrow sectarian sense conceived by Western writers, which the great Vikramâditya inaugurated. It was a revival of Aryan culture and of Aryan polity, which, owing to the disturbed condition of Hindustan and the corruption of Aryan ideals, were becoming decadent and stood in need of revision. The profound peace which a firm central government established opened the highways of commerce, promoted a great activity in all the arts of peace, and brought about a general revival of Aryan learning—philosophy, science, poetry, and the drama—all

PLATE XXXV

VISHNU TEMPLE, SIRPUR, CENTRAL PROVINCES: DETAILS OF BRICKWORK

of which sectarians include under the vague designation of "Hinduism."

The travels of the Chinese pilgrim, Fa-Hien, have given to the world some very interesting glimpses of India in the early part of the fifth century A.D., from the sectarian point of view. The object of his journey was to obtain copies of the Vinaya-pitaka, or rules of discipline of the Buddhist Sangha, and his chief interest as he went through the land of the Lotus of Good Law was to follow the footsteps of the Master, to recount the wondrous legends of His life, and to describe the great monasteries and temples built in His honour. What struck him most in secular matters was the security and tranquillity in which the people lived, their prosperity, piety, and benevolence. The great towns of Magadha, famous in Buddhist history, were mostly deserted or in decay; others rich and prosperous which had sprung up in other places did not interest him. Buddhism as a sect was declining, but the spirit of the Master's teaching prevailed everywhere.

This is a picture of India as seen by a fifth-century Chinese globe-trotter: "Throughout the whole country people do not kill any living creature, nor drink intoxicating liquor, nor eat onions or garlic. The only exception is that of the Chandâlas."[1] The administration of justice was mild and humane. The law was generally maintained without decapitation or severe corporal punishment. Only in repeated attempts at rebellion the right hand of criminals was cut off. The king's officials received regular salaries and did not vex the people. The latter "have not to register their households, or attend to any magistrates and their rules; only those who cultivate the royal land have to pay a portion of the gain from it. If they want to go, they go; if they want to stay on, they stay."[2]

[1] Fishermen and hunters.

[2] Fa-Hien's Travels, Legge's translation, p. 42.

Here is the explanation why Vikramâditya was and is remembered as the great hero of Hindustan, while the very name of his father, Samudragupta, was forgotten.

General Cunningham, Dr. Burgess, and others have laboured assiduously to reconstitute from buildings, which from inscriptions can be dated about the fifth or sixth centuries, what they call a "Gupta style," and cite instances to prove the popular archæological thesis that whenever Indian art was great it was owing to contact with Europe. It need not be disputed that Vikramâditya, like the Mauryan and Mogul emperors and their modern Viceregal representatives, might have had an architectural hobby, and that in riding it he may have made use of foreign as well as native craftsmen who were attracted to his court. But that his dilettante efforts affected in the smallest degree the general character of Indian building there is not the slightest proof; nor is it at all probable that this was the case.

The archæological evidences put forward to support the case are as irrelevant as any of Fergusson's stylistic classifications. If anything can be safely asserted about the temples which the Guptas built and of those which were characteristic of the period, it is that they would be dedicated to Vishnu, the Ishta-Deva of the Gupta dynasty. But in General Cunningham's analysis of the characteristics of the "Gupta style" the first and principal item is "Flat roofs, without spires of any kind," *i.e.* the instances cited are all Siva temples! Further comment is needless.

As an architectural landmark the Gupta period, so far as the north of India is concerned, must be identified with the beginning of that great epoch of Vishnu temple[1] building which, both before and after the Gupta dynasty ended, produced many

[1] The reader must always carefully distinguish between a Vishnu temple as a symbol and a Vaishnava temple belonging to the Vaishnava sect.

PLATE XXXVI

A VISHNU TEMPLE, CHAMBA CITY

splendid shrines in Orissa, Rajputâna, Khajurâho, and many other places in Central India. The râjasic Aspect of Ishwara—Vishnu—was the dominant cult of the Gupta period, as the sâttvic Aspect—Buddha or Brahmâ—had been the prevailing cult in the Mauryan period. The holy Mount of Vishnu therefore became the usual temple symbol within the boundaries of Vikramâditya's empire instead of the glorified stûpa which marked the orthodox philosophy of the Buddhist and Saivaite cults.

I have little doubt that when archæologists turn back from the blind alley into which Fergusson led them, a great deal more material will be found to fill up the blanks in Indian architectural history. In the meantime the great temples of Bhuvaneshwar in Orissa may be taken to represent very accurately the real characteristics of the "Gupta style."

But as Vikramâditya was no more a religious bigot than Asoka had been, and every sect was free to follow its own way of thinking, building activity in the Gupta period was not confined to one type of religious edifice. The almost unbroken peace and prosperity which Hindustan enjoyed for nearly a century under the Guptas seems to have extended over the whole of India, and no doubt stimulated the arts of the builder in the provinces beyond Vikramâditya's dominions.

In A.D. 455, when Europe was being desolated by wild hordes of Asiatic nomads, Vikramâditya's grandson, Skandagupta, once more upheld the banner of Aryan civilisation against the Turanian invader, and stayed the savage descent of the White Huns into the Indus valley, after they had overrun the Kushan dominions. The struggle continued at intervals until about 495. Then the Gupta power was broken for a time by the Hun leader, Torâmana, who became the ruler of Mâlwâ in Central India, apparently without destroying the political institutions which he found there, as he assumed the Indo-Aryan title of "King of Kings."

But the savagery of his successor, Mihiragula, drove the clans into revolt, and a confederacy under Narasimha-gupta of Magadha and Yasô-dharman of Central India defeated the Hun tyrant, who was taken prisoner. The magnanimity of the Aryan race was shown in the way they treated the bloodthirsty enemy of their Dharma, whose fiendish cruelty, especially to Buddhists, had exasperated the clans. He was only banished from Aryâvarta, and a younger brother was allowed to succeed him.

Various dynasties then shared between them the sovereignty of Vikramâditya's dominions until A.D. 606, when Harsha Vardhana, of Thanesar, famous in the Mahâbharata as the land of the Kurus, repelled another Hun invasion, and reconstituted the supreme government of Aryâvarta in a new confederacy, with Kanauj as its capital, which covered most of the territory formerly ruled by the Guptas. His reign is memorable in history for the visit to India of another famous Chinese pilgrim, Hiuen-Tsang, who, like Fa-Hien, left a record of his adventures, incidentally throwing much light upon the state of India at the time in its political, social, and religious relationships.

The principal purpose of Hiuen-Tsang's mission was to study the science of Yoga, which, although regarded as heretical by Buddhists of the old school, was generally accepted by Mahâyânists. From very early times Indian philosophers had laid down the theory that knowledge was of two kinds: The first, *sruti*, acquired by intuition, was that which was revealed by the Higher Intelligence which governs the universe; the second, acquired by the reasoning faculties, was scholarship or traditional learning (*smriti*).

In its earliest conceptions the practice of Yoga in India probably consisted only of the rhythmical physical exercises with which the Kshatriyas, like their Hellenic brothers, maintained a *mens sana in corpore sano*. The next stage of Indo-

PLATE XXXVII

A VISHNU TEMPLE, AHMADNAGAR DISTRICT, BOMBAY

Aryan culture was the consecration of mind and body for communion with the Higher Intelligence by a special series of exercises, both mental and physical. Patanjali was the chief exponent of this science of mysticism, which gradually became one of the fundamental doctrines of Indo-Aryan religion. The miraculous powers attributed to those who were expert in the science naturally led to much charlatanism and abuse; and even the most saintly of Hindu men and women have sometimes failed to recognise that, just as Reason without Intuition may tend to spiritual blindness, so the finest intuitive faculties without the complementary reasoning intelligence may be as a sharp razor in the hands of a child.

Harsha emulated Vikramâditya in his zeal for fulfilling the duties of an Indian King of Kings, as laid down in the most ancient Hindu codes of law, and in the great Aryan epics—the science of government which every youthful Indian aristocrat was taught as the Dharma of his caste. The imperial revenue, according to ancient Aryan custom, was derived first from the cultivation of the Crown lands, a certain proportion of the common lands of the Aryan community which belonged to the Kings of Kings by right. They were leased out at a fixed rent, reckoned upon the produce[1]; the cultivation being superintended by one of the imperial officers. The next source of revenue was the *vali*, or customary offering, which was due from every village to the Râja or the head of its tribe. The latter had also a share of the common lands for the maintenance of himself and his retinue, and passed on to the Mahâ-Râja—the head of a confederation of tribes—the

[1] In the Kautilîya-artha-sâstra, one of the earliest manuals of Indian political economy, the proportion was as follows: One-fifth of the grain grown by manual irrigation; one-fourth of the grain irrigated by water carried on the shoulder; one-third of that irrigated by pumps; and one-fourth of that irrigated by water derived from rivers, reservoirs or wells, with an additional one-fourth or one-fifth of the total produce ("Antiquities of India," by Dr. L. D. Barnett, p. 102).

proportion of the vali due to him. The vali payable by a village was generally reckoned at one-sixth of the agricultural produce. Mines, and also the manufactures derived from them, were an imperial monopoly; but they were sometimes leased to private persons in payment of rent and royalties. Subsidiary revenue was derived from duties on pearls, corals, shells, salt, and tolls upon other merchandise collected by a Department of Commerce, which fixed prices and arranged suitable markets. A Department of Navigation and Fisheries controlled the traffic by sea and river, collected harbour dues, ferry tolls, and a vali of one-sixth upon the fisheries. Forests were also included in the imperial domains; special officers were in charge of their conservation, and supervised the cutting of timber and the use of it for defensive and other purposes. Elephant forests were specially protected. Two other very important departments were those of Irrigation and Roads, for the chief function of the Head of the State, after the charge of military defence and the administration of justice, was to provide for and keep in order public reservoirs and other irrigation works, to maintain the King's highway, and protect travellers upon it.[1]

The effects of the Hun invasions were still evident in Harsha's reign in the greater severity of the punishments awarded to criminals and in the unsafe condition of some of the public roads. As in Fa-Hien's time, the slaughter of animals and the eating of flesh was forbidden to the higher castes. Hiuen-Tsang found also public hospitals and rest-houses, at which necessitous travellers could obtain gratuitous medical aid and food and drink.

[1] All of these details are not mentioned by Hiuen-Tsang, but it may be taken for granted that the chief duties of Indo-Aryan kingship, as stated by Hindu law-givers, were fulfilled by Harsha as they had been by Asoka, Vikramâditya and other great Aryan sovereigns.

PLATE XXXVIII

PORCH OF VISHNU TEMPLE, PATHARI, BHOPAL

Harsha, like the Guptas, was a great patron of letters, and himself an author of high distinction. He was devout in religious matters, and, as a pious Hindu ruler, paid respect to all sects, and listened to the arguments of all the schools of philosophy which conformed to the rules of logic prescribed by the Sâstras. As a Kshatriya warrior his Ishta-Deva was Vishnu, but this did not prevent him from revering the other Aspects of the One. The most interesting of the Chinese pandit's experiences was the great religious festival which he attended by Harsha's invitation, at Prayâga (Allâhâbâd), the confluence of the two sacred rivers, the Ganges and the Jumna.

It was doubtless one of the most ancient of Aryan rites which was being celebrated, as it still is on the same spot, only under Harsha's patronage the ceremonies were of unusual magnificence; for the festival was attended not only by the Sovereign Paramount, but by all the Mahâ-râjas and Râjas tributary to him, and by crowds of pilgrims, Brahmans and devotees of every sect, numbering about half a million, from all parts of Hindustan.

The first three days of the festival were consecrated to the worship of the Trimûrti. It is significant that in the seventh century (A.D. 644) the Saint of Bodh-Gayâ was still venerated by this great concourse of Indians of all sects as representing the sâttvic principle, or the first Aspect of Ishvara; for it was the Buddha's image which was set up on the sands at Prayâga and worshipped there. The next day Sûrya, as Vishnu the Preserver—Harsha's own Ishta-Deva—was worshipped as the second Aspect of the Deity; and on the third day, Siva, the tâmasic Aspect of Ishvara, received the adoration of the whole multitude. The pious Chinese pilgrim was pleased to note that in the distribution of the imperial bounty which followed each day's ceremonies the presents which were consecrated to the Buddha on the first day were double the amount of those given on the two following days; but his somewhat narrow sectarian view did not permit him to understand the religious spirit which animated Harsha and the great multitude worshipping the Buddha as an incarnation of Brahmâ, the Creator.

The rest of the festival, which lasted seventy-five days, was devoted to the distribution of all the surplus of Harsha's treasury which had accumulated since the last festival had been held, five years before. Everything except what was required "for maintaining order and protecting the royal estate" was given away; first to members of the Buddhist Sangha, then to Brahmans, then to Jains and devotees of various minor sects, and lastly to the poor and destitute generally. Harsha set the example of benevolence by giving away "his gems and his goods; his clothing and necklaces; ear-rings, bracelets, chaplets, neck-jewel and bright head-jewel"; and when he had nothing left he put on a mendicant's robe which he had begged from his sister, and paid worship to all the Buddhas, rejoicing that "his treasure had been bestowed in the field of religious merit."

Hiuen Tsang, taking with him all his treasures of Buddhist relics, images, and manuscripts which he had collected, besides costly presents from Harsha, who sent a royal escort to accompany him to the frontier, shortly afterwards left India on his way back to China.

Indian historians have always felt it superfluous for the study of their civilisation to follow the whole succession of kings and dynasties throughout the centuries; they rightly considered chronology and events the most illusory factors in history. I will not therefore trouble the reader with the names and dates of other rulers in Northern India who followed Harsha in fulfilling, more or less successfully, the duties of Indo-Aryan kingship. From the seventh century until the

VISHNU TEMPLE (RAJARANI), BHUVANESHVAR, ORISSA (ELEVENTH CENTURY)

conquest of Babar, the first of the Great Moguls, the political history of northern India was a continuation of the struggle of Indo-Aryan civilisation to maintain itself against the hordes of Huns, Arabs, Pathâns, Mongols, and other more or less civilised nomads who were tempted to plunder and devastation by the wealth and prosperity of India under her Aryan constitution.

The particular cult of Indo-Aryan religion favoured by individual sovereigns of the different dynasties is also a matter of minor interest. The epoch from the beginning of the fourth to the end of the eighth century A.D., which was the golden age of Indian literature, when, as is generally believed, the great Indo-Aryan epics were given their present literary forms, and the Bhagavad Gîta, India's Bible, was written as a synthesis of the religious teaching of the time—an age when the classics of Indian drama, poetry, painting, and music were produced, brought to a close by the appearance of the great philosopher of the Vedânta, Sankarâcharya—will be most fitly summarised architecturally by a description of the rock-cut vihâras and chaitya-houses of Ajantâ, which formed during this period one of the famous universities of India.

CHAPTER XI

ANCIENT INDIAN UNIVERSITIES—THE UNIVERSITY OF AJANTÂ—VISHNU'S LAST AVATAR

THE universities of India were not, however, a creation of the Gupta period. Even as far back as the time of Buddha, Taksha-silâ, the capital of Gandhâra—now a heap of ruins near Rawalpindi—was a famous seat of Indo-Aryan learning. Chânakya, the famous Brahman statesman who was Chandragupta Maurya's War Minister and most trusted counsellor, and Pânini, the great Sanskrit grammarian, graduated there.

Two more of its *alumni*, Gobharana and Mâtanga, in A.D. 67 carried Buddhist learning into China, and in the Gupta period crowds of Chinese students were flocking to its halls. Kâsî (Benares) also, in the Buddha's time, was as now a stronghold of Brahman philosophy. Nâgârjuna, the Brahman protagonist of Mahâyâna Buddhism, founded the university at Sûdhanya Kataka, on the head waters of the Krishna River. He himself resided at Nâlanda, the famous university of the Magadha country, near Rajgriha, which in the seventh century was attended by ten thousand learned monks and scholars. Hiuen Tsang, who lived there for five years, describes its towering monastic walls, resplendent with colour and sculpture; its eight quadrangles and lofty enclosing walls; its pavilions "like pointed hill-tops, its soaring domes and pinnacles which seemed to be lost in the mists of the morning." "From their windows," he said, "one could watch the movements of the

PLATE XL

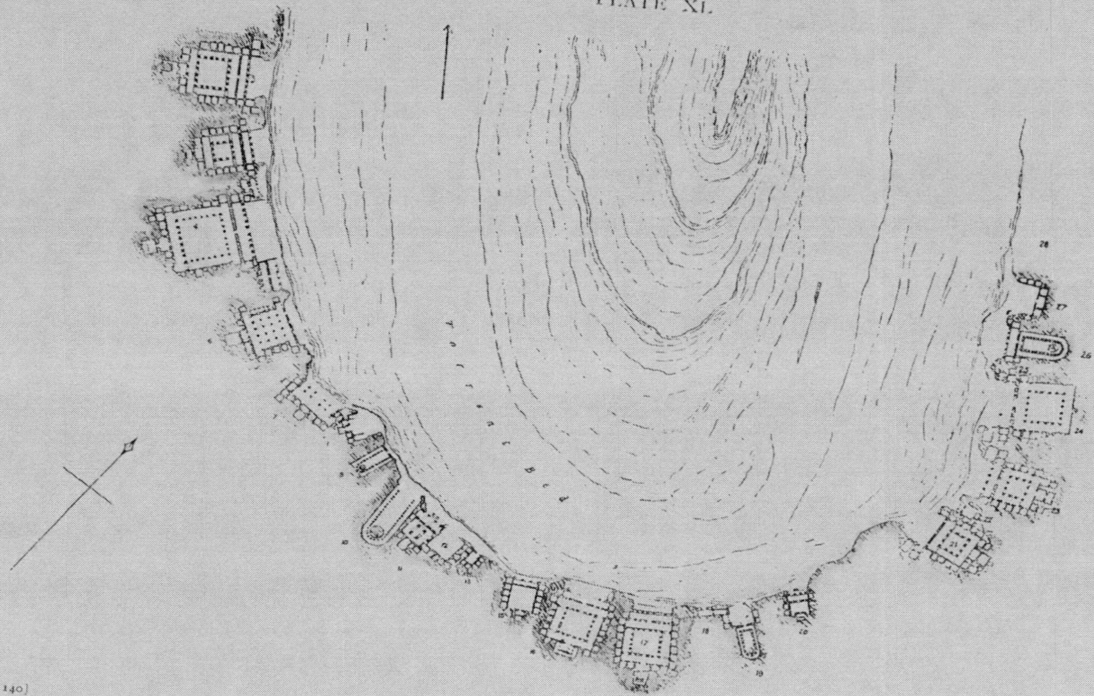

PLAN OF AJANTÂ

PLATE XLI

FAÇADE OF COLLEGE HALL NO. I, AJANTA

winds and clouds, and above their lofty roofs the sun and moon can be seen in conjunction."

He was delighted with its shady groves and gardens; the pools of translucent water shining with the open petals of the blue lotus flowers; the kanaka trees with deep red blossoms, and the pleasant retreats under the dark-leaved mango trees. "There were thousands of Sanghârâmas in India," he wrote, "but none equal to this in majesty or richness or the height of their construction."

The universities were richly endowed by royal and other benefactors, and all of them had free hostels for the maintenance of poor scholars who paid no fees. Some of them, like Takshasilâ and Nâlanda, were universities in the larger sense, where many schools of thought were represented: at Nâlanda there were a hundred professors for expounding the recognised systems of Indo-Aryan philosophy. The larger ones taught secular sciences, such as mathematics and astronomy, as well as metaphysics and religion. Nâlanda was the royal observatory, and its water-clock, says Hiuen Tsang, gave correct time for all Magadha. They were also schools of arts and crafts; for both Brahman and Buddhist monks were skilled in sculpture and painting of icons and in temple decoration, though the former would generally look with contempt upon secular handicraft.

Ajantâ, carved out of the rocky scarp of the Wâghorâ torrent in the upper basin of the Tâptî River, was probably one of those of a strictly sectarian character, devoted to the propagation of a special cult. In some remote time before the Christian era, perhaps, it was only a retreat for a few Buddhist recluses who might have found some natural caves in this wild ravine—curved like the crescent moon and remote from the haunts of men—and made themselves a hermitage looking down upon the torrent which had carved a passage through it, like the holy Ganges rushing out into the plains at Hardwar. Higher up the ravine ends as a precipice, over which the torrent pours from the wooded heights above in seven falls (*sât kund*), as Gangâ leaps through the matted locks of Siva's hair in the forests of Himâlaya.

Gradually the fame of these saintly men spread over the country side. Ajantâ became a place of learning, and many pious benefactors helped to cut monastic halls and chapels deep in the hard trap rock. According to the Western scientific way of writing history, there are four series of excavations, representing as many successive periods. The Indian historian would classify them differently, but we will begin with the Western method. The first to be excavated were the monastic halls now known as Nos. XIII, XII, XI, and VIII, and the chaitya-houses Nos. IX and X, which belong to the second and first centuries B.C. Their axes point to the north or north-east, for they were the dwellings of an austere community of monks who did not adore the Buddha as the rising sun, but meditated upon his Pari-Nirvâna, associated with the north side of the Aryan village, which symbolised the night sky. Their asceticism is further reflected in the simplicity of the pillars of the Sangha in the chaitya-houses (fig. 30), which are plain

FIG. 47.—Hînayâna Sun-windows, Chaitya-house No. IX, Ajantâ.

PLATE XLII

VERANDAH OF COLLEGE HALL NO. II, AJANTÂ

octagonal shafts, without caps or bases, and in the absence of any elaborate sculpture except some of later date than the original excavations. Fine craftsmanship, however, is shown in the polished walls of the small vihâra, No. XIII. Both chaitya-houses had painted decoration, renewed at various times.

To the east of this early group, occupying the centre of the "digit of the moon,"[1] comes the second one, including the vihâras numbered XIV to XVIII and the chaitya-house No. XIX, which embrace a period commencing about the second century A.D. and ending about the fifth. Vihâra XV can be definitely dated *circa* A.D. 185, and XVII and XVIII come within the reign of Vikramâditya of Magadha, an inscription showing that it was dedicated by the king of the Vâkâtakas, whose queen was a daughter of the great Gupta emperor.

FIG. 48.—Monastic Hall or College No. VII, Ajantâ.

On the other side of the earliest group, or at the western tip of the moon's crescent, are the monastic halls numbered I to VI, most of which belong to the seventh century, and right opposite to them, at the other extremity, is the fourth group, standing apart from the other three and facing the setting sun. This includes the vihâras or colleges numbered XX to XXV and the magnificent chaitya-

[1] See preface to Professor F. W. Bain's delightful Hindu romance. The disc of the moon is divided into sixteen parts, called "streaks" or digits; a beautiful woman being called "a digit of the moon."

house XXVI, which are the last and most elaborate of the four groups; some of them remained unfinished.

The whole of this splendid series, therefore, is a record of Indian architectural design from about the time of the Kârlê Chaitya-house to the break-up of Harsha's empire in the middle of the seventh century.

It is unnecessary to go again over the ground covered by the preceding chapters, so we will begin by comparing the finest of the monastic halls, Nos. I and II, in the third group (Pl. XLI—XLIII) with the Gautamîputra monastery at Nâsik (Pl. XXII), in order to show the development of the Indo-Aryan architectural tradition in the Gupta period. The plan of the Ajantâ hall, fig. 50, is practically the same as the one at Nâsik, only, instead of a simple stûpa symbol on the walls of the cells, a great image of the Buddha as the Teacher is sculptured within a cubical cell on the side facing the entrance. The verandah front (Pl. XLI) is supported by six massive columns, as at Nâsik, but an entrance porch had been added in the middle of it. This unfortunately has completely fallen away.

FIG. 49.—Monastic Hall or College No. VI, Ajantâ.

Archæologists have remained completely in the dark as to the connection of the Ajantâ craft tradition with that of Kârlê, Nâsik, and the earlier Hînayâna school. Dr. Burgess only repeats Fergusson's puerile remark that the beautiful "Perse-

PLATE XLIII

INTERIOR OF COLLEGE HALL NO. II, AJANTÂ

politan bell-shaped" capitals are superseded at Ajantâ by a "pudding-shape." The explanation of the symbolism of Indian pillars given above will enable the reader to see that the Ajantâ type is also the traditional Vishnu pillar. Considering the difference of age—about four and a half centuries—there is comparatively little change in the forms, only at Ajantâ there is a more voluptuous feeling for beauty, more classic refinement of detail, and a closer searching for just proportions. The Kârlê and Nâsik monasteries belong to the epic age—the art of the Mahâbhârata and Râmâyana; the Ajantâ monasteries and chaitya-houses, from the fourth to the seventh centuries, belong to the later Indian classics—the age of Sakûntala.

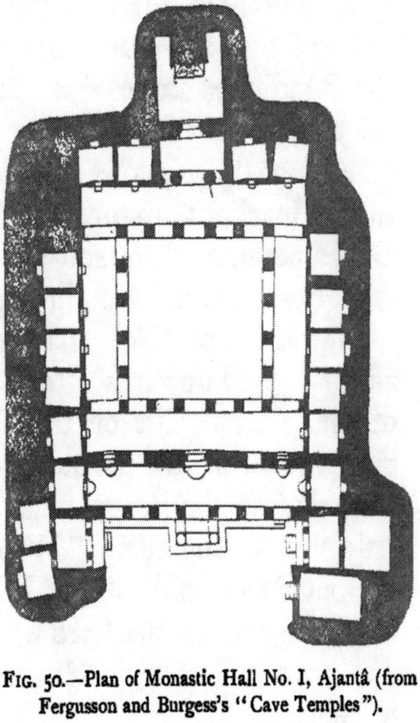

FIG. 50.—Plan of Monastic Hall No. I, Ajantâ (from Fergusson and Burgess's "Cave Temples").

The symbolism is the same as at Kârlê and at Nâsik. The Silpa-sâstras will help us to understand the ideas conveyed by the Ajantâ variety of the Vishnu pillar. Instead of Lakshmî's jar of plenty, the bases of the pillars are square—*Brahmâ-kantha.* Higher up they change into an octagonal section—*Vishnu-kantha.* Still higher the shaft becomes circular or sixteen-sided, with flutings: the technical name for this is *Rudra-kantha.* So the whole shaft symbolises the Three Aspects of the One.

The capital consists of the traditional amalaka, the water-lily fruit (Fergusson's "pudding"). This, as at Kârlê, supports a Vedic altar with four legs, only the succession of thin slabs is reduced to a plain square abacus, and the legs which enclose the amalaka are carved with the greatest skill into little fat men—Indian trolls—or *pisâchas*. Ushas, the Dawn-maiden, Indra, and other Vedic deities are no longer seated on the altar. Their place is taken by images of the Buddha, attended by Devas, carved upon the massive bracket capital.

In Hînayâna architecture one would find the Vedic rail used to decorate the architrave above the pillars. Here it is replaced by a sculptured frieze showing incidents in the life of the Buddha or stories from the Jâtakas. Above this frieze is the chhaja, ornamented as usual with miniature sun-windows. In each of the windows a head appears. We have seen before, in the Bharhut sculptures (Pl. III, A), representations of men or Devas peeping out of sun-windows. Who can this be? That is a question which Buddhist pilgrims, accustomed to the plain sun-windows of Hînayâna symbolism, might well have asked as they gazed upwards, after following with eager eyes the story of the Master's life on the sculptured frieze. On a Vishnu or Siva shrine the devout would know at once that within a sun-window the image must be either Brahmâ or Siva, the rising or setting sun. "What do our gurus mean by this?" the pilgrims would ask. "It is Avalokiteshvara," the monks would answer—"the Lord who looks down from Heaven upon us; not the Tathâgata Himself, but a Bodhisattva, a Buddha in being."

[1] I had identified Avalokiteshvara with Brahmâ by this process of reasoning before I noticed that Colonel Waddell had arrived at the same conclusion by a comparison of the attributes of Brahmanical and Buddhist images. M. Foucher's objections ("Étude sur l'iconographie Buddhique," p. 173 n.) can, I think, be easily met. Avalokiteshvara has a sâttvic as well as a tâmasic aspect, according as he is related to the rising or the setting sun. In the former case (as in Nepal) his image is red; in the latter white. The eleven-headed Avalokiteshvara is derived from the five-headed Brahmâ or Siva symbol, representing the five cosmic elements.

PLATE XLIV

PRINCE SIDDHARTHA, FRESCO PAINTING, AJANTÂ

PLATE XLV

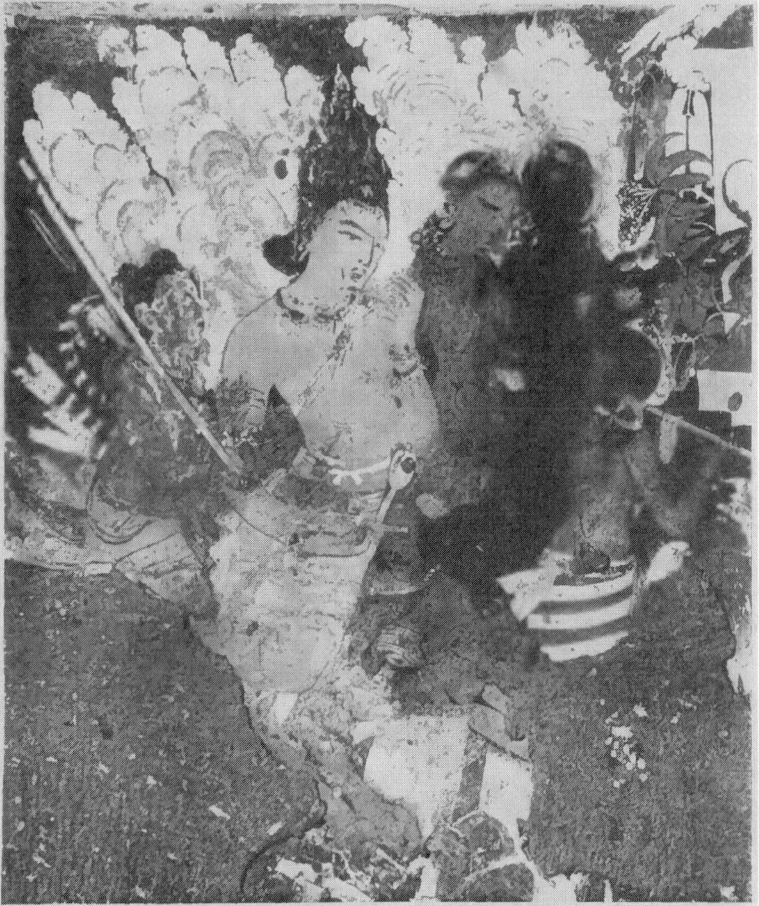

DEVAS AND ATTENDANTS, FRESCO PAINTING, AJANTÂ

Thus Mahâyâna Buddhism transformed into Bodhisattvas, to be worshipped by the faithful as Buddhas that are to be, the Devas who watched the Hînayâna service at Kârlê and Nâsik, and at the older chaitya-houses of Ajantâ, just as they had watched the Vedic sacrifices of old. The bright nature-spirits of the Vedas remained for ever impressed upon the Indian mind; transformed into concepts of philosophy, they became the gods of Brahman theology and Bodhisattvas of the Buddhists.

Above the chhaja is another sculptured frieze occupied mostly by scenes in the Buddhist heavens, and panels in which the sacred goose (*hamsa*), a symbol of the parting soul, is used as a decorative motif. On a narrow band above it, supported by heads which seem to be those of the bats which infest the caves, is a small Vedic rail transformed into a chequer pattern.

The inside of the verandah of the second monastic hall with the remains of its fine painted ceiling is shown in Pl. XLII. The next plate gives a fine impression of the stately magnificence of the interior. The pillars which support the roof are similar to those of the verandah, only the proportions are more massive. It is somewhat smaller than the first hall, being only 48 feet square instead of 64 feet, the dimensions of the former, but the arrangements are similar. The sanctuary with an image of Buddha is on the side facing the entrance, with a smaller cell for another image on either side of it. The scholars' or neophytes' cells, ten in number, are placed along the two sides of the hall at right angles to the shrine. Two larger cells at each end of the verandah provided accommodation for the Abbot and his deputy. The arrangements of the first monastic hall (fig. 50) are nearly the same, but on a somewhat more ample scale.

The chief glory of Ajantâ is in the frescoes, which are now nearly all that remain of the greatest pictorial art of India, but barbarously mutilated and ruined both from lack of care and by inept attempts at conservation. Very rarely in the world's history has there come together that true symphony of the three arts—painting, sculpture, and architectonic design—creating the most perfect architecture, which are so beautifully harmonised at Ajantâ. By a fortuitous circumstance a large fragment of one of the finest frescoes, and one of the greatest masterpieces of any age, in the first monastic hall, is one of the best preserved.

It is painted on the wall to the left of the principal shrine. The central figure is of a youth crowned with a royal tiara and holding Vishnu's blue water-lily in his right hand. A water-lily is also fastened on either side of the tiara, and the long black curls falling over his shoulders are garlanded with jessamine. He is looking downwards in a pensive mood, as if filled with the presentiment of coming sorrow (Pl. XLIV).

On either side a youthful attendant carries the insignia of royalty, a sword of State, and the yak's tail fly-flap. On his left side a young princess, similarly crowned, accompanies him. Close to her in the background is a building, no doubt the royal palace, from which the party is coming. Behind on a mountain-side *gandharvas* and *kinnaras*, the heavenly musicians, are discoursing sweet music. Siva sits conversing with Parvati (fig. 51), and the Devas are watching with interest the great event in the world below.

No doubt the subject is the marriage of Prince Siddhartha—one which a Buddhist artist would paint as a parallel to the old Aryan myth of Siva and Parvati, or of the marriage of Vishnu with the Dawn-maiden. And considering that this monastic hall is one of those which inclines most towards the east, it is easy to understand that the motif of the Dawn-maiden, symbolised in every Vishnu shrine by the large sun-window placed in the front of the sikhara, would be the first to suggest itself to

PLATE XLVI

FAÇADE OF CHAITYA-HOUSE XIX, AJANTÂ

PLATE XLVII

FAÇADE OF CHAITYA-HOUSE XXVI, AJANTA

the mind of an Indian painter. The noble head of Prince Siddhartha finds an exact parallel in another wonderful masterpiece of Indian art, the Vishnu Aspect or central head of the Trimûrti[1] at Elephanta (Pl. LVI). The tiaras (*mukutas*) in both are identical in design, and the head, both in the fresco painting and the sculpture, evidently belong to the same traditional type, though the more youthful Christ-like face of Prince Siddhartha fitly expresses the distinction between the two conceptions.

FIG. 51.—Siva and Parvati. Painting in Cave I (from a copy by Mr. Nanda Lal Bose).

Another superb fragment of painting (Pl. XLV) appears to be also a Vishnu motif. This is painted on the walls of the verandah in the monastic hall No. XVII, which has a northwest aspect; but here it is not the principal subject of the picture, as in the other hall, which is open to the rising sun. This is Vishnu as a Bodhisattva,[2] accompanied by Lakshmî, as Târâ, flying down from heaven to attend some event in the life of the Buddha. The animation of the heavenly beings, expressed by this Indian Tintoretto with an amazing display of

[1] This has always been mistaken for Brahmâ. Dr. Coomaraswamy, in his "Arts and Crafts of India and Ceylon" (Pl. 33), gives the head of Parvati as that of Vishnu.

[2] The Buddhist adaptation of Vishnu as the deification of the Sangha seems to have been the Bodhisattva Visvapâni, whose other name was Akâsa-garbha, the Container of Akâsa (ether)—this being also an attribute of Vishnu as the power which maintained the equilibrium of the cosmos.

technical power, is a great contrast to the serene composure, tinged with sadness, so masterfully rendered by the forgotten Perugino of Ajantâ in the first monastic hall. Only the dullest artistic comprehension will refuse to place these Ajantâ frescoes in the same category as the greatest masterpieces of Italian art. That they have been so long unappreciated by European artists is due in great measure to the miserably inadequate reproductions of them by which they have been hitherto known. The uninspired copies made by the Bombay School of Art, where the minds of Indian students are still drugged with the dull academic formularies of Europe, give no indication of the technical power and transcendent genius of the Ajantâ painters. But for the fact that since these copies were made many of the original frescoes have been shamefully destroyed or ruined by neglect, their destruction by fire would have been no loss to art.

Apart from their artistic value the Ajantâ frescoes have an extraordinary historical interest for the light they throw upon the evolution of Mahâyâna Buddhism; but the full elucidation of them must be left until the publication in "Ars Asiatica" of the results of the complete photographic survey of the paintings with which M. Victor Goloubeff has followed up the devoted labours of Mrs. Herringham and her Indian collaborators.

Of the many chaitya-houses which were the chapels of the University of Ajantâ the two which represent the great epoch of Indian architecture from the fifth to the ninth centuries are those numbered XIX and XXVI.

The latter is the largest and finest in design, for the figure-sculpture on the façade of XIX (Pl. XLVI), though fine as craftsmanship, is not happily conceived architecturally. It is very likely, as Sister Nivedita has suggested,[1] that these sculptures were the work of Gandharan craftsmen, driven to find a

[1] "Footfalls of Indian History," p. 52.

PLATE XLVIII

INTERIOR OF CHAITYA-HOUSE XXVI, AJANTA

PLATE XLIX

PILLARS AND TRIFORIUM, CHAITYA-HOUSE XXVI, AJANTA

shelter in the cloisters of Ajantâ when the Buddhist monasteries of North-west India were ravaged and burnt by the tyrant Mihiragula in the middle of the sixth century. It is quite possible, indeed, that this front is a sculptured palimpsest, executed by two different generations of craftsmen; for it is unusual to find in this great epoch the clumsy spacing of decoration, contrasting so curiously with the fine design of the architectural detail. But it would be easily explained by assuming that some of the colossal figures were sculptured on the original façade long after the chaitya-house was finished.

The façade of XXVI (Pl. XLVII) is much finer as an architectonic unity, though unfortunately the roof of the verandah in front has gone and only a few fragments of the supporting pillars remain. This chaitya-house, indeed, ranks with that of Kârlê as one of the two finest in India.

Both of these Ajantâ chaitya-houses are inclined towards the setting sun, the quarter of Siva is his tâmasic Aspect. This accounts for the tâmasic heads of Avalokiteshvara carved in the little sun-windows on the chhajas, and for the close connection between the chaitya in XXVI and the Siva shrine, known as Arjuna's Rath, at Mâmallapuram, which has been already alluded to (p. 104). It also accounts for the head of the fish dragon (*makara*), the symbol of the clouds gathering at sunset, at the springing of the great sun-window which lights the nave of the chaitya-house; and for the grinning head of the eclipse demon, Râhu, at the pipal-leaf crown of the arch.

The three entrance doors to each chaitya-house are finely carved. As explained above (p. 73), the central door opening to the nave was for the members of the Sangha. At the Ajantâ University it would no doubt be used for the Abbot and his monks; the two side doors—on the left for entrance and the right for exit—being for the scholars, or neophytes, who attended the service in the aisles.

The entrances to a house, temple, or shrine are always in India consecrated places, only second in importance to the sacred image itself; it is therefore here that the highest art of the master-craftsman is shown. Volumes might be filled with examples of Indian doorways of the classic age which reveal the fountain-head of the inspiration of Chârtres, Rheims, and Bourges. Ajantâ has some of them, but other parts of India can show more perfect door-sculpture. Plates L and LI are superb examples from Vishnu temples in Central India, probably contemporary with the latest period of Ajantâ. There one can see that Gothic art of India which in the three centuries of its zenith in India (A.D. 400–700) was the parent tree from which all its Eastern and Western grafts were taken.

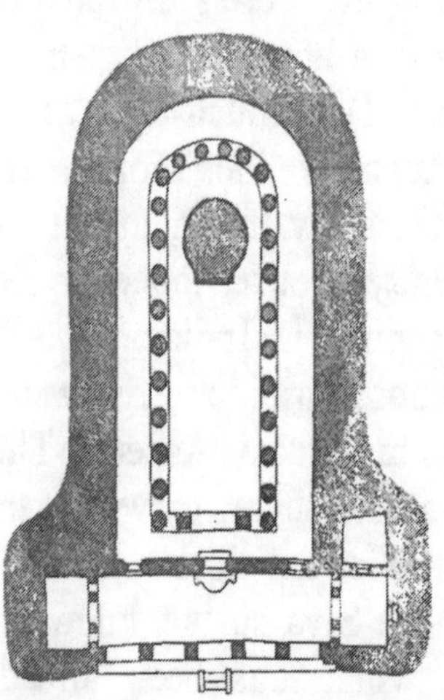

FIG. 52.—Plan of Chaitya-house XXVI, Ajantâ (from Fergusson's "Cave Temples").

Fig. 52 shows the plan of the chaitya-house. The dimensions of it are nearly 68 feet in length, 36 feet in breadth, and the height of the nave to the centre of the roof 31 feet. It is therefore little more than half of the Kârlê chaitya-house; it is a university chapel, and not a cathedral, like the latter. The difference between the chaitya as at Kârlê and Ajantâ shows how Indian Buddhism of the second or third century B.C. differed from that of the seventh or eighth century A.D. At Kârlê the chaitya is a reliquary and a symbol. At Ajantâ it is a shrine for the sacred image which, lighted up by the golden rays of the setting sun through the grand sun-window of the nave, was adored as a mystic vision of the Messiah (Maitreya) who is yet to come. The pillars of the Sangha which divide

PLATE L

CARVED TEMPLE DOORWAY, DHAMTARI, CENTRAL PROVINCES

the nave from the aisles are of the same type as those already described in the first college hall facing the chaitya-house on the opposite bend of the torrent. The symbolism remains the same as at Kârlê. On the architrave, or triforium, above the capitals there is a richly sculptured frieze (Pl. XLIX), and images of the Buddha are placed in exquisite shrines along the walls of the side aisles where the scholars worshipped. All the sculpture at Ajantâ was finished with a fine coat of polished clumam, of the thickness of an egg-shell, which served as a ground for discreet touches of colour; but very little of this now remains.

Some of the latest sculpture at Ajantâ is evidently done by ivory carvers, or goldsmiths, and Cellini's chisel never surpassed the beauty and finish of the bracket capitals from some of the college halls shown in Plate LII. In the lower figure of the plate the amalaka of the capital is converted into Lakshmî's jar of plenty—a favourite device in Indian medieval architecture—the legs of the Vedic altar being converted into floral devices growing out of this cornucopia.

Having thus briefly described the principal architectural details of this wonderful university of ancient India and stated its chronology according to the scientific method, I will attempt to sum up its history from the Indian point of view. Let us try to see it as the Indian artists who created Ajantâ saw and felt it. The Western scientific method ignores the Indian way of thinking and does nothing to light up the obscurity of Indian history: it tells the facts, but leaves Ajantâ to the bats and owls.

Ajantâ is a microcosm of ancient and medieval Indian history, but Indian historians would divide it into three epochs instead of four. The first was the sâttvic cycle; the age of quiet meditation, beginning with the time of the Saint Asoka, whose peaceful edicts proclaimed the Blessed One's message of peace and love throughout the land of Bharatavarsha. Then some pious members of the Sangha carved out of this digit of the moon—Siva's crest—the middle section (Pl. XL) facing north, the region of the moonlit sky, and taught the Buddha's doctrines with the simple austere ritual of the Hînayâna school.

The second was the râjasic cycle—the age of passion, action, and energy—when the hero Vikramâditya ruled the land with justice and wisdom, drove back the Hun invaders, and recovered Lakshmî's jar of plenty by the churning of the Ocean of Time. It was then that the college halls were carved on the western tip of Siva's crest, and there the scholars worshipped God in His râjasic Aspect, taking as His symbols the dawn and the rising sun.

Then, when dark clouds began to gather over Bharatavarsha, when the black plague was raging, and savage hordes of barbarians poured down the Indus valley in the darkest days of the Kali age,[1] began the tâmasic aspect of Ajantâ's life. It is then that the divine powers of destruction, death, and re-birth should be worshipped in fear, but with hope and faith. That was the time when the eastern tip of Siva's crest became the lodging-place of the scholars of Ajantâ; there, in those splendid chaitya-houses, they worshipped the Lord who looks down with infinite love upon His children, even when His work of destruction is going on. He knows there is no death!

And so, at last, the sun of Ajantâ set. The long-expected Messiah did not come. The exact time the sacred spot hallowed by associations of a thousand years was deserted is

[1] Indian chronologists divide the life of the universe into four ages, the Krita, Trêtâ, Dwâpara, and Kali. The commencement of the latter is reckoned at 3102 B.C., and towards the end of it the last incarnation of Vishnu, Kalkin, will appear to restore peace and righteousness on earth.

PLATE LI

CARVED TEMPLE DOORWAY, SIRPUR, CENTRAL PROVINCES

CARVED BRACKET CAPITALS, AJANTA

not known—probably about the tenth century, when the sword of Islam descended to complete the havoc which the Hun barbarians had begun. For centuries the college halls and chapels have been the haunt of venomous snakes and of the wild beasts of the neighbouring jungle; myriads of bats have fouled them, and vast swarms of bees have blackened their lovely painted ceilings with their nests. Since they were discovered at the beginning of the last century, vandals have desecrated them, obsequious officials have cut out sections of precious frescoes to present to "distinguished visitors" as curiosities, and blundering antiquarians have helped to complete the ruin.

Will there come another dawn when they will be filled again with teachers and scholars inspired by the noblest traditions of the noble Aryan race, and feeling the undying poetry of the place? For now once again gods and demons are churning the Ocean of Time, and clouds of poisonous vapours—ignorance, greed, sectarian and racial hatreds—confuse the contending hosts, so that friends and foes mistake each other. But God still holds the churning stick and watches overhead—lest the Devas weaken in the struggle—to see that truth and right prevail. And though the darkness sometimes seems to thicken, the dawn will come at last.

Maitreya did not come. But there is an ancient Indian prophecy that at the end of the Kali age, when the new day begins to dawn, Kalkin, Vishnu's tenth Avatar on earth, will come riding on a white horse, sword in hand, to restore the Law of Righteousness and to rule the Aryan lands. Who was this Avatar the Indian mystic saw? Was it a vision of St. George of Merrie England—when England shall be Merrie once again?

CHAPTER XII

THE GREAT TEMPLE OF ELEPHANTA—THE TRIMÛRTI

AJANTÂ is only one splendid episode in the history of the classic age of Indian art—an age so rich in achievement and so pregnant in inspiration for the whole civilised world that it would be quite impossible in one volume to more than briefly summarise it. Ajantâ reveals the wreck of the great masterpieces of Indian painting. The contemporary Siva temple at Elephanta, a rocky island overlooking the harbour of Bombay, possesses the fragments which now remain of the achievements of India's Michelangelo—her Pheidias and Praxiteles.

Archæologists have been undecided as to the age of this temple, but I am convinced that both Fergusson and Dr. Burgess are very much at fault in attributing it, from evidence of "style," to the eighth or beginning of the ninth century of our era.[1] It is certainly more than a century earlier than Chaitya-house XXVI at Ajantâ, which they date *circa* A.D. 600—but that date is probably a century too early. I think it would be safe to assume that the great sculpture of the Trimûrti had been completed a century before Harsha of Thanesar celebrated the feast of the Indian Trinity on the sands at Prayâga, which Hiuen Tsang attended in A.D. 644. It was probably known in the seventh century as a famous masterpiece throughout Western India, so that the artist of Ajantâ had it in his mind when he painted the wonderful

[1] "Cave Temples," p. 467.

PLATE LIII

CENTRAL AISLE, ELEPHANTA TEMPLE

head of Prince Siddhartha on the walls of the first college hall, about the beginning of the seventh century.

Elephanta was the name given to the island by the Portuguese on account of a great stone elephant which formerly stood near the landing-place on the south side of the island. Its Indian name is Ghârâpurî, which seems to be a corruption of Ghârîpurî, "the town of the Ghârîs, or Guruvas," who are people of the Sudra caste performing priestly duties at Saivaite temples. Probably at one time the island, which contains several other rock-cut shrines besides the great temple, was a sacred city dedicated to the cult of Siva. It is still visited by pious Hindu pilgrims on the occasion of the great Saivaite festival in February, but no regular service has been held at the temple since it was desecrated in the sixteenth century by the Portuguese, who are said to be responsible for most of the barbarous mutilation of the sculptures.

The island, which is formed of a species of hard trap-rock about four and a half miles in circumference, consists of two long hills with a narrow valley between them. The great temple is carved out of the western hill, at a height of 250 feet above high-water level. It has three entrances: the principal one, opening to the central aisle (Pl. LIII), the end of which is filled by the Trimûrti, faces north—like the first cycle of monastic halls at Ajantâ. This northern aspect commands a splendid view over the sea and mainland, with the silhouette of the Western Ghats bounding the horizon.

Fig. 53 shows the plan of the temple. Excluding the pillared porticoes which form the north, east, and west entrances, and the shrine of the Trimûrti which fills the place of the southern porch, the interior of the temple is a pillared hall about 91 feet square, the roof being supported by six rows of pillars with six pillars in each row, except for the space occupied by the Brahmâ shrine (Pl. LIV), which takes the place of four pillars. If the temple had been a structural one, it would therefore have been itself a Brahmâ shrine, with entrances on each of the four sides opposite the cardinal points.

In classic dignity and restraint these massive Vishnu pillars, with their usual amalaka capitals, contrast strongly with the rich elaboration of the first two college halls at Ajantâ,

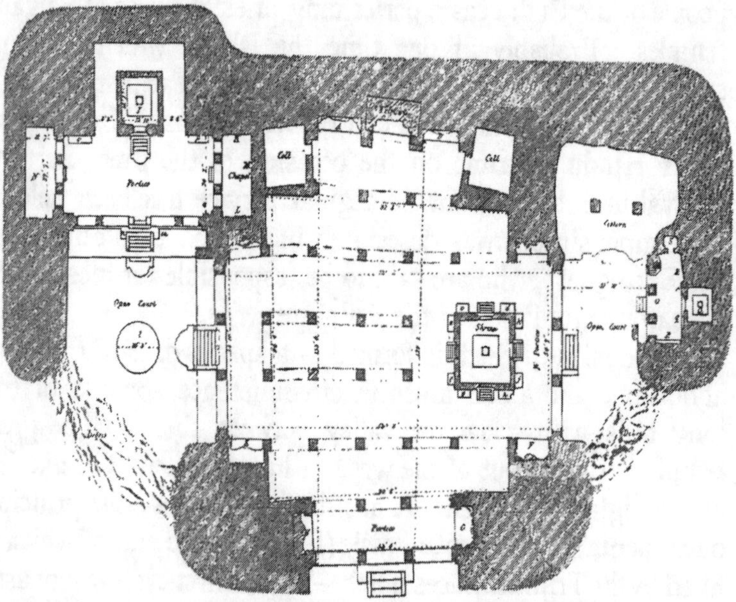

FIG. 53.—Plan of the Great Temple at Elephanta (from Fergusson's "Cave Temples").

though the symbolism is precisely similar. They resemble rather closely the pillars of No. VII (fig. 48), and it may be assumed that the Elephanta temple is of about the same age as the latter.

Entering at the northern entrance, and passing up the central aisle, attention is first arrested by the wonderful Brahmâ shrine on the right (Pl. LIV), placed near the entrance, so that the glow of light from the western court falls upon it. It is a

PLATE LIV

THE BRAHMA SHRINE, ELEPHANTA

cubical cell—a symbol of the universe—pierced by four doors, the ends of the four arms of the cosmic cross, each guarded by two colossal regents of the quarters, like gods of Olympus, which are among the most striking of the Elephanta sculptures. The shrine now contains only the modern lingam of Siva, placed there probably to placate the iconoclasts in early Muhammadan times, or perhaps after it had been desecrated by

FIG. 54.—The Mahâyânist Brahmâ Stûpa.

FIG. 55.—The Stûpa Anthropomorphosised. (The Brahmâ Image of Elephanta restored.)

the Portuguese, when the magnificent Brahmâ image (Pl. LV) for which it was designed was knocked down and flung into the adjoining courtyard. It remains there, I believe, until the present day.

Here is plain evidence of the form which Siva's lingam took about the sixth or seventh century A.D. It was a Brahmâ image, which at this time took the form of an anthropomorphosised stûpa : *i.e.* the early stûpa of the Mahâyâna type (fig. 54), with a square or octagonal base and the four shrines—the symbol of the universe, or Brahmâ's temple—was converted into the four-headed image of Brahmâ, in which the dome of the stûpa remained as the top of his *mukuta* or tiara (fig. 55). When the Muhammadan iconoclasts came, the Brahmâ symbol reverted to its ancient aniconic form, and, the original symbolism having been forgotten in the decadence of Hinduism which set in after the Muhammadan conquest, the phallic ideas now popularly connected with it were read into it by the low-caste guardians of Siva temples.

This grand sculptured symbol of the cosmic forces conveys a vivid impression of another great masterpiece of the Aryan genius—the Hermes of Praxiteles. The two might appropriately be placed side by side to show the similarity in artistry and the difference in spiritual insight of the two schools of Aryan sculpture; for they sum up the highest art of the Western naturalist and of the Eastern mystic.

Some day, perhaps, if the Eastern masterpiece still exists and when the Aryan of the West has begun to understand the art which belongs to him better, reproductions of it may be made for a museum in which Indian art will take its proper place side by side with that of Hellas. The Hermes of Elephanta will not suffer by comparison with that of Praxiteles.

Elephanta is India's Parthenon, and when the eye has become accustomed to the dim light of the interior, the colossal bust of the Trimûrtî (Pl. LVI), carved in the rocky wall which ends the central aisle, will be seen looming out through the mysterious gloom. But it is difficult in the present state of the great temple to realise how awe-inspiringly beautiful it must have been when lighted up by the glow of the bronze temple-lamps and the silver shimmer of the snow-white pillars, finished like marble with the finest polished plaster, and when

PLATE LV

IMAGE OF BRAHMA, ELEPHANTA

the chanting of that great Hymn of the Rig-Veda (X. 129) echoed through the aisles:

There was neither Existence nor Non-Existence;
The Kingdom of Air, nor the Sky beyond.

What was there to contain, to cover in—
Were there but vast unfathomed depths of Water?

There was no Death there, nor Immortality;
No Sun was there, dividing Day from Night:

Then was there only THAT, resting within ITSELF;
Apart from IT there was not anything.

At first within the Darkness veiled in Darkness,
Chaos unknowable, the All lay hid:

When sudden from the formless Void emerging,
By the great power of Heat was born that Germ.

Thereafter came Desire, the primal root of Mind;
Being from non-Being proceeded—this our Rishis know:

What was the Cause—above, below?
What vital force impell'd this parting here?

Who knows whence this was born, or how it came?
The Gods themselves are later than this time:

He only, the Creator, truly knoweth this;
And even He, perhaps, may know it not.

The Indian conception of the Trimûrti, the Three Aspects of the One, may be considered from many different standpoints. Originally, like all other Indo-Aryan conceptions, it was derived from the life of the ancient Indian village community. The first Aspect was Brahmâ, the Creator, whom all Aryans worshipped as the Cause of all things; or Buddha, the great Aryan Guru. It was the symbol of the spiritual wisdom of the Aryan race. The second Aspect was Justice, the pillar of Aryan society, represented by the village council, or by the head of the tribe. The third was the Dharma, the Law spiritual and temporal, revealed and recorded by the Vedas. And as all three Aspects were interchangeable, and manifestations of the universal Law, together they represented God, as Three in One, or One in Three.

As an abstract or philosophical concept the Trimûrti represented the Vedantic theory of the Evolution of the Universe from the Absolute or Unknowable Brahman—the first manifestation of which is Ishvara, or God, likened to the passing of a human being from a state of profound sleep into a state of dreaming and then of awakening. From Ishvara is then manifested Purusha, or Spirit, and Prakriti, the Essence of Matter; and through the divine power called Sakti, the female principle, Purusha causes Prakriti to take form as the Trimûrti.

The latter symbolises two groups of cosmic conceptions. As related to Purusha, the Soul Force, it stands for the spiritual powers, Sat-Chit-Ânandam; or Being (connoting the power of truth and goodness), Thought-power, and Bliss. As related to Prakriti, the Nature-force, it represents the three *gunas*, Sattvam, Rajas, Tamas, or the conditions of creating, equilibrium or preservation, and dissolution or darkness.

In a more popular or mythological sense the Trimûrti stands for the three chief divinities of the Hindu pantheon—Brahmâ the Creator, Vishnu the Preserver, and Siva the Destroyer, who were represented in Mahâyâna Buddhism by the deification of the Buddha, the Sangha, and the Dharma. These three divinities, or Aspects of Divinity, may again be considered from the Western scientific standpoint as solar myths, or symbols of the sun in its three aspects: at rising, at the

PLATE LVI

THE TRIMURTI, ELEPHANTA

zenith, and at setting, which are the three times at which every orthodox Brahman recites his daily prayers.

Though a Siva temple, Elephanta is, as I have said, the Indian Parthenon; for in the Trimûrti sculpture Brahmâ's place is taken by Parvati, as Creatrix, just as in Mahâyâna Buddhism it is taken by the Buddha. The legend of the marriage of Siva and Parvati—the springtime of the Himâlayas, whose loveliness lures once a year the Great Ascetic from his meditation on the snow-clad mountain peak—as told by Kalidâs in the poem of the Birth of the War-God, fills one of the sculptured panels in an adjoining aisle; and her head in the Trimûrti, mistaken by archæologists for Vishnu, is the one on the right of the spectator, or facing west.

The central head, majestic and calm in expression, has always been mistaken for Brahmâ, the Creator; but it is really the râjasic Aspect of the Trimûrti, Vishnu the Preserver, with the shining symbols of His three footsteps [1] upon the splendid jewelled crown, the holy Mount Meru. He wears also His necklet of pearls, the worlds innumerable in the making [2] which are strung together on their orbits in His firmament—and the glorious panch-ratna collar of gold glittering with His jewels [3]—ether, air, fire, water, and earthy matter.

Siva, with frowning brows, parted lips, and protruding tongue, holding the Serpent, a symbol of life, death, and re-incarnation, is the third or tâmasic Aspect of the Trimûrti. His tiara contains a human skull, and floral emblems which belong to Saivaite ritual are wreathed in it. [4]

[1] The three positions of the sun.

[2] The pearl is the symbol of the cosmic element *akâsha*, ether, and thus also of the planets which are born from it; Vishnu being known as Akâsha-garbha, Container of Ether.

[3] The precious stones which symbolise the elements are pearl, sapphire, ruby, emerald, and diamond.

[4] These include the trefoiled leaf of the bel tree (*Cratæva religiosa*), and that of the nirgundi (*Vitex trefoliata*).

Dr. Burgess states that behind the mukuta of Siva the rock is cut away into a recess in which two persons could lie stretched out at length without being seen from below. The Trimûrti of Elephanta was probably the Delphic Oracle of Western India!

It is difficult to compare the magnificent sculpture of the Elephanta temple with any of the masterpieces of the West, for it belongs to a plane of æsthetic thought, not entirely peculiar to India, but one in which Indian artists were supreme. Greek art had its centaurs, fauns, and satyrs, and its pantheon of deified heroes, but left the profoundest mysteries of creation to the speculation of philosophers. Egyptian art, marvellous as it is, can only be regarded from a philosophic standpoint as glorified totemism. Indian philosophy, rising to a far higher intellectual plane, seems to take the monumental art of Egypt at the point where it stopped short, and to raise it, with an equivalent power of technical expression, to the loftiest heights ever yet attained by human thought. The mystics of India reconciled the aims of the artist and philosopher, which Greece and Italy were content to regard as belonging to different planes of thought.

If the Brahmâ image might have been created by the chisel of Praxiteles, it seems as if a reincarnation of Pheidias, inspired by the profound philosophy of the Upanishads instead of by the child-like conceptions of the Homeric Olympus, had been born again to carve this masterpiece of Indo-Aryan genius at Elephanta. There are other great sculptures at Elephanta; but the art of the unknown sculptors of the Brahmâ shrine and of the Trimûrti stands out from the rest, as Valmiki and Kalidâs shine pre-eminently in Indian poetry and drama.

And it is impossible to doubt that these great artists, though their names were consigned to oblivion through the contempt of Islam for the sculptor's art, were in their day held in as high honour as the poets and dramatists of Vikramâditya's court, and as the miniature painters whom Akbar and Jahângîr counted among their intimate friends. Great art like this could hardly have been created under the social stigma which now attaches to the master-craftsmen of India. The blindness of Anglo-Indian critics has not allowed them to perceive the wide gulf which separates the fine sculpture of the Indian temple images from the popular art of ordinary architectural decoration—a gulf fully as wide as that which separated the great masters of Europe from the apprentices or common craftsmen of their guilds.

It is almost miraculous that, in the wholesale destruction of works of the classic age of Indian art, which went on unchecked for centuries after the Muhammadan conquest, any of those which must have been once counted the most precious of them all should be amongst those which have suffered least from the blind fury of the iconoclast. But one sculpture like the Trimûrti of Elephanta and one painting like the Prince Siddhartha suffice to show that Indian artists may stand among the greatest of the world.

Orientalists, looking only at the outside of things, have worked with untiring zeal to show Greek influence in Indian art and literature, as a mark of Western superiority, without being able to realise where the true resemblances lie; just as the secret links which bind Greek and Gothic art together remain hidden from the book-learned student who sees the form but fails to grasp the inner spirit.

Indo-Aryan art was Greek because it was born of the common parent of European and Indian civilisation. Greek art remained a child always, with childish dreams of life and beauty. Let us ever cherish those dreams of childhood which belong to the springtime of humanity. But the art of India grew to maturity and put away childish things. The art of Gandhara was her plaything as a child.

CHAPTER XIII

THE DYNASTIES OF SOUTHERN INDIA—ARYAN CIVILISATION IN THE SOUTH—THE FIVE GREAT ASSEMBLIES—LOCAL SELF-GOVERNMENT IN THE TENTH CENTURY—SIVA TEMPLES AT BÂDÂMI—TEMPLES AT PATTADAKAL—THE VIRÛPÂKSHA TEMPLE—THE EVOLUTION OF TEMPLE PLANNING

So far we have left out of account the history of the dynasties which carried on the Indo-Aryan tradition in the Dekhan and in Southern India, after Asoka's great empire had resolved itself into different dynastic factors. The history of Indian civilisation is little concerned with the martial exploits of the different warrior kings who disputed for the headship of the Indo-Aryan communities in different parts of India, but a general outline of the dynastic record is useful for the framework of it.

The most powerful people with whom the early Aryans first contended for the possession of Indian soil were probably the Nâgas, who figure so conspicuously in ancient Indian sculpture with their remarkable serpent crest, or headdress. They must not be confused with the mythical people, with bodies half-human, half-snake, inhabiting rivers, lakes, and seas and also the sky and the regions below the earth, which appear in the same sculptures. The origin of the Nâgas is as yet unknown: possibly their choice of a snake totem indicates that they were originally mariners and came to India oversea. After they had been driven out of the valley of the Ganges and the

Jumna by the Aryans, they probably remained as the principal power of the Dekhan for many centuries. They were among the first of the non-Aryan people to come under the influence of the Buddha's teaching, which must have brought them within the pale of Aryan civilisation; but except for some indefinite poetical allusions to them in the Mahâbhârata and the Râmâyana nothing has been recorded of their history.

The period when Aryan civilisation began to extend over Southern India is also a matter of uncertainty, though the poetical account of it is given in the Râmâyana. As in the north, it invigorated and supplemented, but did not entirely supersede the older states of culture which existed before the Aryans entered India. Asoka sent his younger brother, Mahendra, to lead the Buddhist mission in the south; but even before the third century B.C. Aryan institutions had existed there, and the three principal dynasties—the Pândya, Kerala or Chera, and the Chola—claimed descent from the five Pândava heroes of the Mahâbhârata, who founded a kingdom with its capital at Indraprastha, one of the old Delhis.

The first of these three dynasties was the southernmost, extending over the present Tinnevelly and Madura districts; the Keralas ruled the western districts; the Cholas the eastern and the central districts, now known as Mysore. Originally the latter had their capital at Uraiyûr, the modern Trichinopoly.[1] In the early centuries of the Christian era, and probably long before that time, the southernmost point of India was a place of pilgrimage for Brahmans from Benares.[2] In very remote times Southern India came into contact with the West through its great maritime trade. Gold and silver, pearls, coral and precious stones, pepper and other spices were sent by way of the Red Sea ports and the Nile to Alexandria. Pliny com-

[1] Vincent Smith, "Early History of India," p. 415.

[2] V. Kanakasabhai, "The Tamils 1800 Years Ago," p. 21.

plained of the drain upon the resources of the Roman Empire on account of the wealth which went to pay for these luxuries. One of the Pândyan kings sent embassies to Augustus at Rome, and Græco-Roman mercenaries were employed in the armies of the Tamil kings.[1]

There are some general descriptions of splendid cities and royal palaces in the earliest Tamil literature. Such details as are given indicate a close resemblance to the architecture of the north, and the employment of "skilled artisans from Magadha" in the construction of them is sometimes mentioned.[2] But the real architectural history of the south, or Tamil-speaking country, does not begin much before the seventh century, when the principal "Raths" at Mâmallapuram previously described were sculptured. This almost coincided with Hiuen Tsang's visit to Southern India (A.D. 640), where he stayed for a time at Conjeveram, then a large city and capital of the kingdom called Drâvida, which was ruled by kings of the Pallava dynasty who rose to power about the third century A.D., and for five or six centuries afterwards disputed with the three older dynasties for supreme rule in the south.

The dynastic history of Drâvida in the seventh century is mostly concerned with the constant wars between the Pallava kings and the Chalukyan rulers of the Dekhan who had succeeded the Andhras about a century previously. The Chalukyans seem to have been of Rajput origin. Both Ajantâ and Ellora were situated in their dominions. The most powerful of Chalukyan kings was Pulakêsin II, whom Harsha of Thanesar, *circa* A.D. 620, endeavoured to subdue; but after a severe repulse he was constrained to leave him undisputed master of the Dekhan. Hiuen Tsang was also a visitor at Pulakêsin's Court at Nâsik, and another record of his reign remains in a fragmentary painting in the first monastic hall at

[1] V. Kanakasabhai, "The Tamils 1800 Years Ago," p. 37.

[2] *Ibid.* p. 25.

Ajantâ, which is believed to represent the reception of an embassy which Khushrû II of Persia sent to the Indian king.[1] It is impossible to follow Mr. Vincent Smith in the inference he draws from the painting of this event by Indian artists that "it proves, or goes a long way towards proving, that the Ajantâ school of pictorial art was derived directly from Persia, and ultimately from Greece."

Though the Dravidians of the Dekhan and the south were not of Aryan race, and though they were to a certain extent civilised before Vedic culture began to influence them, it can hardly be disputed that at a very early time they, like the Nâgas, had adopted Aryan political and religious institutions, and that all the higher culture of Southern India was dominated by Aryan thought in much the same way as Roman culture was impregnated with that of Greece.

The "Five Great Assemblies" which Megasthenes mentions as restraining the power of the southern kings must have been modelled upon the traditional Council of Five which controlled the affairs of the Aryan village, in order to maintain the privileges of the people against abuse of regal authority. All the higher philosophy and religion of the South were likewise Aryan in inspiration, though Dravidian culture had a robust local character, typical of the race, and was not purely imitative. Only in that sense can the architecture of the South be called Dravidian; for all its derivation, structural and symbolic, was Aryan, and its traditions were those of the craftsmen of Magadha who followed in the train of Asoka's missionaries. The "Dravidian" temple was, as I have explained, a glorified stûpa; no element in its design can be said to be of local origin, and there is no evidence of the existence of any great architectural tradition among the Dravidians before Aryan civilisation penetrated into the south.

[1] Vincent Smith, "Early History of India," p. 384.

Aryan culture, indeed, seems to have gathered new strength from its transplantation into southern soil; just as Hellenic culture, when it was decadent in the land of its birth, acquired new vigour in Italy. Sankarâchârya, who relighted the torch of Vedic philosophy in the asrams of the north, and Râmanûja, the exponent of Vaishnavism, were born there. When Northern India was being overrun by the Muhammadan invaders, the south remained the bulwark of Aryan institutions for several centuries, and many of the most important records of Aryan polity and culture are found there.

The organisation of the Aryan village community remained intact in Southern India until the days of British rule. Râm Râz compiled his invaluable notes on Indian village and town planning from the traditional canons of South Indian craftsmen, and to the present day the art of Southern India, decadent as it generally is, yet retains more of the virility of the classic Indo-Aryan period than is generally found in those parts of India which remained longer subject to Muhammadan influence.

The earliest Tamil literature confirms the accuracy of Megasthenes in reference to the "Five Great Assemblies." The members of them took precedence in royal processions after the king's principal officers of State.[1] Of the different classes composing the Assemblies, the representatives of the people safeguarded the popular rights and privileges which Indo-Aryan institutions bestowed upon them; the priests controlled all religious ceremonies and the administration of temples; the physicians directed State sanitation; the astrologers fixed auspicious times for public ceremonies and foretold coming events; the State officials attended to the collection and expenditure of revenue and the administration of justice.[2]

A considerable number of inscriptions of the Pallava period discovered by the Archæological Survey of India refer to the

[1] V. Kanakasabhai, "The Tamils 1800 Years Ago," p. 143. [2] *Ibid.* pp. 109–10.

system of local administration by the Councils of Five. But the most interesting and detailed in its information are two which are inscribed on the walls of a Vaishnavaite temple in the Madura district. They belong to the early part of the tenth century A.D., when a Chola king, Parântaka I, had possessed himself of Madura, the Pândya capital. The inscriptions relate to the king's intervention in the affairs of a municipality in his dominions, called Uttaramêru-Catur-Vêdimangalam, which was evidently of considerable size, as it was divided into thirty wards like the city of Pâtaliputra in the time of Chandragupta.[1]

The circumstances recorded in the inscriptions show that an appeal had been made to the king on account of the maladministration of municipal affairs. The laws had not been observed; there had been embezzlement of communal funds, and the officials responsible had not rendered their accounts. The king thereupon (A.D. 918-9) sent one of his Court officials, a Sudra, to inquire into the matter, and the first inscription relates to the arrangements made as the result of his conference with the local Assembly. The form in which it is set forth shows that the royal envoy acted solely in an advisory capacity, and not as a dictator of the king's commands: "We, the members of the Assembly of Uttaramêru-Catur-Vêdimangalam made this settlement—Tattanûr Mûvendavêlân sitting with us by royal order—in order that the wicked men of our village may perish and the rest prosper," etc.

As it was a Brahman community it was not surprising that the Sudra official's visit did not result in a satisfactory settlement. The next year, apparently, another appeal was made, and this time the king sent a Brahman to assist the distracted municipality with his advice. The second inscription which records the result is equally explicit as to the relationship between the local Assemblies and the Supreme Government. The arbitrator

[1] *Supra*, p. 24.

sent from the royal Court in drafting the final settlement refers to the members of the Assembly with the honorific *Tiruvadiyâr* (their Majesties), and it is by their command and not by royal mandate that the rules approved of are promulgated: "At the order of the great men sitting in the Assembly, I, the Arbitrator, Kâdadippôttan Râjumalla-mangala-priyan, thus wrote the settlement."

Sir C. Sankaran Nair has written an interesting analysis of the settlement,[1] a full translation of which is printed in the Report of the Archæological Survey of India for 1908. The main purport of it was the election of five committees of the General Assembly—namely, the Annual Committee, the Garden or Park Committee, the Tank or Water Committee, the Gold or Finance Committee, and the Panca Vara Committee to regulate the affairs of the commune.

The nominations for the committees were to be made at a meeting of the householders of each of the thirty wards. The qualifications for membership were:

1. He must own more than a quarter *veli* of tax-paying land. But in the case of a Brahman who was learned in one Veda and one of the four Bhasyas, one-eighth *veli* of land was sufficient qualification.

2. He must be the owner of a freehold house and live in it.

3. He must be above 35 years of age and below 70.

4. He must know and be qualified to teach the Mantra Brâhmana.

The latter rule, Sir Sankaran Nair observes, placed the administration of the communal affairs entirely in the hands of Brahmans, or of those versed in Brahmanical philosophy; but it should also be mentioned that Uttaramêru was a Brahman community, as the affix -Vêdimangalam implies.[2] The election

[1] "Village Government in Southern India," *Modern Review*, Calcutta, March, 1914.

[2] See *supra*, p. 14.

rules were made to suit local circumstances; for other inscriptions show that cultivators and merchants were on the voters' register in other villages.

The settlement enjoins that of those possessing the above qualifications only those who are well conversant with business and are virtuous shall be nominated, and that preference should be given to anyone "whose mind is pure and who possesses honest earnings, who had not served on any of the committees in the previous three years."

The disqualifications for membership are then stated. Nepotism was guarded against by the rule that none of the near relatives (a long list of whom is given) of any nominee for office shall be eligible. Anyone who had been outcasted, or was a "foolhardy" person, or who had committed incest or theft, or had become a "village pest," was to be permanently disqualified.

The names of the nominees for each of the thirty wards were to be inscribed on voting tickets, and on the day of election a meeting of the General Assembly was convened by the Finance Committee of the current year at the principal temple. All the priests attending the temple were expected to be present in the inner chamber (*antarâla*). The nomination tickets for each ward were tied up in separate packets and placed in a jar or voting urn. Then the eldest of the temple priests held up the jar before the whole assembly, and one of the packets was drawn at random by any young boy who stood near. The packet thus drawn was placed in another jar, and from this the boy drew one nomination ticket and handed it over to the arbitrator, or returning officer, who was to receive it "on the palm of his hand with the five fingers open." The arbitrator then read out the name on the ticket and it was handed on to be read out in turn by all the temple priests present. One nominee for each of the wards was similarly drawn and declared duly elected for the ensuing year of office.

From the members thus elected, twelve of the oldest and most learned, or those who had previously served on the Park and Water Committees, were selected for the "Annual Committee." Twelve of the rest were chosen for the Park Committee, and the remaining six formed the Water Committee. The term of office for each committee was one year; but any member guilty of misconduct was to be removed at once.

There were separate nominations for the Panca Vara Committee, which apparently checked the work of the other four; and also for the Finance or "Gold Committee." The elections for these committees took place in the same manner as that prescribed for the other three. A sixth committee, "For the Supervision of Justice," is mentioned, but the mode of its election is not specified. It may have been nominated by the king, who was presumed to be the incarnation of justice and who represented the final Court of Appeal.

The settlement concludes with rules for the appointment of the local accountant. He had to prepare his own accounts and submit them to the "Great Committee" for audit at the expiration of his term of office; his honesty must be vouched for by the Committee before he could be reappointed.

Other South Indian inscriptions record the interesting fact that women were eligible for membership of these committees; mention is made of one who served on the Committee of Justice.

Hiuen Tsang's record of his travels gives us information of the different religious sects existing in Southern India in the seventh century. The Jains were numerous and flourishing, but Buddhism, as a sect, had álmost ceased to exist. According to tradition, the Jains are said to have gone south owing to a great famine in Northern India in the first century B.C. The old Jain temple at Aihole has already been described,

PLATE LVII

SIVA TEMPLE AT BADAMI

and also the characteristic roofing of Canarese Jain temples, the form of which was dictated by local climatic reasons. Jainism cannot be said to have created a special architecture of its own, for wherever they went the Jains adopted the local building tradition. In Northern India Jainism followed the Vaishnava cult in building, and their *tîrths*, or places of pilgrimage, were the sacred hills, like Palitâna, Girnâr, Âbû and Pârisnath, upon which they built "cities of the gods" consisting of innumerable temples crowned with the symbol of Vishnu's holy mountain, the sikhara, and grouped together on a regular plan like a village. In Southern India they adopted the "Dravidian" or Siva type of temple; only using the Vishnu symbol in sculpturing colossal images of their Tîrthankaras as Pillars of the Universe. These temples mostly belong to a later chapter of Indian architectural history which does not come within the scope of this book.

The Saiva cult, after the decline of Buddhism, took deep root in Southern India, and even when a Vaishnava propaganda was successful there it had little influence on the local architectural tradition, for the Vaishnavaite temple differed only from the Saivaite in the symbolism of the sacred images which were worshipped.

As in the north, the period from the seventh to the tenth centuries was a great architectural epoch in Southern India. The most characteristic of the Mâmallapuram monolithic shrines which belong to the beginning of this epoch have been described in a previous chapter. In the neighbourhood of Bâdâmi, situated in the Bijâpûr district of the Bombay Presidency, there is a small but exquisite temple of the same age, known as the Mâlegitti Sivâlaya temple, which shows South Indian art in its perfection. It is built of stone finely jointed without mortar, and is one of the earliest structural temples of the Siva type now known. It is placed on the summit of a rocky hill with surroundings of similar character to those of Ajantâ. The cubical shrine with its pyramidal tower (Pl. LVII) closely resembles that of Arjûna's Rath at Mâmallapuram, but the entrance faces the rising instead of the setting sun, as it is dedicated to the benign aspect of Mahâdeva. It differs from the Mâmallapuram temple in having a mandapam, or hall of worship, about 20 feet square added to the antarâla of the shrine. This has a terraced roof surrounded by sculptured monastic cells used only symbolically. The walls which enclose the mandapam have two windows on the north and south filled with perforated stout lattices. In front of the mandapam there is an open porch supported by four massive pillars.

The classic proportions of the whole structure and the exquisite taste of the sculptured ornament of this little temple will be a revelation to European artists who only know Indian architecture from the over-laboured craftsmanship and redundant decoration of the decadent period. A smaller shrine in the same neighbourhood (Pl. LVIII) and of about the same age reveals the unerring judgment of the Indian master-builder in choosing his site and adapting his structural design to the formation of it. It seems almost as if the Divine hand which piled up this steeple of living rock above the river bank had also sculptured the temple as its finial, so cunningly has the craftsman adapted the canons of his art to the place chosen for the shrine of the Deity.

Not far from Bâdâmi, in the ancient Chalukyan territory, is Pattadakal, a place as yet unheard of by most European students of architecture, but remarkable for some of the finest and most interesting structural temples in India. It is not far from Aihole, a little to the south of Bijâpûr, famous for its great mosques, tombs, and other buildings of the Muhammadan period. The Virûpâksha temple, the largest of

PLATE LVIII

SIVA TEMPLE AT BADAMI

them, has a definite date, an inscription showing that it was built by a king of the Chalukyan dynasty, Vikramâditya II, who ruled from 733 to 747. It is of the Siva type of design, and, were it not for Fergusson, who classifies the one as "Dravidian" and the other as "Indo-Aryan," there could be no question but that the supplementary Vishnu temple adjoining it (Pl. LIX) is of the same style and period, built to represent the Vaishnava or râjasic Aspect of Mahâdeva. There are several similar pairs of temples in the neighbourhood of Pattadakal.

The archæological explanation of the "style" of the Vishnu temple, as given by Dr. Burgess in the "Imperial Gazetteer of India," is that perhaps some northern king coming to Pattadakal on a pilgrimage had this temple of the "northern style" built by the side of the "Dravidian" temple as a memorial of his visit. This hardly explains how similar pairs of temples came to be built near Sennacherib's palace at Nineveh with the symbols of life and death planted beside them on the sacred hill, nor other coincidences of the same kind in many other places in India. Kings do not generally build temples in the territories of other potentates whom they visit in a friendly way.

It is a somewhat remarkable circumstance that the earliest known temple architecture of Southern India appears in the seventh and eighth centuries in the perfectly developed state shown by the temples of Bâdâmi, Mâmallapuram, and Pattadakal, and that there seems to be no extant record of the many centuries of growth which led up to this perfection. It has been assumed that the use of wood and other impermanent materials accounts for the historical hiatus, but I do not think that this is altogether a sufficient or convincing explanation. In many localities in India stone must have been the usual building material for centuries before the temples of Aihole and Bâdâmi were built and before the granite rocks of Mâmallapuram were sculptured. The real explanation is, I believe, to be found in the study of the planning of the great cathedral temples of India, such as the Virûpâksha temple at Pattadakal.

The great temples of India were rarely, if ever, built for their own sake, to make a place known as a religious centre. They grew gradually out of the sacred associations of the sites which they occupied. Pattadakal must have been noted as a place of pilgrimage for many centuries before the Virûpâksha temple was built: some yogi of great fame may have lived there under his chosen Bodhi tree, growing where the natural formation of the ground suggested a symbol of his cult, or where the beauty of the prospect inspired pious thoughts. When the yogi died, his stûpa would be raised near the same tree, and pilgrims would flock to worship at the shrine Vishnu the Preserver and Siva the Lord of Death. When the tree died, another shrine crowned with Vishnu's sikhara would be built to mark the place where it grew. The two shrines would remain perhaps for many centuries quite insignificant in size and with no architectural pretensions, until some royal devotee or wealthy merchant would pay for enclosing the holy places in splendid caskets of sculptured stone, and for the accessory buildings which provided accommodation for the priests and pilgrims who worshipped there. An inscription would record the donor's name and the date of this devotional act; the previous history of the shrines would remain only as a tradition in the minds of the people. To the outside observer, who saw only the buildings, it would remain a blank.

This is the story which the plan of the Virûpâksha temple (fig. 56) tells us. The nucleus of the plan originally was a plain cubical cell covered by a dome like the buildings shown in the Nineveh relief (fig. 40). At first, perhaps, it was built only of

PLATE LIX

TEMPLES AT PATTADAKAL, GENERAL VIEW

rough stones or of bricks. When it fell into ruin, another one, still small in size but of better material and construction, was built in place of it. The magnificent pile of the eighth century was the casket of sculptured stone which enclosed one of the earlier shrines, leaving a path for the pradakshinâ rite all round it.

The details of the Virûpâksha temple have never been adequately photographed, but the design of the whole tower built over the holy of holies can be seen in the illustration of another Siva temple at Pattadakal (Pl. LX): it differs only in minor details from the Virûpâksha temple.

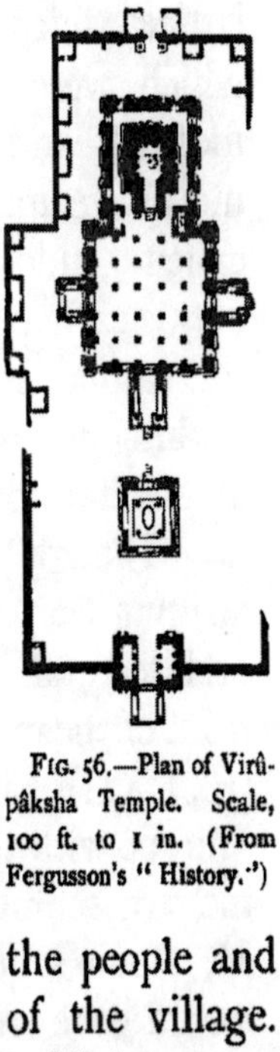

FIG. 56.—Plan of Virûpâksha Temple. Scale, 100 ft. to 1 in. (From Fergusson's "History.")

The structural principle of its design has been already explained (p. 120). It closely resembles the Bâdâmi temple and Arjûna's Rath at Mâmallapuram (Pl. XXVIII); but the roof of the antarâla is built up higher, and a large sun-window filled with a sculptured shrine in miniature occupies the front of it. It corresponds with a similar one which appears over the antarâla of the adjoining Vishnu shrine.

In front of the antarâla—the hall of the priests—is a pillared mandapam, the hall of the people and the meeting-place of the General Assembly of the village. The tradition of Aryan village life was linked with its structure by the pillars supporting it, symbolising the sacred grove which was the general meeting-place in the absence of a building; by the gopurams, the cow-gates which formed its entrances, and by the "embattled fret" in the plan of the walls which enclosed it. Only, instead of Kshatriya warriors, the shrines of the gods protected the villagers within the sacred enclosure. The shelters of the fighting men upon the walls became monastic cells.

The mandapam of the Virûpâksha temple is of the same design as that of the temple of Bâdâmi described above, but it is more than double the size of the latter—*i.e.* about 50 feet square. The roof is supported by sixteen monolithic pillars with sculptured bracket capitals, and the enclosing walls on each side are pierced by four windows. The pierced stone lattices which fill the latter (Pl. LXI) are the prototypes of those which were so conspicuously beautiful in Muhammadan mosques and tombs at Ahmâdâbâd and elsewhere. All the motifs, geometric as well as floral, used in what are wrongly called "Indo-Saracenic" lattices are found in Indian temples of this early period. Except for the substitution of Arabic texts for animal and human forms as decoration, Islam brought nothing new to the masonic craft of India. Indo-Muhammadan architecture belonged root and branch to India's own tree.

Though in a bad state of preservation, one of the most striking features of the Virûpâksha temple is a masterpiece of architectural sculpture, the detached Brahmâ shrine placed in front of the mandapam enclosing Siva's symbol, the bull Nandi (Pl. LXII). It combines the stateliness of the classic design of Europe with the fervid imagination of Gothic art. The finest modern sculpture of Europe has a close kinship with it. If M. Rodin's genius had been devoted to building design, he would have created architecture like this.

It would be a mere solecism to compare these Indian Siva shrines with Renaissance buildings like St. Paul's in London or St. Peter's in Rome. The Indian builder was too sincere in his religious feelings to try to amuse the eye with meaningless "effects" of line or form, or to exhibit for public applause his cleverness as a composer of "style." The temple was not an archæological essay, but a sermon in stone, suggesting in

PLATE LX

TOWER OF SIVA TEMPLE, PATTADAKAL

its symbolism the rhythm of the cosmos, teaching the lessons of the universal life, and recording the sacred traditions of the Indian people. There is, nevertheless, a closer æsthetic affinity between these South Indian temples and the Parthenon of Greece than in any of the buildings of the Renaissance of Europe.

Pl. LIX gives a general view of the two temples,[1] but

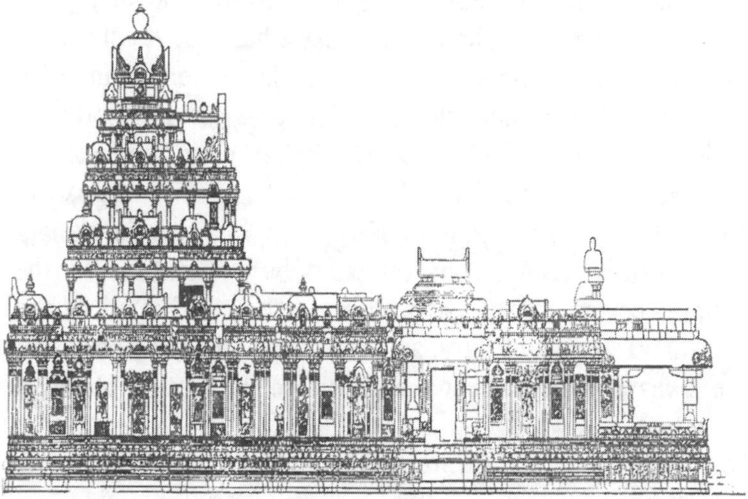

FIG. 57.—Virûpâksha Temple at Pattadakal, South Elevation (from a Drawing by Mr. H. Cousens). Scale, 20 ft. to 1 in.

the fine proportions are considerably marred by the fact of the sculptured plinth upon which they both stand being buried underground.

Mr. Cousens' drawing of the south elevation (fig. 57) represents the plinth of the Virûpâksha temple after excavations have been made. Possibly these have not yet been carried down to the original ground level, for the famous sculptured Kailâsa temple at Ellora, which is almost a duplicate of the Pattadakal

[1] From Fergusson's "Mysore and Dharwar."

temple, has a lower plinth with a high dado of magnificently sculptured elephants in high relief (Pl. LXVIA), which adds greatly to the grandeur of the design. The Pattadakal original of the Kailâsa temple has not yet received the attention due to it as one of the master-works of the classic period of Indian architecture. Fergusson's meagre description does scanty justice to it.

The Vishnu shrine adjoining it is shown in the foreground of Pl. LIX, on the right. The sikhara has lost its crowning member, which Fergusson assumed to have been an amalaka, like those of the Orissa temples. The vagaries of the archæological stylist are difficult to follow, for there seems no reason to suppose that it was different from other temples of this part of India, styled "Chalukyan" by Fergusson, in which the sikhara is crowned by a stûpa dome instead of by the amalaka; for the temples belong to the Saiva cult, and are dedicated to the Vaishnava Aspect of Siva, as Mahâdeva. The four sides of the sikhara are ornamented with projecting vertical bands of miniature sun-windows in the middle; the corners show horizontal mouldings in which the amalaka motif alternates with sun-windows.

The plan is similar to that of the Virûpâksha temple, only on a much smaller scale. The roof end of the antarâla is ornamented with a large sun-window, used as a shrine for the image of Siva in his mystic dance of the cosmic rhythm. The mandapam has a flat roof supported by four pillars. The sculptured bull of Siva stands in the open facing the mandapam, the shrine enclosing it having fallen into ruin.

The Virûpâksha temple, which has an easterly aspect like the contiguous Vishnu shrine, was walled in by a great quadrangle, with the principal gopurams on the eastern and western sides. Under the shelter of the walls accommodation was provided for Brahmans and their scholars, and for pilgrims.

PLATE LXI

STONE LATTICES, VIRŪPĀKSHA TEMPLE, PATTADAKAL

Many of the great South Indian temples repeat the plan of the Indian village in their enclosing walls, with gopurams on all four sides. This is not so frequent an occurrence in Northern India, which was so much more completely under Muhammadan domination, probably because the Muhammadan rulers razed the outer defences of Hindu temples for military reasons; but it may be seen in the plan of the Mârtând temple in Kashmir (fig. 46), where the lines of the two main streets of the village plan are also repeated.

When a famous shrine like the Virûpâksha temple attracted more pilgrims than could be accommodated under the walls, or when a pious king wished to increase the endowments of Brahmanical learning which belonged to the temple, the difficulty of enlarging the original sacred structure was overcome by the expedient of enclosing the first quadrangle with a larger one, the gopurams of the latter being correspondingly greater in width and height. The temple of Tiruvallûr (fig. 58) is an example of this natural process of organic growth in building which Fergusson, with curious inconsistency, criticises as a "false system of design." To satisfy architectural theorists, the builders should have pulled down the innermost shrine, with all its immemorial traditions, and rebuilt it on a larger scale according to the "true principles" of design.

As a matter of fact, in every South Indian temple which was completed according to the intention of the original builders, the tower of the holy of holies always dominated the gopurams of the mandapam and those of the walls of the quadrangular enclosure, as it does in the Virûpâksha temple. The great temple at Tanjore, completed about the beginning of the eleventh century, is a conspicuous example of this rule. The expedient of making the outer gopurams the principal structural features was only adopted when some ancient and highly venerated shrine already existed on the site, and it might be considered desecration to touch it or to disturb the meditations of its pious custodians.

This system of adding enclosure to enclosure gradually created the best known of the great temples of Southern India, like those of Srirangam, Râmêsvaram, and Madura, with their towering gopurams forming landmarks for many miles around

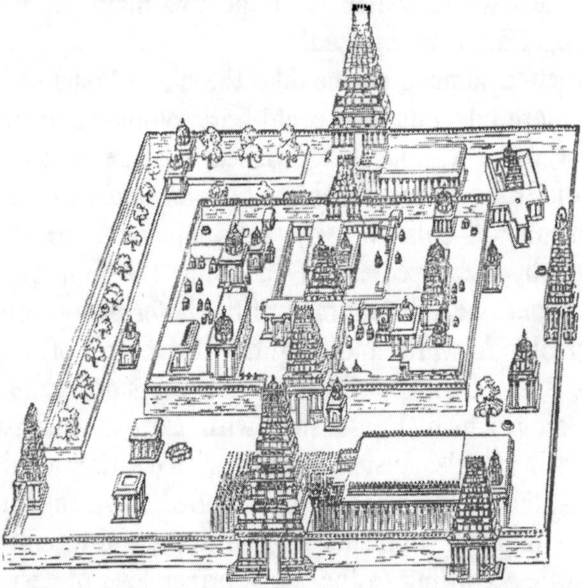

FIG. 58.—Temple at Tiruvallûr (from Râm Râz's Essay on the Architecture of the Hindus).

them. Within the outer courts numbers of subsidiary shrines, bathing tanks, and "halls of a thousand pillars," representing the parks or groves of the Indo-Aryan village, were built to provide for the vast crowds of pilgrims which congregate there at the time of great festivals, while numerous bazaars supply them with food and other necessaries.

In most cases the existing outer enclosures are additions or restorations made since mediæval times; but it must be

PLATE LXII

184] NANDI SHRINE, VIRŪPĀKSHA TEMPLE, PATTADAKAL

understood that the traditions which ascribe great antiquity to the temples cannot be dismissed as Brahman fables. The nucleus of the temple may be an ancient structure associated with the first penetration of Aryan religion into Southern India. The successive enclosures are the record of the unbroken tradition of the Indo-Aryan buildingcraft from remote antiquity to the present day.

CHAPTER XIV

THE TÎRTH OF ELLORA—THE VISVAKARMA CHAITYA-HOUSE—THE DUMAR LENA TEMPLE—THE RAMÊSVARA TEMPLE—THE KAILÂSA TEMPLE—THE INDRA SABHÂ AND JAGANNATH SABHÂ

WITHIN the territories of the Chalukyan kings where Bâdâmi, Pattadakal, and Ajantâ were situated there was another place, now known as Ellora, around which the associations of Aryan piety had gathered from time immemorial. Ellora, which is now within the Nizam's dominions, is not far to the south of Ajantâ, and the amenities of the place which made it sacred to religious devotees of every sect were likewise Siva's moon-crest, the bend of a rushing torrent, overhung by a rocky hill, and a waterfall. Ajantâ was a university, Ellora a tîrth, or place of pilgrimage. Tradition does not record what yogi's wonder-working austerities first brought pilgrims to the place, but it is known at the present day as one of the twelve sacred tîrths to accomplish which is the desire of every sâdhu or sannyâsin.

According to the strict rule of his caste every Brahman, when he has fulfilled the duties first of a Brahmachârin, or student, and afterwards those of a father and householder, should on the approach of old age hand over charge of his family to his son, and, following the example of the Buddha, shave his head, discard the sacred cord which is the symbol of his order, and take the vow of a sannyâsin. Then with a pilgrim's staff and water-vessel, and with begging-bowl in hand,

PLATE LXIII

FAÇADE OF THE VISVAKARMA CHAITYA-HOUSE, ELLORA

he should go forth into the world as a mendicant and spend the rest of his life in wandering from one sacred tîrth to another. At this stage the Brahman's only spiritual exercise is meditation, and he is absolved from the routine of religious ceremonies and ritual.

The Brahman, as a sannyâsin, is one of a Sangha or spiritual brotherhood in which caste restrictions are unknown. His body is held to be no longer subject to defilement, and to become so free from the gross attachments of the flesh that on his death it does not need the purification of fire. As in the days of the Buddha, this brotherhood is open to all castes, though non-Brahman mendicants, or sâdhus, are supposed to need the help of religious exercises, other than meditation, to enable them to rise to a higher spiritual grade.

FIG. 59.—The Waterfall at Ellora, from an engraving by F. J. Havell, after a drawing by W. Havell (1782-1857).

The choice of tîrths for pilgrimage depends upon the Ishta-deva of the pilgrims, whether they be sannyâsins, sâdhus, or belonging to the lay community. There are tîrths for pilgrims of all sects; others which are considered as specially Jain, Saivaite, or Vaishnavaite. All sects have their sacred hills or mountains, rivers and waterfalls. Other places are sacred as being associated with the events of the Mahâbhârata or Râmâyana. Some pilgrims will elect to follow the course of the wanderings of

Râma and Sîtâ in exile, others the last journey of the Pândava heroes; or to visit the birthplace of Krishna, or the places where portions of Umâ's body fell upon the ground as Siva bore it sorrowfully away to his Himâlayan retreat.

There are places, like Benares, which provide for those who are unable to accomplish the greater ones a series of miniature tîrths which are believed to possess all the efficacy of the originals. But in all cases it is the place and its associations which are in the pilgrim's mind, not the temples which have been carved or built as a tribute to the sanctity of the ground. And wherever the tîrth may be, from Cape Comorin to the Himâlayas, it is always associated in some way with the sacred soil of Aryâvarta and the traditions of the Aryan race. In this way of thinking all India is one, so perfect is the bond of spiritual sympathy between all the diverse sects and races which came within the Aryan pale and under the spell of the Aryan genius.

The scarp of the rocky hill at Ellora, over which in the rainy season several torrents leap down into the watercourses at its foot, for over a mile in length is sculptured into shrines and monasteries belonging to different sects, but most of them face the setting sun and thus are dedicated to the tâmasic aspect of the Trimûrtî. The chief exception is the small group of Jain temples at the northern extremity of the line, including the Indra Sabhâ and the Jagannath Sabhâ which face the south. From this one may conclude that they were not devoted to the austere meditative cult of the Jain ascetic, but that some wealthy Jain merchants were showing their gratitude to Lakshmî for success in business by having these splendid shrines carved in her honour; the Dawn-Maiden, as the bringer of prosperity, being associated with the quarter from which the monsoon rain-clouds come.

The sectarian dedication of Ajantâ kept its architectural

PLATE LXIV

FAÇADE OF THE RAMESVARA TEMPLE, ELLORA

character within one very well defined type. At Ellora, which was and is a place of pilgrimage for all India, the imagination of the artist had wider scope; and there could hardly be a grander opportunity for sculpture on a titanic scale than the cliffs of Ellora afforded. So far as archæological investigation goes, the group of monasteries and an important chaitya-house, now known as the Visvakarma jhôprâ, at the south extremity of the line, are assumed to be the earliest in date, because they are Buddhist; but the system of chronology based upon the hypothesis that Brahmanical architecture is derived from the Buddhist is wholly unreliable. There is very little doubt that Ellora was a resort for devotees of all sects from a remote antiquity—Buddhists, Jains, and sâdhus and sannyâsins of the orthodox schools living side by side, worshipping together the aspect of the Divine manifested in the wonderful natural phenomena which attracted them to the place, but every sect representing a different philosophical school or a different theory of the divine nature.

The command of an unlimited number of skilled craftsmen which the affluent Buddhist sect had for centuries after Asoka's conversion naturally gave Buddhism greater architectural opportunities. But in every period of Indian history it was only the popular side of Indo-Aryan religion that was represented by the sculptor, painter, and architect. The higher philosophy of every sect ignored the aids to contemplation and the gorgeous ritual which popular feeling demanded. The lonely forest, the mountain cave, the quiet river-bank were more to the philosopher than the most splendid shrine ever made by the hands of men. So at Ellora and every other sacred tîrth the centre of interest to the pilgrims would often be, not a magnificent chaitya-house, temple, or splendid monastery, but a roughly hewn cave or a natural grot, where a yogi lived whose inspired sayings were treasured up in the people's mind and added to the storehouse of Indian wisdom. Archæology can give a date to the work of the painter, sculptor, and architect; but the antiquity of the hermit's cave, which to the Indian historian may be a record of far higher significance, must always remain a matter of conjecture.

Ellora was never at any time, like Ajantâ, appropriated by any particular sect, as archæological classification might lead one to suppose. The chief architectural or sculptural antiquities of Ellora which can be approximately dated all come within that epoch of Indian history so graphically described by Hiuen Tsang, when Buddhists, Jains, and orthodox Brahmans joined together in divine worship at public festivals, and were more or less equal sharers of state patronage.

The Visvakarma[1] chaitya-house, if the local tradition preserves its original dedication, may have been the chapel of the guild of masons who were working at Ellora, and some of the adjoining monastic halls may have been their residences. A place like Ellora, where splendid shrines and monasteries were continually being carved out of the cliffs on either side of the great waterfall, would doubtless have a colony of skilled masons permanently residing there, and their services would be utilised for any religious sculpture required, whatever its sectarian character might be. The same masons who sculptured the Visvakarma chaitya-house, or their descendants, may have assisted the Saivaites at the Dumar Lena—a reproduction of the Elephanta temple—and later on at the Kailâsa temple, which is almost a copy of the Virûpâksha temple at Pattadakal, and also the Jains in sculpturing the Indra Sabhâ and the Jagannath Sabhâ. In the same way, in later times, Hindu craftsmen of every sect worked for the Muhammadans in building their mosques and tombs, for no

[1] Visvakarma was the craftsman's synonym for Brahmâ, as the Divine Artificer, or the Architect of the Universe.

"Saracenic" builders came into India with the Muhammadan conquerors.

The Visvakarma chaitya-house is larger than any of the Mahâyânist chapels at Ajantâ, its length being over 85 feet and breadth 43 feet, but it is by no means so impressive, either externally or internally. It is chiefly interesting for the novelty of the design of the façade, Pl. LXIII. When a chaitya-house faced the west, as in this case, the usual proportions of the great sun-window which lighted the nave would be inconveniently large, although the set-back of the front wall and the use of curtains tended to mitigate the glare. In the Visvakarma chaitya-house the traditional design of the façade is altered by an arrangement which might have been called "Renaissance" in style, had it been seven or eight centuries later in date, in order to reduce the size of the openings. The effect is not altogether pleasing, and the Visvakarma chaitya-house, on the whole, is lacking in the fine inspiration of other great works at Ellora. There is a certain dryness and formality in the design of the whole front, although it has the negative merit of not being overcrowded, like some of the Ajantâ work.

According to archæological convention, the Buddhist group is placed first in chronological order; but the probability is that the Saivaites, or followers of orthodox Brahmanism, were the first to occupy the site, for they held all the places adjoining the waterfall and Siva's crescent which made Ellora holy ground. Both the Jains and Buddhists would seem to have been allotted their respective stations to the north and south of the Saivaite group at a later date. On both sides of the ravine above the waterfall there is a series of simple excavations of no architectural pretensions, but they may possibly have formed the original asrâma, or hermitage of Ellora, before it became famous as a place of pilgrimage.

Adjoining the waterfall the scarp of rock on the southern side is cut into a group of three comparatively small and simple shrines [1] which also belong to the period before the seventh century, when the quiet of the hermitage was as yet undisturbed by the excavation of the magnificent temples upon which the Chalukyan kings lavished all the resources of their treasury. The Dumar Lena temple, close to the waterfall on the northern side of the ravine, seems to indicate the beginning of the bestowal of royal bounty upon the asrâma of Ellora. In plan it is almost an exact reproduction, on a somewhat larger scale, of the great temple at Elephanta; but it is oriented differently, as the four entrances of the Brahmâ shrine, instead of fronting the four quarters, turn to the intermediate points of the compass. The entrances correspond with those of the shrine—that which overlooks the waterfall is south-east. Probably this orientation was arranged so that the main axis of the temple should follow the direction of the stream at the point where it stands.

The principal subjects of the sculpture are a repetition of those at Elephanta, but none of it has the wonderful inspiration of the original. The Dumar Lena might be dated roughly at about the seventh century, at the time when Harsha of Thanesar, Pulakêsin II, and the Pallava dynasty of the south shared between them almost the entire sovereignty of India. Both Ellora and Elephanta were within the Chalukyan king's dominions, and possibly one or both of the temples may have been executed under his patronage.

The next group, farther to the south of the waterfall and having the same orientation as the Dumar Lena, marks the increasing fame of the Ellora tîrth. The eight shrines in the group, now numbered 24 to 17, are of about the

[1] According to the arbitrary scheme of numbering adopted by Dr. Burgess, these are Nos. 27, 26, and 25.

PLATE LXV

TRANSVERSE SECTION, KAILASA TEMPLE, ELLORA

same age as the Dumar Lena. The most remarkable of them is known as the Ramêsvara temple; its noble sculptured front is shown in Pl. LXIV. Opposite the entrance Siva's bull, Nandi, is raised on a richly carved pedestal. Though very different in proportion and effect to their prototypes in the Kârlê chaitya-house and the Gautamîputra monastery at Nâsik, the decorative motifs of the massive dwarf pillars of the façade are the traditional ones derived from ancient Aryan symbolism. Lakshmî's water-jar, the cornucopia of India, is used for a capital as the alternative of the amalaka; the legs of the Vedic altar which it was meant to support are here transformed into sculptured figures. The panelled treatment of the low screen-wall connecting the pillars is evidently a reminiscence of the Vedic railing, and the same motif in a modified form appears in the sculptured frieze above the pillars. The two columns in front of the shrine are of the same type as those at Elephanta, and the craftsmanship throughout the temple evidently belongs to the same virile school as the latter, representing the period when the principal seat of the Chalukyan government was at Nâsik instead of at Bâdâmi.

Farther south along the line we come next to the chief glory of Ellora, and in some ways the most wonderful *tour de force* achieved by Indian sculptor-architects—the Kailâsa temple. The history of the temple has been ascertained with tolerable certainty. About A.D. 754 Dantivarman, one of the minor chiefs of the Dekhan and the head of the ancient Râshtrakûta clan, overthrew Kîrtivarman II, the descendant of the great Pulakêsin, and assumed supreme power in the Chalukyan territory which his dynasty enjoyed for two and a half centuries.[1] He was soon afterwards deposed by his uncle, Krishna I, who extended his nephew's conquests and, apparently to celebrate his triumph, had this magnificent Siva

[1] Vincent Smith, "Early History of India," p. 256.

temple carved out of the living rock. As Krishna's capital was at Bâdâmi it was natural for him to choose the neighbouring temple of Virûpâksha at Pattadakal as the model for it.

The Kailâsa temple has the usual orientation of a Siva shrine, that is, its entrance faces the setting sun. It derives its name from the Himâlayan mountain which was Siva's mythological paradise; for Siva, like Vishnu, as a nature symbol is a mountain deity, and the high pyramidal towers which covered Siva shrines were meant to represent Kailâsa, just as the sikhara of Vishnu shrines represented Mount Mandara, or Mêru. The distinction between the two symbols was that Siva's mountain was the rugged, white snow-capped peak, soaring above the clouds, where nature was quiescent and as if wrapped in meditation. The cubical cell where the yogi sat in thought alone with the universe was the symbol of it. Vishnu's symbol was the fruitful mountain, whose rounded summit was crowned with deodar or cedar, and the tree- and flower-clad hill glad with the song of birds and teeming with joyous life, like a lotus-flower with turned-down petals offering its nectar to the bees.

The dedication of the Kailâsa temple to Siva's Himâlayan paradise was not an arbitrary choice; for it had a particular significance in reference to the tîrth of Ellora, which in the imagination of the pilgrim was a sacred place because the rocky hill and its watercourses seemed to reproduce in miniature the Himâlayan mountains and the holy rivers which had their sources there. The army of skilled masons Krishna I had at his command set themselves a gigantic task, which at that time was also a novel one. Instead of merely hollowing out the interior of a temple in the scarp of a hill, or sculpturing one in miniature from a boulder of granite, they cut down into the rock and, quarrying a pit from 50 to 100 feet deep, 250 feet in length, and 160 feet wide, carved out of the middle of it a full-size double-storied temple, considerably larger than the structural

PLATE LXVI

THE KAILASA TEMPLE, ELLORA: GENERAL VIEW

PLATE LXVIa

THE KAILASA TEMPLE, ELLORA. SOUTH ELEVATION

one which was its model, adding to it a series of magnificent chapels and monastic halls which were cut deep into the rock on three sides of the quarry, as shown in the transverse section of the temple, Pl. LXV.

The comparative dimensions of the Kailâsa temple and the Virûpâksha temple at Pattadakal can be seen in figs. 60 and 56, which are drawn to the same scale. The general view of the former from the north-west is given in Pl. LXVI. The block in front is the outer gopuram, or entrance, with a fragment of the adjoining walls crowned with the lotus-leaf battlement which is so conspicuous in later Muhammadan fortresses, mosques, and tombs. The first part of the temple inside the gopuram is the two-storied Brahmâ shrine for Siva's bull, connected with the gopuram by a bridge cut into the rock. On either side of this shrine are two fine dhwaja-stambhas, nearly 50 feet high, surmounted by Siva's three-pronged ensign, the trisula, the symbol of the three Aspects. Another bridge connects the Nandi shrine with the splendid porch, or gopuram, which is the front entrance to the twelve-pillared mandapam leading into the antarâla and the holy of

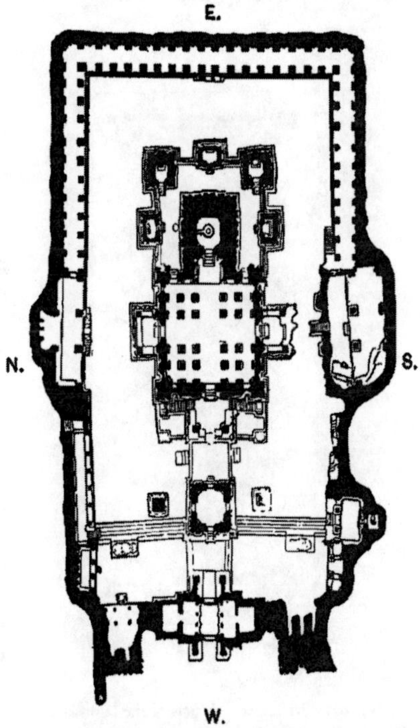

FIG. 60.—Plan of Kailâsa Temple, showing the Cloisters and Side-chapels at Ground Level, and the Temple at the Upper-floor Level. Scale, 100 feet to 1 inch. (From Fergusson's "History.")

holies. The section given in Pl. LXV through the corresponding north and south gopurams shows the arrangement of the interior of the mandapam. It closely follows the design of the Pattadakal temple, but it is considerably larger and more ornate. It is lighted by the gopuram doors, by two other doors opening into the terrace surrounding the vimâna, and also by six windows of almost the same design as those of the Virûpâksha temple which have been already illustrated. The walls of the mandapam on the north, south, and west are decorated with panels of figure sculpture illustrating various mythological subjects, such as that of Dûrgâ slaying the buffalo-demon Maḥishâsura, probably an allegory of the return of clear weather in Northern India, when the bright sunshine dispels the miasma and oppressive atmosphere which accompany the cessation of the monsoon rains. But hardly any of the figure sculpture at Ellora is specially remarkable; it is more the stupendous *tout ensemble* of the Kailâsa temple which is so amazingly wonderful.

FIG. 61.—Perforated Window of the Mandapam, Kailâsa Temple. (From a drawing by the Archæological Survey of India.)

The roof of the antarâla, according to the usual design, rises above the terraced roof of the mandapaṃ, and the gable of it is sculptured with a large sun-window filled with a figure of Siva, seated in yogi attitude, with the right hand raised in the dharma-chakrâ mûdra, or the gesture of teaching. The

PLATE LXVII

KAILÂSA TEMPLE, ELLORA: ENTRANCE PORCH OF MANDAPAM

pyramidal tower of the holy of holies is of the Siva type, based upon the piling up of the yogi's cubicle, as before explained, the crowning member being the stûpa dome. The whole of the main block, including the vimâma, the antarâla, and the mandapam, rests upon a basement, about 27 feet in height, sculptured with a magnificent dado of elephants in very bold relief which seem to be supporting the temple on their backs. The large intervening panels beneath the north and south gopurams of the mandapam are filled with groups of figure sculpture. The fine one under the south gopuram, illustrating the legend of the demon king, Ravana, being imprisoned by Siva under Kailâsa when he impiously attempted to remove it bodily to Ceylon, is shown in the frontispiece.

This great sculptured basement, unfortunately now much mutilated, provides a raised terrace for the circumambulation of the holy of holies, the entrance and exit being through the mandapam on either side of the antarâla. At the corners and in the middle of the three sides of this terrace there are five small shrines forming a group round the principal one. The first one, on the north side, is dedicated to Ganesa, the elephant-headed son of Siva, symbolising the reasoning faculties, who must always be first invoked before the Great Spirit is addressed. The next, at the north-east corner, is the shrine of Bhairava, or Rudra, Siva's tâmasic or destructive aspect. The third, immediately behind the holy of holies, belongs to Pârvatî, Siva's sakti or nature-force. The fourth belongs to Chanda, the scavenging deity who purifies the foulness caused by the processes of involution, and thereby prepares for the next turn of the wheel of life. The fifth is dedicated to the Sapta-Mâtris, the seven Mothers of Creation.

As will be seen in the plan, fig. 60, and the transverse section, the Kailâsa temple is surrounded on three sides by cloisters and chapels cut into the faces of the quarry which has this glittering marvel in the centre of it. If the temple were detached from its surroundings and stood in the open, like the Raths at Mâmallapuram, it might be compared unfavourably with the simpler and more stately craftsmanship of the Pattadakal temple. But with a rare inspiration of genius the sculptors of Ellora threw into striking contrast the effect of the jewel-like brilliance of the temple—built as it were of white marble, coruscating with the sunlight reflected on every facet and elaborated with the finesse of chased silver—and the broad surfaces of smoothly dressed stone on the sides of the quarry, the noble simplicity of the massive piers of the side-chapels cut into the rock and the mysterious gloom of their deep recesses. Part of the cloisters which surround the temple and the front of the Lankêsvara chapel above them are illustrated in Pl. LXVIII.

In accordance with the usual Indian practice, the finished surface of the Kailâsa temple and its surrounding chapels were coated with fine white polished plaster, suggesting the Great Yogi's snow-capped Himâlayan hermitage. In the interior of the mandapam the plaster was used as a ground for fresco painting. The cloisters on the ground-level and the chapels facing the north and south gopurams of the mandapam formed an outer pradakshinâ path, the sides of the cloisters being sculptured with a great series of reliefs illustrating the whole mythology of the Trimûrti for the edification of pilgrims. The series of chapels or monastic halls on the south side (Pl. LXV) rise in three stories above the cloisters, the intention being to cut right through the upper surface of the rock, so as to form a sky-light. This part of the scheme was never completed.

The outer circuit of the temple commenced at the north-west corner with the delightfully sculptured shrine (fig. 62) of the sacred rivers, which, flowing from the Himâlayas through

PLATE LXVIII

LANKÉSVARA CHAPEL, KAILÂSA TEMPLE, ELLORA

Siva's matted locks, were here appropriately worshipped at the gates of his paradise. The goddess Gangâ, standing on a makara, is in the centre; on her right is Sarasvatî with a lotus flower as a pedestal; and the goddess Jumna standing on a tortoise holds the left. The seven sculptured panels on the

FIG. 62.—Shrine of the Sacred Rivers, Kailâsa Temple.

architrave above probably represent others of the fertilising rivers which water the holy land of Aryâvarta, and the water-jars above them doubtless have a similar significance. The symbol of the rain-cloud, Indra's elephant, stands detached in front of the shrine, and is matched by another one on the opposite side, in front of the small chapel which completed the outer circuit.

It is reasonable to suppose that several generations of craftsmen were employed in completing the whole scheme of the Kailâsa temple. At the same time it is evident that the additions made by Krishna the First's successors were not haphazard, but were part of a skilfully co-ordinated traditional plan which the original designers had in view, if they did not actually lay it out. In fact we have in the Kailâsa temple a complete reproduction, so far as different technical conditions allowed, of one of the great structural temples of that epoch, including the surrounding walls, accessory chapels, and monastic buildings. The temple enclosure, as in structural examples, repeated the plan of the Aryan village, the mandapam in the centre standing for the assembly hall, the Lankesvara chapel on one side and the corresponding chapels opposite to it representing the north and south cow-gates, and the battlements of the screen walls on either side of the entrance gopuram exactly reproducing those of a fortified town or village.

The cliffs between Kailâsa and the Buddhist quarter of the tîrth is occupied by the Das Avatâra Temple, so called from its sculptures of the ten incarnations of Vishnu, and by the Ravana-ka-khâi, both of which are planned on similar lines to the monastic halls of Ajantâ and were probably Brahmanical adjuncts to the Kailâsa temple. The Buddhist quarter begins with the great three-storied monastery now known as the Tîn Tal cave.

Though the most splendid of the temples and monasteries at Ellora belong approximately to the same period (from the sixth to the ninth centuries), the location of the different sects points to the conclusion that the orthodox Brahmans and their followers were the first to constitute Ellora as a tîrth and that they always had a priority of claim, signifying in this case the choice of sites nearest to the torrent and waterfall which represented the source of the Ganges. The relegation of the Jains

PLATE LXIX

THE INDRA SABHÂ, ELLORA, FROM THE ENTRANCE

PLATE LXX

LONGITUDINAL SECTION OF THE INDRA SABHA, ELLORA

and Buddhists to the places farthest from the chief attraction of the tîrth shows that they were the last comers and had to content themselves with inferior stations. When the Jains began to add to the architectural splendour of the place, about the ninth century, the best available site was on the northern side of the "Ganges source," and at a considerable distance from it, where the two fine temples already alluded to, the Indra Sabhâ and the Jagannath Sabhâ, are located.

The names of the two temples and the orientation of their shrines indicate that, unlike most of the other shrines at Ellora, it was not the tâmasic aspect of the Trimûrti that was here invoked, but the blessings of the Rain-god, represented by Vishnu the Preserver and his sakti, Lakshmi, the bringer of prosperity. Only, as the temples belonged to the Jain sect, they appealed specially to their saints, the Tîrthankaras, to whom analogous divine powers were attributed. With this qualification the symbolism of the structure and ornament has the same significance as in Brahmanical and Buddhist temples.

The entrance to the Indra Sabhâ (Pl. LXIX) is completely sculptured out of the living rock, like the Kailâsa temple which it resembles in many respects, though on a considerably smaller scale. It is approached through a gopuram with the usual guard-house sculptured in miniature on the top of it. Immediately within the walls stands the Jain equivalent of Siva's Nandi shrine. The cubical cell is of the Brahmâ type, with a door on each of the four sides, and the square block of stone in the centre of the shrine, sculptured on each side with a figure of Mahavîra, the Jain contemporary of the Buddha, stands for the four-headed Brahmâ symbol as seen at Elephanta. The roof of the shrine is of *panch-ratna* or "four-jewelled" type—that is, a yogi's cell, covered by the stûpa dome in the centre, with four similar ones of smaller size placed at the corners of it. Variety is given to the traditional design by adding a porch, or antarâla, with its deep chhaja to each side of the shrine and corresponding sun-windows or gables filled with sculpture on the roof.

On the west side of the court, in front of one of the side-chapels, there was, as shown in the illustration, a very splendid Vishnu pillar 31½ feet in height, crowned by a Brahmâ symbol represented by four Jain figures in yogi attitude. The pillar collapsed many years ago. The main block of the Indra Sabhâ consists of a two-storied temple cut into the rock for a depth of over 100 feet, as shown in the section, Pl. LXX. Perhaps the most remarkable of the sculpture of the Indra Sabhâ is the strikingly beautiful and original façade of the side-chapel on the western side of the main temple (Pl. LXXI), the richness of which contrasts so admirably with the larger surfaces of the grand chhaja shading the main front and the magnificent profile of the elephants kneeling above it, seen on the right of the illustration.

Adjoining the Indra Sabhâ is another Jain temple of a similar type, but smaller in size, called the Jagannath Sabhâ, the front of which (Pl. LXXII)—a splendid example of the skilful artistic treatment of masses of living rock—shows the practical effect of the massive chhajas in giving protection from the heat and glare of the Indian sun.

PLATE LXXI

SIDE-CHAPEL OF THE INDRA SABHA, ELLORA

PLATE LXXII

FAÇADE OF THE JAGANNATH SABHÂ, ELLORA

CHAPTER XV

THE HINDU DECADENCE IN THE NORTH OF INDIA—THE TEMPLES OF KHAJURÂHO—THE DOMES OF MANDAPAMS—SANKARÂCHARYA AND HIS MISSION—SOUTHERN INDIAN ARCHITECTURE IN THE TENTH AND ELEVENTH CENTURIES

THE Kailâsa temple at Ellora, magnificently conceived and superbly wrought though it was, must always rank lower as an artistic achievement than the great temple of Elephanta. The eighth century in the north of India was artistically and politically the beginning of the Hindu decadence which continued its downward course until, after several centuries of ineffectual struggles against the Muhammadan invader, India at last, under the great Akbar, once more enjoyed the blessings of a lasting peace, and a renaissance began of which Hinduism, purified and strengthened by the ordeal of fire and sword, was again the moving spirit. Politically, the decadence began with the death of Harsha in A.D. 647, soon after the return of Hiuen Tsang to China, when one of his ministers, Arjuna or Arunâsra, seized the throne. Shortly afterwards, owing to his ill-treatment of an envoy sent by the Emperor of China, a Tibetan army invaded Magadha and the usurper's career was cut short by a disastrous campaign in which he was taken prisoner and sent off to China in the train of the imperial envoy he had insulted. Harsha's empire was then broken up.

Except the Chalukyan king, Krishna I, whose reign was made memorable by the Kailâsa temple, there is hardly a name of distinction in the next three and a half centuries among the rulers of the numerous kingdoms, great and small, into which India was divided, until Mahmûd of Ghaznî began his series of ferocious raids which ended with the capture of Somnath and the destruction of the famous temple in 1026. The dynastic history of this period, so far as it has been ascertained by patient research, is a tedious record of petty internecine warfare caused by the rivalries and quarrels of kings and chieftains, who, except for the record of conquest or defeat, seem to have very little claim to be remembered by posterity.

But during this long period India remained free from the ravages of foreign invasions, and owing to the solidity of the Indo-Aryan social fabric these constant local wars probably affected the economic condition of the country far less than might be supposed. Fighting was the business of the Kshatriya caste alone, and when there was no vital national interest at stake, the wars which were the outcome of dynastic jealousies were only gladiatorial contests on a large scale in which none but the combatants and their relatives were deeply interested. The other three castes, Brahmans, Vaisyas, and Sudras, went on with their respective occupations as philosophers, traders, and husbandmen, and looked for protection from the winners in the game, whoever they might be. The description given by Megasthenes of men ploughing and digging the soil in perfect security, while close at hand armies in battle array were fighting desperately, may seem highly coloured, but it gives an insight into social conditions which prevailed in India under the caste system for many centuries after the time of Chandragupta.

The causes which led to the spiritual and intellectual degradation of India in this period were those which affect every state of culture too long confined within itself and deprived of the stimulant of new ideas which enable it to readjust itself to changing conditions of life in every age. Indo-

PLATE LXXIII

GOPURAM OF THE MADHAVA PERUMAL TEMPLE, GANDIKOTA, CUDDAPAH DISTRICT

Aryan religion, which was based upon a profound philosophy of life, physical and spiritual, became bound up with the personal interests of a corrupt priestly caste which exploited the instinctive piety of the people, and the original simple meanings of its formularies were buried under a mass of ritualistic mummery. The respect paid by the people to monasticism led thousands to adopt it solely for the easy life and prospects of worldly advantages which it held out to its votaries. Philosophy, losing touch with realities, stultified itself with hair-splitting dialectics, and as in the Middle Ages in Europe, religion, superstition, and rascality too often went hand in hand. As a religion Buddhism had become infected with the prevailing sacerdotal vices against which the original teaching of Sâkiya Muni was a protest. His ethical doctrines had long since become the common property of Hinduism, and the Buddha himself was acknowledged as one of the ten incarnations of Vishnu; but as a sect Buddhism was fast declining in the land of its birth, although in China and the Far East it was gaining many adherents.

But neither the spiritual and intellectual degeneracy of the times nor the frequent local wars caused any diminution in the activity of the builder. On the contrary, the enormous increase of monastic institutions and the encouragement of superstition by a crafty priesthood gave a great impetus to religious foundations, while the constant fighting made the fortification of towns and villages a necessity. Temple building also, by the very degeneracy of religious teaching, received an enormous increase. According to the true spirit of Indo-Aryan religion there were certain worshipful places marked out by nature as the dwellings of the gods, and the temples built there by man were but symbols of the divinity that was immanent in the site. But superstition encouraged the belief that temple building had a virtue of its own, and that the presence of the gods could be compelled by establishing earthly thrones for them in places where their presence was most needed. So every petty Râja who busied himself in robbing and killing his neighbour invoked the blessing of God upon his undertakings by providing sumptuous temples in his capital, or at the tîrth which his Brahman counsellors advised him to patronise, or by providing accommodation for the crowds of monks who were the parasites of every royal court.

It is the architecture of this decadent period, labelled "Puranic" or "Hindu" by antiquarians, which the European student has been taught to believe is most typical of the Indian mind. The art of every country has passed through the same phase of deterioration when its vital creative energy begins to wane. The undiscerning critic is unable to see that the defects of the qualities of Indian art do not represent its highest ideals. Most of the great temples of India with which Europeans are more or less familiar belong to the period of decadence, either before or after the Muhammadan invasions. Though many of them certainly can stand by themselves as splendid monuments of art, it is impossible to appreciate them rightly without a careful study of the classical models which furnished the motifs of their design. From about the eighth or ninth century, until the time of Akbar, the creative energy of the Indian master-builder kept to the beaten track of Hindu tradition and did little but elaborate upon old ideas.

In Northern India one city after another grew in architectural splendour with the rise of new dynasties and the creation of new kingdoms. Kanauj had been Harsha's capital, and its fine gardens and public bathing-tanks attracted the notice of Hiuen Tsang. In the ninth and tenth centuries it became still grander as the capital of the Panchâla kingdom, and when Mahmûd of Ghaznî captured it in A.D. 1018, his iconoclastic fury vented itself upon the destruction of its temples, which were said to number ten thousand. In 1193 Shihâbu-d-Dîn, the first of the Ghûri line which succeeded Mahmûd's dynasty, completed its ruin, and only the mosque which he built with the masonry borrowed from its temples remains to witness its departed glory.

Gaur, which under the name of Lakhnautî succeeded Pâtaliputra as the principal city of the Magadha country, became one of the capitals of the Pâla and Sena kings of Bengal. It was likewise sumptuously laid out with parks and bathing-tanks and extended for about nine miles along the bank of the Ganges. In 1194 it shared the fate of Kanauj when the last of the Sen dynasty was overthrown by one of Kutbu-d-Dîn's generals, and thereafter its craftsmen were employed in reconstructing its innumerable temples to suit Muhammadan ritual. Thus though the style of the mosques and other buildings which now remain is essentially Hindu and in no sense "Saracenic," as understood architecturally, there is nothing left of the architecture of the place belonging to the period treated in this volume. Benares and Ujjain, though historically two of the oldest and most famous cities of India, and even now of great architectural interest, contain few important buildings of the pre-Muhammadan period, most of them having fallen under the mailed fist of the iconoclast Aurangzîb in the seventeenth century.

In spite of the wholesale destruction which went on almost unchecked for several centuries, there are still remaining enough of the great buildings of the Hindu decadence to make the architectural reputation of any country. The immense building activity of the period was by no means confined to temples and monasteries. India had always been famous from the days of Chandragupta for its great public highways with fine bridges and sumptuous rest-houses for travellers. The earliest Muhammadan visitors to India, like Alberuni, were amazed at the magnificence of the irrigation works built of massive masonry, and all that was done subsequently by the Mogul rulers was but a revival of the Buddhist and Hindu tradition. It is, however, impossible to treat this part of the subject satisfactorily in the present work; but as there was never any distinction in India between civil and ecclesiastical architecture, the study of temple craftsmanship gives the key to all the rest. The great irrigation works of India were also a part of the temple stapathi's work. Temple building was the artistic synthesis of Indian daily life and the stapathi was both engineer and architect—a master-craftsman to whom art was both religion and the science of practical work.

We have already discussed the development of the great Siva temples in the south of India up to the eighth century. The colossal gopurams which distinguish them in the present day are nearly all additions of comparatively modern date. Besides being landmarks for pilgrims, the gopurams doubtless served their original purpose as watch-towers; also the battlements of the walls enclosing the temple courtyards were not mere ornaments, but would be used for defensive purposes in time of war. Pl. LXXIII will enable the reader to appreciate the fine design of some of these temple gopurams, although the roof of it has fallen.

It remains now to compare the great Siva temples of this period with the analogous Vishnu temples, built by Jains, Saivaites, and Vaishnavaites in Northern India. The simplest type of a Vishnu temple, consisting only of the shrine, or vimâna, and the antarâla provided for the priests, has been sufficiently illustrated by the examples given in Pls. XXXIII to XXXIX. The splendid temples at Khajurâho, the ancient capital of the Chandêla dynasty, whose dominions covered the districts now known as Bundelkhand of the Native States and the Central Provinces of British India, are typical of the archi-

PLATE LXXIV

KANDARYA MAHADEVA TEMPLE, KHAJURAHO

tecture of the middle period of the Hindu decadence which was shortly before Mahmûd of Ghaznî's raids. They were probably built, together with a number of magnificent reservoirs formed by building great embankments of masonry across the valley of Bundelkhand, in the course of the century beginning with A.D. 950, when the Chandêlas, who had for a long time been petty feudatory Râjas, became powerful independent sovereigns who played a considerable part in the attempt to repel the Muhammadan invasions. The temples of their capital, now a deserted place lying about 150 miles south-east of Gwalior, escaped entire destruction, and about thirty of them still remain more or less intact. Though the sectarian dedication of them differs, some being Jain, others Saivaite and Vaishnavaite, they are nearly all of the Vishnu type of design, but elaborated with extraordinary richness.

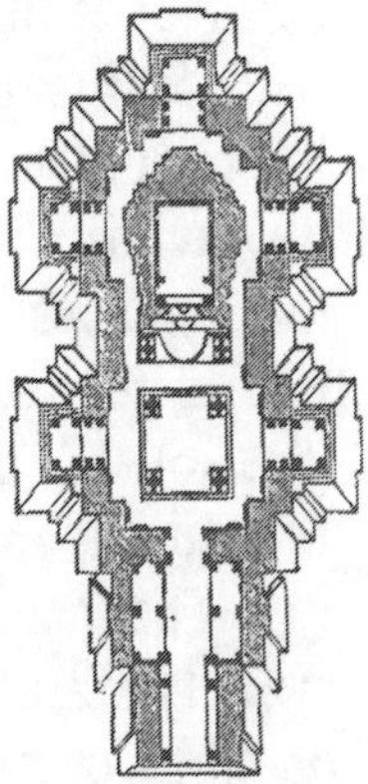

FIG. 63.—Plan of Kandarya Mahâdeva Temple, Khajurâho. (From Fergusson's "History.")

Pl. LXXIV, a view of the sikhara of the Kandarya Mahâdeva temple, will show with what magnificent imaginative power and technical skill pinnacle upon pinnacle, crowned with Vishnu's lotus emblem, are piled round the central tower of the shrine to give the impression of the holy mountain upholding the highest heavens. The sculpture in itself is not of the finest art, but nothing could surpass the skill with which details of bewildering complexity are coordinated together in masses so as to form a perfectly balanced architectonic unity.

The plan of the temple (fig. 63) points to the probability that the structure is not all of the same age, but that the sanctum and perhaps the inner four-pillared mandapam belong to a more ancient shrine which was enclosed in the tenth century by the wonderful casket which now forms the exterior, on the same principle as the great Siva temples of Southern India were gradually built round a nucleus of a simple yogi's cell.

The view of the Chutterbhuj temple (Pl. LXXV) shows the external effect of the three successive mandapams through which the inner shrine is approached, and the section of a Vishnu temple (Pl. XXXI) will explain the arrangement of the interior. The Chutterbhuj temple is of the *panch-ratna* type, being built like the Tâj Mahall on a high platform of masonry with four smaller shrines at the corners of it. It is also interesting to notice that adjoining it a Siva, or so-called "Dravidian" temple, built on an extension of the same platform, makes a symbolic pair with it in the same way as the pair of temples at Pattadakal and those in the Nineveh relief (fig. 40). A distant view of this temple, called the Mritanga Mahâdeva, appears in the illustration on the right.

The mandapams of these temples and many others of the same type are distinguished by their splendid domes supported on eight or more pillars and built up in concentric rings of masonry, sculptured internally with endless variation of detail, but always to represent the mystic lotus flower which encloses "the beautiful circle of earth." Externally the courses of masonry are extended into a square pyramidal form, like the tower of a Siva shrine, so that the three different parts of the structure of the temple stood for the Three Aspects—the cell of the vimâna with its four porches representing Brahmâ; the sikhara, Vishnu; and the roof of the mandapam and also the internal dome of the vimâna, Siva. Sometimes a hollow space was left between the internal and external courses of masonry—a practical arrangement for keeping the mandapam cool inside.

These great domed mandapams were no doubt built in place of the more ancient flat terraced roofs panelled internally

PLATE LXXV

CHUTTERBHUJ AND MRITANGA MAHADEVA TEMPLES, KHAJURAHO

with lotus flowers (fig. 13), in order to provide an open floor space in the centre of the pillared halls for the convenience of public meetings, musical entertainments, nautches, etc., which were held at the temple. Sometimes, as in the larger temples at Khajurâho, separate mandapams were provided for music and dancing. The mandapam, the fine interior of which is shown in Pl. LXXVI, belongs to the Khanwar Math at Khajurâho. The crown of the dome with its carved pendant has fallen in. The next plate illustrates the very beautiful marble dome of the Vimala Saha temple at Mt. Âbû, a building of the eleventh century. The sculptured figures, though here they serve no structural purpose, are reminiscences of the ribs of wooden domes. The ribbed dome came into practical use again in Muhammadan times. The so-called "Pathan" domes and all the great domes of Bijâpûr and elsewhere were entirely of Hindu craftsmanship, and were directly derived both as regards symbolism and structure from the domes of Indian mandapams.

The decorative sculpture on the temples at Khajurâho and elsewhere is sometimes grossly obscene, a fact which might mislead Europeans into forming a wrong judgment of the ethics of Hindu religion. It is no doubt true that some Hindu sects, especially in the decadent period, indulged in the most depraved ritualistic practices, but Indo-Aryan religion should not be convicted of immorality on that account. There must naturally be a different outlook in sexual matters among a community which regards marriage at an early age as a social and religious duty than there is in Europe, where it is usually deferred to much later in life and where a considerable proportion of both sexes remains celibate. A Vishnu temple was a symbol of the active or dynamic principle of nature, and most of the external sculpture was popular art interpreting vulgar notions of the philosophic concept, but not necessarily implying any moral depravity. The indecency was generally introduced on account of the popular belief that it was a protection against the evil eye. There was never any obscenity in the sculpture of the sacred images worshipped within the sanctum and elsewhere. The imagers, being often Brahmans, were much more highly cultured than the ordinary craftsmen, and their art was the authorised interpretation of the esoteric philosophy of Hinduism.

The temples of Khajurâho may be regarded as typical both of the greatness and weakness of the architecture of the north of India in the period immediately preceding the Muhammadan conquest. In the south the decadence was deferred for at least two centuries later, for South Indian architecture hardly passed its zenith before the end of the tenth century. The demoralising effect of the Hun invasions and of Mahmûd of Ghaznî's devastating raids did not penetrate into Southern India, and probably on that account Aryan culture there retained its vitality much longer. The eighth century in the south was the beginning of an intellectual revival heralded by the appearance of the great philosopher Ṣankarâcharya, the protestant reformer and defender of Vedic religion. His mission, like that of the Buddha, was to free Indo-Aryan religion from the superstitious abuses which had accumulated round it and to propound a new philosophical synthesis of all the spiritual wisdom of Hinduism. But while the Buddha's doctrines were agnostic, Sankarâcharya's religious teaching was essentially pantheistic and his philosophy set forth a rationalistic theory of the First Cause based upon the teaching of the Upanishads and of the Bhagavad Gîta.

Both on religious and philosophical grounds he was an uncompromising opponent of the Buddhism of his day, though it differed fundamentally from the original creed of the Hînayâna school; but he sought to reconcile the differences of

PLATE LXXVI

DOME OF MANDAPAM, KHANWAR MATH TEMPLE, KHAJURÁHO

PLATE LXXVII

DOME OF MANDAPAM, VIMALA SAHA TEMPLE, MT. ÂBÛ

all the Brahmanical sects which took their stand upon the Vedas. Sankarâcharya may be regarded as the founder of the modern Saivaite cult, as Râmanûja, his opponent in the twelfth century, was the protagonist of modern Vaishnavism.

Sankarâcharya was a Brahman of the Nambudri class, and is supposed to have lived about the end of the eighth and beginning of the ninth centuries. His birthplace according to one account was in a village of the Malabar district, according to another at Chidambaram. There are numerous legends of the miraculous events attending his birth and early years. After some years of studentship at an âsrama on the banks of the Narmada under a famous Guru called Govinda, he renounced marriage and the life of a householder and took the vow of a sannyâsin. Then, like the Buddha, he went to Benares, where he gathered round him a number of disciples and probably wrote his most important works, the commentaries on the Upanishads and the Bhagavad Gîta. He was still a young man when, accompanied by great numbers of his chelas, he started on his great pilgrimage throughout India, preaching the philosophy of the Vedanta, denouncing the immoral ritualistic practices of the Saktas and other sects, and refuting the arguments of the pandits of different schools who opposed him. To establish his teaching on a permanent footing he organised an order of sannyâsins open to all castes, after the model of the Buddhist Sangha, which was divided into ten grades, and with the help of his many royal adherents he built and endowed a number of monastic institutions as training centres for the exponents of reformed Hinduism. The chief Guru of the Sringeri Math, the most famous of his monasteries in Southern India, continues to be regarded as the spiritual head of the Saivaite cult to the present day. When Sankarâcharya's mission had been thus accomplished, he retired to the Himâlayas, and, according to tradition, died at Kedarnath, one of the most venerated of the Siva tîrths, in A.D. 828, at the age of thirty-eight.[1]

As before mentioned, the architecture of Southern India from the ninth to the eleventh centuries bears witness to the vitality of Indo-Aryan culture at this period, and Sankarâcharya's influence was so lasting that even when Râmanûja subsequently succeeded in creating a diversion in favour of Vaishnavism, the temple buildings of the south continued to adopt the Saivaite forms of architecture in preference to the proper symbolism of the Vaishnavaite sect. Thus the great Vaishnava temple of Srirangam and the Vaikuntha Perumal temple at Conjeveram[2] are designed entirely as Siva shrines, and differ only from the traditional type in the symbolism of the images worshipped there.

The records of the Chola king of the tenth century, Parântaka I, in connection with the mode of election for village councils, have already been mentioned. The most powerful king of his line, Râjarâja the Great (A.D. 985–1018), conquered Ceylon and became suzerain of nearly the whole of Southern India. He built the stately Siva temple at Tanjore to commemorate his victories, but other temples of lesser note belonging to his or his son's reign are more interesting on account of their superb sculpture. Pls. LXXVIII–IX illustrate some of the wall shrines of a temple at Gangaikonda-cholapuram in the Trichinopoly district which show South Indian sculpture at its finest. The magnificent bronze images of this period, examples of which are preserved in the Madras Museum, are among the greatest achievements of Indian art.

The classic dignity of the mandapam of the temple at

[1] For further details of Sankarâcharya's life and work, see "Sri Sankarâcharya," by C. N. Krishnasamy Aiyar, M.A., and Pandit Sitanath Tattvabushan's explanation of his philosophy (Natesan & Co., Madras).

[2] See Fergusson's "History" (revised edit.), vol. i. pp. 359 and 371.

PLATE LXXVIII

A. THE DANCE OF SIVA

B. GANESA

SCULPTURED PANELS FROM TEMPLE AT GANGAI-KONDA-CHOLAPURAM, TRICHINOPOLY DISTRICT

Dârâsuram in the Tanjore district (Pl. LXXX) may be said to reflect something of the austere intellectuality of Sankarâcharya's teaching. The strength and simplicity of the structural design and the comparative reticence of the ornament stand in striking contrast with the almost riotous profusion of the Khajurâho temples, though the magnificent *tout ensemble* of the latter may be more impressive. These two buildings are contemporary documents which give a faithful record of the life of the times when the intellectual and spiritual centre of Aryan India had moved from the northern to the southern provinces.

It is to this period that Fergusson assigns the most delusive of all his classifications of Indian architecture, the "Chalukyan style." His definitions of it are so vague that it is difficult to make anything intelligible out of them. He is nearest the mark in describing it as being locally "halfway between the Dravidian and northern styles," for most of his examples are a composite form of Vishnu and Siva temples—that is, the Vishnu sikhara is crowned by the Siva dome instead of by the amalaka—a natural consequence of the fact that the districts in which he locates the style lie just between the special spheres of influence of the Vaishnavaite and Saivaite cults in the north and south of India respectively.

The temple at Ittagi in the Hyderabad dominions (Pl. LXXXI), which Fergusson cites as one of the most typical of the style, is evidently only an elaboration of the Vishnu temple at Pattadakal (Pl. LIX), which he labels "Indo-Aryan." The "star-shaped" plan of some of the vimânas given as examples is also only an elaboration of the circular plan of the stûpa and a structural application of the symbolism of the eight- or sixteen-petalled lotus. The circular vimâna, technically called *vesara*, was by no means confined to the provinces described as the location of the style.

Nor are richly carved doorways and pillars a peculiarity of these provinces, and if technical distinctions like that of pillars turned in a lathe are to be catalogued, every one of the provinces of India must be assigned its own style, for every locality had its own school of craftsmanship with certain technical traditions peculiar to itself. In this case the local school developed a special skill in turning massive stone columns upon a vertical lathe, and consequently every temple in those districts was ornamented with elaborately turned pillars as specimens of its skilled craftsmanship. The mandapam of the temple of Rangaswami in the Dharwar district of the Bombay Presidency (Pl. LXXXII) is a fine example of this local peculiarity; but though admirable as a technical achievement, it is not altogether an artistic success on account of the bewildering repetition of circular mouldings by which the craftsmen sought to display their skill in turning.

When the fundamental ideas which underlie the structure and symbolism of Indian architecture are properly understood, it will be easy for the student to analyse the innumerable variations of traditional themes which are to be found in other great buildings and which must be left unnoticed in this work. India, in spite of its heterogeneous sectarian and racial composition, is spiritually and intellectually one country. That is a fact clearly stated in its architecture. The artificial boundaries which antiquarians have sought to establish are academic conventions which leave the heart of the matter untouched, for they are without either æsthetic, scientific, or historic foundation. The Indian synthesis must be understood before any of the elements of its composition can be intelligently analysed.

PLATE LXXIX

SIVA AND PARVATI, TEMPLE AT GANGAI-KONDA-CHOLAPURAM, TRICHINOPOLY DISTRICT

CHAPTER XVI

THE MUHAMMADAN INVASIONS AND AFTER

MUHAMMADANISM is one of the principal elements which are combined in the Indian synthesis. The fierce struggle which took place before it was fused together with Hinduism was born of racial antipathies and material interests rather than of intellectual or spiritual differences. Ages before the time of Muhammad Hinduism had settled for itself by the peaceful arguments of philosophy all the problems which Islam set out to determine by the sword. The missionaries of Asoka were the first to prepare in Western Asia the soil in which Islam grew. Its iconoclastic madness was only the religious zeal of a primitive, warlike race inspired by the principles of Hînayâna Buddhism as they were re-stated by the prophet of Mecca. The monotheistic idea which Islam propounded was as old as the Vedas, and even Buddhism itself had accepted it long before the Hegira.

Indian literature and science had been eagerly studied by the scholars of Baghdad for centuries before the Muhammadan conquest of Hindustan. The skill of Indian master-builders made Mahmûd of Ghaznî's capital one of the finest cities of the East. Hindu generals fought in the armies of the Muhammadan invaders of India, and when finally the old Hindu capitals, Delhi and Gaur, became the seats of Muhammadan power, Baghdad and Mecca nominally remained the spiritual centres of Muhammadan India, but the culture of

Islamic India was farther removed from its birthplace than the Muhammadanism of Arabia and Turkey from Judaism and Christianity. The philosophical differences between Muhammadan and Hindu thought were no greater than those which existed between the different sects of Hinduism itself. The success of Islam in India from a proselytising point of view was always due to its material inducements and the attractions of a social system which freed the low-caste Hindu from Brahman tyranny, rather than from the spiritual appeal of its dogma.

The "Indo-Saracenic" style of Indian architecture was purely a creation of Fergusson. The Muhammadan invasions made no decisive break in the building traditions of India, except that they brought about a reversion to the ideals of Hînayâna Buddhism. The Indian master-builder continued to build for his Muhammadan rulers according to the Indo-Aryan traditions, just as he had done for Buddhist, Jain, and Hindu. The Indian mosque was the Hindu temple adapted to Muhammadan ritual. Its most typical plan, oriented like a Vishnu shrine, was like that of a Hindu temple, a rectangle with gopurams on the north, south, and west sides, for both the temple and the mosque enshrined the tradition of the Indo-Aryan village. The so-called "Pathan dome," like all other Indo-Muhammadan domes, was the dome of a Hindu mandapam *minus* the external symbolism. The "Indo-Saracenic" arch was the arch of a Hindu vault technically adapted for the wider spans required by the different structural conditions which Muhammadan ritual imposed. No Indian mosque contains a single structural idea borrowed from the Saracenic architecture of Western Asia, Egypt, or Turkey. Muhammadan art in India from its very beginning was, and continued to be, wholly Indian in spirit and in craftsmanship. All the symbolism of its ornament was Indo-Aryan, except that texts

PLATE LXXX

MANDAPAM OF TEMPLE AT DĀRĀSURAM, TANJORE DISTRICT

from the Quran are used in places where the Hindu sculptor would have put symbolic figures or animals.

The story of the Muhammadan conquest, so far as it affected Indian architecture, has been told in another volume.[1] Every one of the local varieties of the so-called Indo-Saracenic style was derived from an adaptation of the local temple craftsmanship. Mosque and temple were both Hindu art, and under such wise and beloved rulers as Husain Shah and Akbar, orthodox Hindus would help to build a mosque in the same spirit as in Asoka's time they would bring votive offerings to the stûpas of Buddhist saints.

Not even in the question of the idolatry which was anathema to the Muhammadan was there any vital difference between the teaching of Hinduism and of Islam. The iconoclast vented his blind rage upon Hindu sculptured symbols without understanding their meaning to prove that he was a true believer. His own intangible idols were sacred things necessary for his soul's salvation. The Muhammadan was no philosopher, and to his practical mind an image of wood or stone, set up for worship as a symbol of God Who is everywhere and in everything, seemed an impious attempt to substitute things of earth for thoughts of heaven. The Hînayâna school of Buddhism had forbidden image worship for a different reason, because the teaching of the Buddha was agnostic and did not recognise the idea of a personal God. But both before and after the time of Muhammad all Hindu teachers were iconoclasts in a spiritual sense, though they did not seek to propagate their culture by fire and sword, and at all times there were among them some who were puritans in the Muhammadan and Christian sense, objecting to any kind of figure symbolism in religious ritual.

[1] "Indian Architecture: its Psychology, Structure, and History, from the First Muhammadan Invasion to the Present Day."

There are numerous temples to be found in different parts of India representative of this puritan phase of Hindu art. Pl. LXXXIII shows the wall sculpture of one such temple in the Dharwar district of the Bombay Presidency, which might belong to a Gothic cathedral. The canopies of the shrines remain as ornaments, but a Vishnu pillar, or a pair of them, used as pilasters take the place of the images.

The whole synthesis of Indian life and thought from the time of Asoka down to the present day is thus written down in its craft traditions, forming a priceless record of a great civilisation to which the whole world is deeply indebted. No civilisation, ancient or modern, has produced a higher culture, no other has succeeded better in making religion the philosophy of life, and on the whole probably no other has contributed so much to human knowledge. All Indo-Aryan religion, deceptive and often degraded though it may be in ritualistic practice, is founded upon the greatest of all scientific truths—the reality of divine revelation or inspiration. That was the great secret of the Rishis which they so jealously guarded for posterity, seeking for humanity's sake to find the way by which the pure in heart may come to drink at the divine well of knowledge the elixir of immortality—the all-pervading truth which must be the mainspring of every right human action. It was therefore that the yogi who believed himself to be in contact with that divine source was regarded as a man of God, and his cell a fit place for worship. And if the yogi often deceived both himself and others, and if human credulity often ascribed to the truly inspired powers equal to the Highest, the divine truth shines none the less brightly behind the clouds of man's follies and weaknesses.

Indo-Aryan sociology as regards the caste system was admirably conceived, under the peculiar conditions in which Aryan society found itself in India, for preserving its higher

PLATE LXXXI

GREAT TEMPLE AT ITTAGI, FROM THE SOUTH-WEST (ELEVENTH CENTURY)

PLATE LXXXII

INTERIOR OF MANDAPAM, RANGASWAMI TEMPLE, DHARWAR DISTRICT, BOMBAY

culture from degradation by contact with the semi-civilised races which formed the substrata of the population. All systems have their abuses, but without the caste system Indo-Aryan civilisation would probably have been obliterated long ago. Whether the rigidity of the system, which became more intense as the forces which tended to disintegrate Indo-Aryan society grew stronger, should under modern conditions be relaxed, is quite another question.

The best testimony to the wisdom of Hindu polity is that the organisation of the village community, which was the bed-rock of Aryan society, remained unshaken for at least five thousand years, until the middle of the last century. Aurangzîb's attempt to uproot it only led to the downfall of his dynasty. From the days of Chandragupta Maurya every empire which remained secure in the affection of the Indian people built upon that foundation. Its solidity preserved Indian culture from all the attacks of bigotry and racial hatred, and maintained the country's economic stability throughout centuries of devastating foreign invasions.

No political system yet devised by the wit of man has succeeded in making the methods of war obsolete; but the organisation of the Indian village republics was a better defence against the vile tyranny of an overgrown militarism than any yet discovered in Europe or in Asia. It failed at times as an instrument of national defence only because the petty jealousies and rivalries of kings prevented India from presenting a united front against the common enemy, but militarism never grew into a menace to the liberties of the people and a danger to civilisation: except when Scythians, Huns, or Mongols thundered at the gates of India, war was the sport of kings which did not very deeply affect the life of the majority of the people who were non-combatants. For individuals it probably secured a larger measure of personal freedom than most governments of modern times in the East or in the West, while it did not prevent the co-operation of national forces for purposes useful to the community at large.

Though her ancient political constitution has been broken up, the heart and soul of India are still in her villages, and if her voiceless millions are ever to become articulate, it must be by restoring the communal life of the Indian village. Only when that is accomplished can it be said that the foundations of the British Raj are well and truly laid; for then it will rest upon the bed-rock of liberty and justice, which in India as in other countries has always been the safest foundation of Empire.

India is loyal to the core; the canker of anarchy bred in the foul slums of cities only penetrates into her village life because the law-abiding instincts of the people are there denied the power of expression. India still has faith in British justice, but the complications of modern administrative methods sow the seeds of discontent and prevent European officials from keeping in touch with popular sentiment. Justice can only serve its purpose when it accords with popular sentiment. The village panchayat may have been crude in its ideas, but the justice it dispensed in its own community was based upon popular tradition and intimate knowledge of the life of each one of its members. Professional litigation, which is the curse of modern India, did not exist under the native system of administration, and perjury, which is rampant in Anglo-Indian courts of justice, was a vice which had little purpose to serve when every witness's previous life and character were known to all the judges.

India is awakening to a consciousness of her past history; it would be folly for British administrators to shut their eyes to the fact or to believe that bureaucratic methods out of all relation with India's past can continue to work without ever-increasing friction. The difficulties and dangers can only be

PLATE LXXXIII

DETAILS OF TEMPLE AT DHAMBAL, DHARWAR DISTRICT, BOMBAY

met by a thorough investigation of the means by which the Aryans of old succeeded in winning the undying affection and devotion of their fellow-men in the East.

Europe is now witness to the demoralising effect upon a great nation of a perverted philosophy which glorifies brute force as a symbol of kingship and manhood, and does not disdain to propagate it by crimes which disgrace the name of civilisation. When the intellectuals of Germany are allowed to see a glimmering of truth they may begin to find the spiritual philosophy of the East of more service to humanity than their poisonous scientific "culture," and recognise in Asoka, Vikramâditya, and Akbar a nobler ideal of kingship than that which is now held up to them.

And when it has shaken off this tyranny of militarism which has fooled and enslaved it, the democracy of Germany may find in the ancient Aryan constitution of India a practical solution of the problem of self-government which stood the test of five thousand years, and might be used still, as in the days of Chandragupta Maurya, "to check the power of kings," and to lay the foundations of a lasting peace in Europe.

Rheims Cathedral, the glory of the Middle Ages, is shattered by twentieth-century savages; but the genius of the Latin race survives and the traditions of Gothic art are still alive in India, the land of its birth. Only a new spiritual stimulus is needed to revive their old creative force, and the comradeship-in-arms of East and West on the battlefields of France will surely be followed again by a closer spiritual fellowship in the arts of peace. So the spirit of Gothic art may be reborn, and East and West may join once more in raising a great monument to the glory of God, in memory of the heroes who have fallen in the fight and of the martyrs who have suffered for the cause of freedom.

INDEX

Printed by Hazell, Watson & Viney, Ld., London and Aylesbury.